KITCHENER

BY
GENERAL C. R. BALLARD

With Seventeen Maps

DODD, MEAD & COMPANY
NEW YORK   1930

COPYRIGHT, 1930
BY C. R. BALLARD

ALL RIGHTS RESERVED
NO PART OF THIS BOOK MAY BE REPRODUCED IN ANY FORM
WITHOUT PERMISSION IN WRITING FROM THE PUBLISHER

PRINTED IN THE UNITED STATES OF AMERICA
BY THE VAIL-BALLOU PRESS, INC., BINGHAMTON, N. Y.

ABBREVIATIONS

The following abbreviations are used in the footnotes for works which have been quoted more than once.

ARTHUR.	*The Life of Lord Kitchener.* By Sir George Arthur.
CHURCHILL.	*The World Crisis.* By the Rt. Hon. W. S. Churchill.
COLVILE.	*History of the Sudan Campaign,* 1884–1885. Compiled for the War Office by Sir H. E. Colvile, K.C.B.
CROMER.	*Modern Egypt.* By the Earl of Cromer (Sir E. Baring).
FRENCH.	'1914.' By the Earl French of Ypres.
HUGUET.	*L'Intervention Militaire Britannique en 1914.* By Général Huguet.
LANREZAC.	*Le Plan de Campagne française et le premier mois de la guerre.* By Général Lanrezac.
MACPHAIL.	*Three Persons.* By Sir Andrew Macphail.
O.H.	*The Official History of the War.* Edited by Brig.-General J. E. Edmonds.
REPINGTON.	*The First World War.* By Lieut.-Colonel C. A'C. Repington.
ROBERTSON.	*Soldiers and Statesmen.* By Field-Marshal Sir William Robertson, G.C.B., etc.
RONALDSHAY.	*Life of Lord Curzon.* By Lord Ronaldshay.

SCOTT-MONCRIEFF.	*Life of Sir Colin.* By M. E. Hollings.
SMITH-DORRIEN.	*Memories of Forty-eight years' Service.* By General Sir Horace Smith-Dorrien, G.C.B., etc.
WILSON.	*Diary of Field-Marshal Sir Henry Wilson, G.C.B., etc.* Edited by General Sir C. E. Callwell.
WINGATE.	*Mahdiism and the Egyptian Sudan.* By Major (now General Sir F. R.) Wingate, G.C.B., etc.

A CHRONOLOGY

1850. June 24. Born at Crotier House, County Kerry.
1868–70. Royal Military Academy, Woolwich.
1871. Jan. 4. Gazetted Lieutenant, Royal Engineers.
1874–78. Palestine Survey.
1878–82. Cyprus Survey.
1883. Jan. 4. Captain.
1883–84. Attached to Egyptian Cavalry.
1884–85. Nile Expedition and Desert Column.
1884. Oct. 8. Brevet Major.
1885. June 15. Brevet Lieut-Colonel.
1886–88. Governor of Suakin. Wounded at Handub.
1888. April 11. Colonel.
1888–92. Adjutant-General, Egyptian Army.
1892–98. Sirdar of the Egyptian Army.
1896. Commanding Dongola Expedition. Battle of Firket.
1896. Sept. 25. Major-General.
1898. April 8. Battle of the Atbara.
1898. Sept. 2. Battle of Omdurman.
1898. Sept. To Fashoda.
1898. Created Baron, of Khartoum and Aspall, G.C.B.
1899. Dec. 23. Lieutenant-General.
1899–1902. South African War.
1900. Feb. 18. Battle of Paardeberg.
1900. Oct. Commander-in-Chief, South Africa.
1902. May 31. Signed Peace at Pretoria.
1902. June 1. General. Order of Merit. Created Viscount. G.C.M.G.
1902–09. Commander-in-Chief in India.
1909. Sept. 10. Field-Marshal. G.C.S.I.
1909–10. Tour of China, Japan, Australia, New Zealand.
1911. K.P.
1911–14. H.M.'s Agent and Consul-General, Egypt.

1914. Aug. 6. Secretary of State for War. P.C. Created Earl Kitchener of Khartoum, Viscount Broome, Baron Denton.
1915. K.G.
1916. June 5. Lost at sea in H.M.S. *Hampshire*.

CONTENTS

PART I EGYPT — 1
- I THE SUBALTERN — 3
- II ENGLAND IN EGYPT — 11
- III GORDON — 20
- IV 1886–1892 — 42
- V THE SIRDAR — 50
- VI THE ATBARA AND OMDURMAN — 62
- VII FASHODA — 79

PART II SOUTH AFRICA — 83
- VIII THE TANGLED MESS — 85
- IX PAARDEBERG — 100
- X PRETORIA — 118
- XI COMMANDER-IN-CHIEF — 128

PART III INDIA — 149
- XII REFORMS — 151
- XIII THE NORTH-WEST FRONTIER — 163
- XIV THE QUARREL WITH CURZON — 172
- XV ROUTINE — 186

PART IV THE WAR OFFICE — 195
- XVI SECRETARY OF STATE — 197
- XVII EXPANSION — 210
- XVIII THE OPENING MOVES — 218
- XIX THE PARIS INTERVIEW — 239
- XX THE MARNE — 248
- XXI THE RIFT WITH G.H.Q. — 255
- XXII GALLIPOLI — 268
- XXIII SHELLS — 284
- XXIV SALONIKA — 302
- XXV THE WINTER OF 1915–1916 — 319
- XXVI THE LOSS OF H.M.S. "HAMPSHIRE" — 331

LIST OF SKETCH MAPS

Only those places are marked which are mentioned in the text.

1	EGYPT	page 10
2	THE SUDAN	28
3	THE ATBARA	68
4	OMDURMAN	72
5	SOUTH AFRICA	86
6	THE MARCH TO PAARDEBERG	102
7	PAARDEBERG	105
8	INDIA: THE DISTRIBUTION SCHEME	160
9	THE STRATEGIC DEPLOYMENT	220
10	THE RETREAT	230
11	AUGUST 23RD, 28TH, 30TH	236
12	THE EVE OF THE MARNE	251
13	THE TRENCH LINE	256
14	GALLIPOLI	269
15	BRITISH ATTACKS IN 1915	290
16	PART OF THE BALKANS	303
17	LOSS OF THE "HAMPSHIRE"	332

PART I

EGYPT

CHAPTER I

THE SUBALTERN

LORD KITCHENER left no memoirs. Sir George Arthur has compiled a full and careful record of his life; as private secretary and close friend this author had great opportunities for knowing what was in the mind of his chief; he had access to State papers and to valuable private correspondence. His volumes must stand as the official account. But they are very official, in the sense that Sir George was evidently determined not to insert anything which could not be verified by chapter and verse.

I have taken licence to go further afield—to the Officers' Mess and Club Smoking-Room in search of those who served under Kitchener. We mixed up facts and conjectures, likes and dislikes; opinions were sometimes highly coloured by personal feeling. Nevertheless such opinions have a real and distinct value of their own. If it is true that no man can be a hero to his valet, still less can a commander be a hero to his soldiers unless he has deserved that honour, and deserved it thoroughly. As a rule subordinates know what has happened in war, and sometimes why it happened; no self-advertising swashbuckler can throw dust in their eyes; they will not accept a retreat "according to plan" when the plan was something else. Their verdict is unsparing but generally very just.

From the earliest days Kitchener's life was strangely unlike that of the average British officer. No public school or cricket field; except for short periods no mess-room or garrison routine; no promotion examinations or Staff College. He was scarcely ever on parade and never attended manœuvres until he became a General.

It would be too much to say that this very solitary life

shaped his character, but there can be little doubt that it left its mark on his manners and habits. Many people thought him a bit of a prig. His closer friends warmly repudiate the suggestion and declare that on the contrary nobody was ever less priggish. I would agree with that opinion, but it is impossible to get away from the fact that he left that impression in some quarters. His inspection of a regiment was confined to business, a short and sharp investigation, some searching questions, remarks few and rarely complimentary. He refused to attend the usual inspection dinners; this rose from a determination not to increase the mess bills of impecunious subalterns—a very sound reason, but they did not appreciate it. The inspection dinner is a fine old army institution where talking shop cannot be allowed; over sherry and bitters the General begins to discuss polo ponies or a local race meeting; by the time the port has gone round he is telling his best stories, which are received with respectful applause; he sits down to the bridge table with the Captain whose company he has been cursing all the morning. In fact, he becomes human, and goes away having learnt a good deal about the inward parts of that very human body known as the British regiment —much more than he had learnt on the parade ground.

But Kitchener could not unbend. If he cared anything for personal popularity he certainly never stooped to court it. To him a regiment consisted of so many officers and men who ought to come up to certain standards. Even the best earned only mild approval. The worst provoked no violent language, but a burst of hot rage would have been less awful than his calm anger. Prowess in sport weighed nothing in the scale against a slack day's work or a big sick list, which was his chief abomination. Though cricket and regimental games were to be encouraged, it was only because they were good for the health of the men. He was fairly liberal about leave, but again only because it would benefit an officer to get away for some months of the hot weather; he took no interest in the subaltern's enjoyment of London town, and having no interest he would not feign any. It was a pity, for Kitchener and the

British subaltern might have learnt a good deal from each other; but between them there lay a great gulf which was very rarely crossed.

His father, Colonel Kitchener, served in the 13th Light Dragoons, and for a short period before retiring had exchanged into the 9th Foot. He held a reputation for a very violent temper and some strong prejudices. The family consisted of four children (three sons and one daughter), of whom the third was Horatio Herbert, born in Ireland, June 24, 1850.

In accordance with one of the Colonel's theories none of the boys went to public schools. The system of private tutors gives close individual attention and, from a purely academic point of view, may be the best means of working up knowledge. The pupil was brilliant at mathematics and mechanics; a couple of years in France and Switzerland added French and German. A short time with London crammers was sufficient to pass him into Woolwich Academy, which he joined as a cadet in 1868. It might have been expected that among his fellow cadets he would lose some of his reserve, but apparently this did not happen. He showed no enthusiasm for games, and riding was his only amusement.

A term was dropped through ill-health and he did not pass out till December 1870. Then came his first connexion with our future brothers-in-arms of France. Colonel Kitchener had settled at Dinan, and the young cadet went there to spend Christmas. During the autumn the German hordes had swept down from the eastern frontier; Woerth and Gravelotte had been fought in August: Metz was invested: the fatal 2nd of September brought about the fall of the Third Empire at Sedan, followed by the siege of Paris. Gambetta escaped from the beleaguered capital in a balloon and struggled to raise troops to keep up resistance. The Army of the Republic, under Chanzy and D'Aurelle de Paladines, was attempting a relief from the south and southwest.

Laval, the H.Q. of General Chanzy, was only about sixty miles from Dinan—and of course the English cadet wanted to see a bit of the fighting. With a companion called Dawson he made his way to Laval, to offer his services as a volunteer. But Kitchener got no further, for he caught a severe chill while ballooning and was invalided home.

Slight as this connexion with the French had been, it nevertheless remained a tie which was not forgotten when forty-four years later the Woolwich cadet had become a Field-Marshal and Secretary of State for War.

He was gazetted lieutenant in the Royal Engineers on January 4, 1871, and in accordance with the custom of his corps the young officer joined at Chatham. Practical work at the School of Military Engineering was thoroughly congenial, and it certainly formed the finest training which the future Sirdar could have found—practical instruction in railways, bridging, building, and all the technical side of his work. But outside this the routine of barrack life was a bore, and soon after he had been posted to a Mounted Troop at Aldershot he applied for an appointment in the Near East.

A Woolwich friend, by name Conder, was employed on a survey of the Holy Land, under the auspices of the Palestine Exploration Fund, a Society which was interested in history, geology, and archæology. Conder knew Kitchener's tastes and qualifications and put his name before the Society; as the War Office made no objection the young Sapper found himself in the Near East at the end of 1874. So for the next eight years we find him chiefly occupied in mapmaking, first in Palestine and later in Cyprus. At first he was in close company with Conder, commander of the little survey camp which moved from point to point.

Kitchener's religious convictions, like his other strong emotions, lay deep beneath the surface; we cannot know how far they were stirred by visions of the Holy Land. But apart from that there was another and obvious interest in those years of toil. Knowledge of the country folk and their languages, Arabic and Turkish, was to be later of even more practical value to the Sirdar than his training as an engineer. Here in the outlying villages he saw fanaticism of the Moslems, tyranny of rulers, ignorance of peasants, deep-rooted traditions, all of which tended to obstruct even the simplest efforts at justice or reform or sanitation. Familiarity with these things tempered the white heat of the reformer with the patience of a far-seeing administrator. Malaria in himself, cholera in other people, and an attack by fanatics on the survey camp were other experiences. In the attack Conder was wounded, and after the two had returned to London to prepare the map for printing he was still too unwell to resume work in the East. Thus when Kitchener went back to Palestine in January 1877 he was in command. Though it was not a big command there were many points which called for careful organization and even diplomacy. Turkey was at war with Russia, the Crescent with the Cross of St. Andrew; the small camp of the white man contained feeble means of defence against a rush, and a false step in dealing with the local Moslems might have led to disaster. But he found that the Arabs of Palestine had very little love for their Turkish rulers, and they remained quiet, except when fighting among themselves.

Having finished the survey in October 1877, Kitchener visited Constantinople on his way back to England. Several months were required to complete the map and reports, which were finally handed over in September 1878.

Affairs in the Near East had resulted in England taking over the administration of Cyprus, and Sir Garnet Wolseley was appointed High Commissioner. By this time the ability of Lieutenant Kitchener as a surveyor and linguist had been recognized, and when the Foreign Office wanted a map of the island it was natural that application should be made for the services of the young expert, who was sent to Cyprus in September 1878. The expert insisted that his map should be compiled in accordance with the correct procedure of Chatham, with base line and trigonometrical points. What the

High Commissioner wanted was a batch of rough sketches of the various villages; this would be cheaper, quicker, and of more immediate and practical value for purposes of administration. Kitchener appealed to the Foreign Office, which upheld him, but the High Commissioner shut down the whole thing on the score of expense. It was a curious little difference between the youthful lieutenant and his chief, and it brings out the fact that the junior was already given to forming strong views which he was not prepared to give up.

The work was stopped, but the expert linguist clung to the Near East and got a job as Vice-Consul in Kastanuni, a province of Anatolia lying on the south shore of the Black Sea, a hundred miles east of Constantinople.

The population of Kastanuni was a mixture of Turks, Greeks, Armenians, Circassians, Jews, the strength of each nationality varying according to the results of massacres and assassinations. Even if the Vice-Consul had possessed supreme powers it would have puzzled him to reduce this mob to order; Turkish Governors solved the problem by doing nothing except extorting bribes and blackmail. At its worst Turkish rule, or mis-rule, is an appalling iniquity, and the extraordinary thing is that after centuries of it there is still any population left to suffer. Like other British officers who have been in Turkey, Kitchener wrote a report which "was read with much interest" in the Foreign Office.

A new High Commissioner in Cyprus, Colonel Biddulph, re-started the survey of the island and called for the expert's return. In the spring of 1880 he was back, with permission to make a map in his own way. Cyprus does not fill up much room in our atlas, a blob of mountains in the Mediterranean, a hundred miles in length and barely fifty across; but it took three years to complete the survey.

Eight years take a big slice out of a young officer's career. Unless on active service the average subaltern spends that period in stumbling along the straight and narrow path of regimental duty. An invitation to appear before the Colonel sends him to the Orderly Room wondering which of his sins have been found out: he accepts the daily reprimand with the light-heartedness of irresponsible youth. His only interest in finance concerns a private overdraft: he dreams of his next leave, of backing a winner, of somebody else's sister. When active service comes along he is a first-rate regimental officer. Kitchener missed the nursery stage. At twenty-six he was running his own little camp, sometimes in places which no white man had ever visited before. He looked on discipline from the point of view not of the slave but of the taskmaster. At thirty he was appealing to Downing Street against the decision of his own chief. Organization, finance, diplomacy, were serious responsibilities. In those days there were no social amusements, and a little rough shooting was the only form of sport. He rarely spoke except to issue orders; there was no one of equal standing with whom plans or views could be discussed; silence grew into a habit. Convictions came from inside and scarcely ever depended upon the opinions of other people. He was saved from boredom by the intense joy he took in his work. Heaven knows what he was dreaming about.

CHAPTER II

ENGLAND IN EGYPT

THE BRITISH occupation of Egypt began in 1882, and before ten years had passed a bankrupt State was transformed into one of considerable prosperity. The steps which led up to the occupation were founded on a mixture of finance, misgovernment, oppression. To describe them in any detail would be impossible, but even a brief outline will be helpful towards an understanding of the great works which were afterwards carried through by Kitchener.

Since the days of the Pharaohs, and presumably for some ages before them, the Nile has risen and fallen with wonderful regularity, bringing from the mountains of Central Africa the water and silt on which life depends. The original mouth of the river had been silted up and consequently the current spread into many channels and formed the rich Delta lying on the triangle between Cairo, Alexandria, and Port Said; each side of this Delta is just over a hundred miles in length. A system of canals distributed and regulated the water supply. A thousand miles south of Cairo lies Khartoum, at the junction of the Blue and White Niles. South of Khartoum the country is something like an inverted Delta, formed by the many tributaries flowing down from Abyssinia on the south-east and the Equatorial Mountains. Between Cairo and Khartoum is practically a desert except where the Nile traces a ribbon of green through the yellow sand.

Until the middle of the nineteenth century the Egyptians had been content with crops of grain. Then, however, it was discovered that cotton and sugar cane could be grown on the fertile soil to an enormous value, which opened prospects of boundless wealth. On the strength of this the Khedive,

Ismail, and his Pashas plunged into an orgy of extravagance, which attracted the attention of European financiers and speculators. These gentlemen soon turned the stream of wealth into their own pockets. Few Orientals can resist borrowing as long as anyone will lend, and there is plenty of money to be lent when interest is high. Between 1850 and 1875 the National Debt rose from £4,000,000 to £100,000,000; the nominal rate of interest was about six to nine per cent, but as the issue had been made at a discount the creditors were actually receiving eight per cent and often more. Up to 1875 the interest was found by the simple method of leaving other debts in arrear. This started the grievance of Pashas and officers, who, receiving no pay, were forced to extract means of subsistence from their inferiors; the system spread and the grievance became general. Worse still, in 1876 it became evident that the taxation would not suffice to pay the interest on bonds, and therefore the financiers had a grievance of their own. Through the money markets of London and Paris pressure was put on the Governments of England and France, who insisted on appointing various Commissions to control the Egyptian budgets. These Commissions soon made themselves thoroughly unpopular by their investigations. They found that the bigger landowners, from the Khedive downwards, were exempt from taxation; that while the officials who did hard work got no pay, there were many who did nothing and drew high salaries; that a large percentage of the taxes never reached the Treasury; that the poorer classes were already taxed into a state of starvation. All of this had been known for some time and had been accepted as the normal condition of government. But when foreigners suggested reform, the traditions of centuries and the patriotism of Egypt were called forth to resist. The Nationalist Party raised the cry of "Egypt for the Egyptians," which would have been all right if the Egyptians had not already sold their birthright to the usurers. Encouraged by the Nationalists, the Khedive Ismail dismissed some of the foreign advisers, and matters were brought to a head in 1879 by a public outbreak in Cairo.

England and France thereupon stepped in and insisted that the Sultan, whose empire still extended over Egypt, should depose Ismail and install Tewfik, Ismail's eldest son, in his place. The new Khedive, a youth of mild temper and pleasant manners, had just sufficient education to see that reform might eventually be profitable, but he had not the energy or power to put it into force. The Nationalists continued their agitation, and in November 1881 a military revolt broke out. A Colonel of the Army, Arabi Pasha, took the lead and became virtual ruler of the country. Most of the foreigners fled to Alexandria, and warships of several nations anchored in the harbour of that town to protect their subjects. Tewfik himself found it necessary to leave his capital and take up residence at Ramleh.

Arabi had little difficulty in attracting followers. The foreigners were not popular; it was commonly said that all Europeans who came to Egypt were "voleurs" except one—Gordon—and he was "fou." Pashas and landowners hoped that the expulsion of foreign control would leave them free to amass fresh debts; peasants who, in imitation of their betters, had borrowed from Greek moneylenders, were equally hopeful; the Army and officials were told that the pay which was due to them had been seized by the rapacious Europeans; and, needless to say, the Moslem religious leaders were violently opposed to the infidel dogs. "Egypt for the Egyptians," when translated into plain language, meant that all debts would be cancelled—an attractive program for a nation of debtors. The Powers called on the Sultan to intervene, and there were several conferences which resulted in nothing. It was quite obvious that nothing could be done except by force, and preparations were made for sending troops from England. Our Government expected that the French, whose financial interests were the same as our own, would join in taking action. But, as the French Chamber refused to vote any money for an expedition, the British had to act alone. Though at the time some complaints were heard that we were pulling chestnuts out of the fire for the benefit of the Paris Bourse, the refusal of the French to take part afterwards simplified matters very much, for it meant that England could carry out the occupation of Egypt without interference.

Arabi sent a considerable force to Alexandria and began to improve the fortifications. The British Admiral, Sir Beauchamp Seymour, warned him to stop. When this warning had been repeated without effect the British Fleet bombarded the Forts on July 11, and afterwards took possession of the town. Arabi withdrew his forces sixteen miles along the railway towards Cairo and there entrenched himself in a strong position.

General Sir Garnet Wolseley and four brigades of British troops arrived in Alexandria during the course of August. Some small demonstrations were made towards Arabi's force. Then three brigades were put back on their transports and moved round to Ismailia, which lies just half-way along the Suez Canal. The move was completed by August 19. From this point a railway runs to Cairo, and as Sir Garnet had very little transport it was all-important to move along a line of rail. A mixed Division arrived from India, which brought the total strength up to 12,000 infantry, 3,000 cavalry, and 60 guns.

At Tel-el-Kebir, 25 miles from Ismailia, the Egyptians had built a very strong line of earthworks, four miles long, covering the station and extending far into the desert on each side. Their strength has been estimated at 20,000 regulars and a force of Bedouins. Wolseley pushed forward and formed a camp about six miles from Tel-el-Kebir. There he halted for some days in order to accumulate a store of supplies. On the evening of September 12, the whole force moved out and made a night march which brought them to the position just before dawn.

The surprise was complete. One rush carried the first line of entrenchments, and though isolated bodies afterwards

ENGLAND IN EGYPT

made some resistance, the Egyptian Army and Arabi hurried to get away. General Drury Lowe and the cavalry made a fine march to reach Cairo the next day. The city was occupied without resistance; Arabi surrendered and was sentenced to exile; the Egyptians disbanded themselves.

The little campaign of 1882 has been thrown into insignificance by great wars; at Tel-el-Kebir our total casualties amounted to 84 killed, 342 wounded; but though the battle ranks as a small affair it started a new page in history. The British occupation had become an accomplished fact.

The form of government which was now installed had to make allowances for various interests. It recognized the Sultan as Suzerain, and the Khedive as his Viceroy. Tewfik returned to Cairo in state, Nubar Pasha became Prime Minister, and a Cabinet was formed consisting entirely of Egyptian-born Ministers; all orders were issued over their seals. But some half a dozen Englishmen were to act as "advisers," and there was an army to see that their advice was taken. For all practical purposes Sir Evelyn Baring, who arrived in September 1883, was ruler of the country; and he served out reforms with a firm and not always a kindly hand. The Pashas wriggled uneasily and even some of his British colleagues, whilst admiring his courage, thought him rough in procedure. Lady Strangford is believed to have been the author of the following epigram:

> "The virtues of Patience are known;
> But, I fear, when it comes to the touch
> In Egypt they'll find, with a groan,
> There's an *Evil in Bearing* too much."

Scott-Moncrieff took over the very important branch of Public Works, and the following extract from his own reminiscences is illuminating:

"Nubar on taking office sent for Vincent, Lloyd, and myself. He explained to us that the Ministers, heads of departments, must be Egyptian subjects. It was against the policy of the British Government to appoint us three as actual Ministers. Then he said he wished to speak to us each separately. What he said to Vincent and Lloyd I do not know, but his conversation with me was something as follows. After repeating that he could not make me Minister of Public Works, and that he must put in a native, he said, "Voulez-vous avoir un homme capable, ou une nullité?" "Une nullité, s'il vous plait, Excellence," I replied. "Ah, mon cher, vous avez raison, vous avez raison, je vous chercherai une nullité." And he was as good as his word, and appointed a very nice old fellow—Rushdi Pasha—to be my nominal chief."[1]

Such was the system in every Government Department. Administration was carried out by Sir Evelyn Baring as British Agent, Vincent in finance, Scott-Moncrieff in Public Works; also by General Sir Evelyn Wood, who, as Sirdar, began to raise a new Egyptian Army. The little band of British reformers had much opposition to contend with. Bondholders still insisted on their pound of flesh and were backed by the French, who now regretted their refusal to assist in suppressing Arabi's rebellion. From having been comrades they became critics. This restricted expenditure even where it was most required. Further difficulties arose through the attitude of Downing Street. Mr. Gladstone had more than once declared that the occupation was a temporary measure to restore order, after which troops and officials would be recalled; the consequence of this declaration was a state of uncertainty. If his intentions were carried out the Nationalists might again be in power; therefore even the most enlightened Egyptians, for their personal interests, were careful to keep a footing in the Nationalist camp and to avoid giving countenance to foreign reforms. Fortunately, however, quick successes in irrigation smoothed the way to peace.

Scott-Moncrieff, a Colonel of Royal Engineers, had for six years been in charge of the great Ganges Canal. He

[1] Scott-Moncrieff, p. 176.

ENGLAND IN EGYPT

knew all there was to be known, and perhaps more, about irrigation. Attention was first turned to the great Barrage. This work spans the two arms of the Nile a few miles below Cairo. It had been started in 1843 by Mehemel Ali, a really able Khedive: the construction was entrusted to a French engineer, Mougel Bey: it cost £1,800,000 besides the unpaid labour of the annual *"corvées."* The huge work was completed in 1863, but several cracks appeared and no money was procurable for repairs; in 1867 the whole thing was abandoned as derelict. Still there remained the framework of valuable masonry. At the small expenditure of £26,000 some patchwork was done in 1884 which raised the water level by seven feet and brought an increase of over a million sterling in the cotton crop. This astounding result put Scott-Moncrieff in a very strong position. The merchants of Cairo and Alexandria were now his fervent supporters; even the French relaxed some of their jealousy. In spite of the low state of the Treasury, Baring managed to extort a million sterling, which was made over to Scott-Moncrieff for further improvements. Temporary patchwork was replaced by permanent repair, and in 1890 the restoration was complete, bringing in an annual increase of two and a half million in cotton. When the Nile is at its lowest there is still ample water for all purposes. The success of the Barrage encouraged the engineers to construct another great dam at Assuan —this, however, was much later and did not reach completion until 1900.

Besides the Barrage, other important works were taken in hand. Four British engineers were brought over from India and began a personal inspection of canals and the system of working them. Scott-Moncrieff says:

"My old friend Rushdi Pasha said he supposed I would have these four gentlemen with their headquarters in Cairo, and that I would send them out *en mission.* I said, "No, these officers (who were called Inspectors) should live in the native towns and villages and not come often to Cairo." This the Pasha did not like. It would pour light into tracts where they preferred darkness. "C'est une révolution que vous proposez." "Justement, Excellence, c'est une révolution," and I had added that, if my officers were not allowed to live out among the villages, we would all go back to India."[1]

The Revolution soon revealed that the system was wasteful of water, of labour, and of human life. Work on the canals and dams was being carried out by a simple system of forced labour. About 85,000 men were employed, each for 160 days, chiefly in removing silt from the canals. They were underpaid, underfed, underlodged; they supplied their own tools. The sheik of each village was responsible for collecting his quota of the working party and, unless he could be bribed, did so with enthusiasm. The tenants of wealthy landowners were excused from the *corvée*, but their lands were enriched by the labour of the poor and unprotected peasants. The system was, of course, iniquitous, and Scott-Moncrieff, who was a practical humanitarian, saw that the abolition of the *corvée* would not only relieve the poor but also, by judicious engineering, enrich the whole country. This was the revolution which he and his assistants carried through.

By payment of six shillings the peasant was allowed to escape the *corvée* and thus had something like 160 days to devote to his own patch. The money thus collected was spent on dredgers which removed the silt much better and more quickly than the thousands of toilers. The success of the first dredgers was as complete as that of the Barrage. Nubar Pasha asked what sum would be required to do all the work formerly done by *corvée;* the estimate was £400,000 a year. This sum was eventually found, and Scott-Moncrieff was able to write:

"So the Egyptian *corvée* was killed, never, I trust to revive. I wish I could say that I was sure that the *corvée*

[1] Scott-Moncrieff, p. 177.

is dead for ever. Were the strong hand of England removed from the Nile Valley I do not like to think what abuses might not spring to life." [1]

These last words deserve to be underlined.

By 1887 Egypt was solvent and the budget began to show a surplus which brought smiles to all faces.

Apart from their new financial prosperity, the Egyptians began to regard their new rulers with a mixture of fear and respect. The British Engineer listened to complaints from the humblest fellah on the Nile bank. If justice were rough and ready it did not extort bribes nor apply torture. For the first time in history the peasants felt something like confidence; this had a considerable bearing on the work which afterwards fell upon Kitchener's shoulders.

[1] Scott-Moncrieff, p. 197.

CHAPTER III

GORDON

WHILE the Revolution was running its peaceful course in Egypt the Sudan had been the scene of a tragedy. "Sudan" means the "country of the Blacks." The natives were in every way different from their Egyptian rulers whom they hated with good reason. They were the blackest of negroes, utterly barbaric, war-like, without organization or fire-arms. Various tribes inhabited the great Province, which spreads southwards from Khartoum, and were constantly at war with each other. The Government at Cairo had not interfered to suppress this natural instinct, but maintained a few garrisons scattered over the country to enforce the collection of revenue.

The Province was wealthy; grass uplands provided pasture for herds of camels and cattle; ivory, gum, and ostrich feathers were exported by traders, who absorbed most of the wealth. An influx of pure Arabs had also been attracted by the rich harvest which could be gathered from the slave trade; superior cunning and a few rifles soon gave them power over the barbaric Sudanese. Thus the country was populated by negroes under the tyrannical rule of slave-trading Emirs, who in their turn were under the loose and corrupt dominion of Cairo.

In 1881 a young Dervish, by name Mahommed Ahmed, began to collect a following. He came from a family of boat builders at Dongola. Wingate [1] says that until he gave way to luxury and sensualism he was a clear thinker of apparently austere habits, with marvellous powers of language, to which was added a mystic personal magnetism. He appealed

---

[1] Wingate, p. 14.

to the fanaticism of the tribes and to their hatred of
the Turks, by which name they knew their Egyptian rulers.
Aided (as was alleged) by the miraculous intervention of
the Prophet the new leader gained some minor successes
over the small garrisons in the south; these gave him a few
rifles and added much to his prestige. He assumed the title of
"Mahdi," the promised successor of the Prophet, the liberator of the Sudan. Many tribes of the south joined or were
forced to join his standard for the Holy War.

In 1883 the Rebellion had reached such proportions that
the Egyptian Government determined to send a strong force
to subdue it. Though the British Government would lend
no help, the Khedive was allowed to do what he could to subdue his own subjects. In September Hicks Pasha, an ex-officer of the Indian Army, started southwards from Khartoum with a force of 8,000 men. As no lines of communication
could be maintained, supplies for fifty days were carried
with the column when it left the Nile and marched westwards towards El-Obeid. Water failed; many died of thirst;
and the remainder were cut to pieces on November 5. A
huge quantity of arms, ammunition, and supplies fell into
the hands of the Mahdi.

The Cairo Government, alarmed lest the rebels should
now be strong enough to invade Egypt, wished to send
another expedition to repair the disaster. But Gladstone,
already pledged to evacuation, would not hear of anything
that might commit us to further action, and insisted that
all the remaining garrisons, including the main body at
Khartoum, should be withdrawn. In January 1884, Lord
Wolseley recommended that Colonel Charles Gordon should
be sent out to arrange the evacuation. Gordon had an interview with the Cabinet on the 18th and started for Cairo
the same evening.

The tragic fate of Charles Gordon established his fame
as a martyr to his sense of loyalty and humanity. But even
before this time he had won a reputation for courage,
originality, and a mastery of other men. As such men

often do, he sometimes went beyond the instructions received from higher authority. He had served with distinction as Sebastopol. In 1863 he commanded a very irregular force in China, and in a campaign of various adventures stamped out the Taiping Rebellion. After a spell of duty as C.R.E. at Gravesend, he went to Constantinople on a commission to improve the navigation of the Danube. While there he was offered an appointment as Governor of the Equatorial Provinces of the Sudan. For six years he lived among the tribes, struggling chiefly to suppress the slave trade. Though the Khedive gave him some support, his policy was not popular with the Pashas of Cairo, and when Ismail was removed Gordon resigned.

One of his many adventures must be recorded. A powerful group of slave traders under a leader called Suleiman raised a standard of revolt. Gordon mounted a camel and rode alone 85 miles across the desert to the rebel camp. His sudden appearance and air of authority over-awed the Dervishes; at his command they dispersed and the Governor returned to Khartoum. It was a real triumph, but perhaps led Gordon to over-estimate his personal power. Later on Suleiman collected a new following, while Gordon was absent in Cairo; an Italian called Gessi crushed this revolt; Suleiman was forced to surrender and suffered death as a rebel.

After returning from the Sudan Gordon was employed in various ways and spent the year 1883 in Palestine. He had undertaken to go to the Congo in the service of King Leopold of Belgium, when the British Government asked him to return to the Sudan. Baring had been consulted, and his opinion is on record.

"The main fact was this—after the defeat of General Hicks's army the Sudan was lost to Egypt beyond any hope of recovery unless some external aid could be obtained to effect its reconquest." [1] "I consider myself largely responsible for initiating the policy of withdrawal." [1]

[1] Cromer, I, pp. 374, 386 and 390.

And Gordon himself wrote a Memorandum in which he shows that at first he shared this opinion—"The Sudan is a useless possession, ever was so, and ever will be so. . . . I think the Government are fully justified in recommending evacuation."

We can now go back to the young surveyor completing his map of Cyprus. On just one point his feelings were those of the normal British subaltern—he was consumed with desire for active service. For some time it had been evident that the Nationalist movement under Arabi would burst into flame, and Kitchener managed to escape from his work on a week's leave which was cleverly timed to fit in with the bombardment of Alexandria. But as he was not on duty with the British forces he could not get permission to join the landing-party. There can be little doubt that he expected the authorities at Alexandria to insist on retaining him; his services as a Sapper or with the Intelligence would have been of real value. Sir Beauchamp Seymour actually wired to Cyprus asking for an extension of the leave. But the High Commissioner had got his back up; when granting leave he had no idea that his surveyor was off to Alexandria, and therefore he flatly refused any extension. By missing the boat by which he ought to have returned, Kitchener granted himself an extra week, after which he reluctantly came back to Cyprus and accepted with bad grace the official reproof. The High Commissioner did not consider that zeal for active service constituted an excuse for absence without leave.

For some time relations seem to have been strained, and Kitchener was held to his work in Cyprus. This was unfortunate, for Wolseley would have been glad to have the Arabic expert for his Tel-el-Kebir campaign. By the end of 1882, the campaign was over, and Sir Evelyn Wood, as first Sirdar, began to raise a new Egyptian Army under a select band of British officers. He telegraphed to Kitchener asking him to come as second-in-command of the

Cavalry. There was no likelihood of further operations, and even if any such operations developed, the raw untrained Egyptian Cavalry would not have any share in them. The Sirdar's offer was accepted, but without enthusiasm. The Cavalry consisted of a single regiment, and the prospect was one of routine work in stables and riding-school, imparting elementary instruction to unsoldierly recruits.

After the suppression of Arabi, social life in Cairo was resuming its normal course. The former inhabitants turned to look after their affairs and were followed by a cosmopolitan crowd of financiers, merchants, hotel-keepers, and tourists. Diplomatists of all nations vied with each other in dispensing hospitality. British troops guaranteed security: British officers guaranteed racing, polo, dancing and club-life.

But the Cavalry "Bimbashi" seems to have busied himself with the recruits at their quarters outside the capital. A prominent civilian who frequented the club and race-course throughout 1883 says he never heard the name of Kitchener till a year later. In November, a couple of months' leave was due, and as Kitchener had not been in England for nearly five years it might have been expected that he would hurry homewards. But a geologist, Professor Hull, was starting on an expedition through the Sinai Peninsula, and easily induced the enthusiastic explorer to join him. They crossed the desert from Suez to Akaba, and then turned northwards to the Dead Sea. There news came in of the disaster to Hicks Pasha, and Kitchener immediately hastened back to Egypt. He arrived in Cairo a month before Gordon passed through.

Gordon, with Colonel Stewart, reached Khartoum on February 18. The only other Englishman there was Mr. Power, Vice-Consul and correspondent of *The Times*. The garrison consisted of 8,000 Egyptian troops of the worst possible quality.

On March 16 Gordon ventured to fight. His men fled like hares before the Dervishes;[1] of the survivors two Egyptian commanding officers were tried for cowardice and shot.

From this moment it was evident that the danger was more serious than Gordon had supposed. With the garrison and some river steamers he might perhaps have made his way to safety, but there were other garrisons further south whose fate was sealed. There was also a crowd of nominal Christians, Levantine traders, and shop-keepers, with wives and families; it was impossible to get them all away, especially at the time of year when the Nile was low. Gordon was now faced with a big question: whether to obey the orders of his Government (which he understood quite well) by cutting his losses and escaping with as many as he could, or to obey the impulse of humanity by hanging on in the hope of relief. An attempt to answer this question would carry me out of my depth, but to a man of Gordon's character there could be only one answer—if indeed the question ever arose in his mind. He made such preparations as were possible for a siege, and sent messages calling for relief, messages which became more violent as the danger increased. The wretched inhabitants trusted the British commander, and he could not desert even the meanest of them. This was the loyalty for which Gordon laid down his life.

But even those who are most fervent in worship of this heroism cannot argue that he was judicious in his attempts to convert the Government to his views. He had gone out pledged to evacuation and confident that he could carry it through; without his own assurances on this point the Government would never have entrusted him with the mission. On arrival at Khartoum it turned out that evacuation was impossible. If he had admitted an error in judging the situation, if he had telegraphed a report, with reasonable suggestions, if he had asked for fresh instructions, no blame

[1] Wingate, p. 110.

could have been thrown upon him, and the suggestions must have been received with consideration. Instead of this he flung out a string of commands and threats; he bombarded Baring with telegrams: and when his views did not meet with immediate acceptance he washed his hands of all responsibility. "I will consider myself free to act according to circumstances"—"The Government will be branded with indelible disgrace." [1]

This was not the best way to attract sympathy or support, and some of the suggestions were too startling for the stately calm of Downing Street. For instance, he proposed that a certain Zobeir Pasha should be sent to assist him, and this was certainly enough to awaken astonishment. Zobeir had been one of the rebels of the southern Sudan against whom Gordon struggled for years—"the greatest slave-hunter who ever existed." He was the father of Suleiman who had been captured and shot by Gessi, Gordon's lieutenant. He had been enticed to Cairo on some pretext and was detained there as a semi-prisoner on very easy terms; he had wealth and influence. It seems that Gordon realized that he himself could not restore order in the Sudan, and an inspiration seized him that Zobeir would be a lesser evil than the Mahdi. He issued a proclamation rescinding his previous orders against slavery, and demanded that the old slave-trader should be sent to Khartoum. Worse still he allowed Power to communicate all this to *The Times*. The British and Foreign Anti-Slavery Society was shocked. The Cabinet could not possibly assent to the proposal.

The next proposal was that a meeting should be arranged with the Mahdi. Gordon had an utter contempt for the Egyptian rulers, and this brought him into a degree of sympathy with the rebels. He was very willing to carry out the orders of Downing Street and abandon the province to the Dervishes, if only some guarantee could be found for the safety of fellow Christians. He believed that by virtue of his former prestige he might again impose his will in a personal

[1] Cromer, I, p. 455.

meeting. Baring, anxious to avoid the commitments which Gordon's opportunism might create, firmly put his foot on this proposal. It was after this refusal that the last wire was received—"I will consider myself free to act according to circumstances."

Gladstone declared fiercely in the House of Commons that Gordon was trying to force the hand of the Government and that the Government would not be forced until independent opinion had been consulted. It must be remembered that rebellion in the Sudan was nothing of a novelty; on the contrary from time to time immemorial it had been the normal state of politics. Rumours were often exaggerated and might be so in the present case. Furthermore, it must be remembered that Gordon had established a reputation for getting into trouble and out again. This reputation now served him badly. The situation certainly looked black, but after all he had been in worse. Even so good a judge as Scott-Moncrieff wrote from Cairo on August 10 when the siege had lasted four months:

"One bold spirit of our corps, Kitchener, with an escort of Bedouins has pressed on single-handed to Dongola and southwards, and if they would only let him I believe he would dash on to Khartoum. Generally there is not much anxiety about Gordon. He was known to be all right up to June 23, and, as one of his old Sudan officers said to me the other day, 'He is just as good a Mahdi as the other fellow.' No one, I think, will be surprised to find him quietly organizing a good government at Khartoum, and loyally served by the people." [1]

In London, however, a strong agitation was kept up in the Press. Gladstone maintained a firm front until the end of July; then some of his own colleagues threatened to resign unless troops were sent out as a relief expedition, and the Prime Minister gave way. In August Wolseley was appointed to the command and started for Egypt.

[1] Scott-Moncrieff, p. 184.

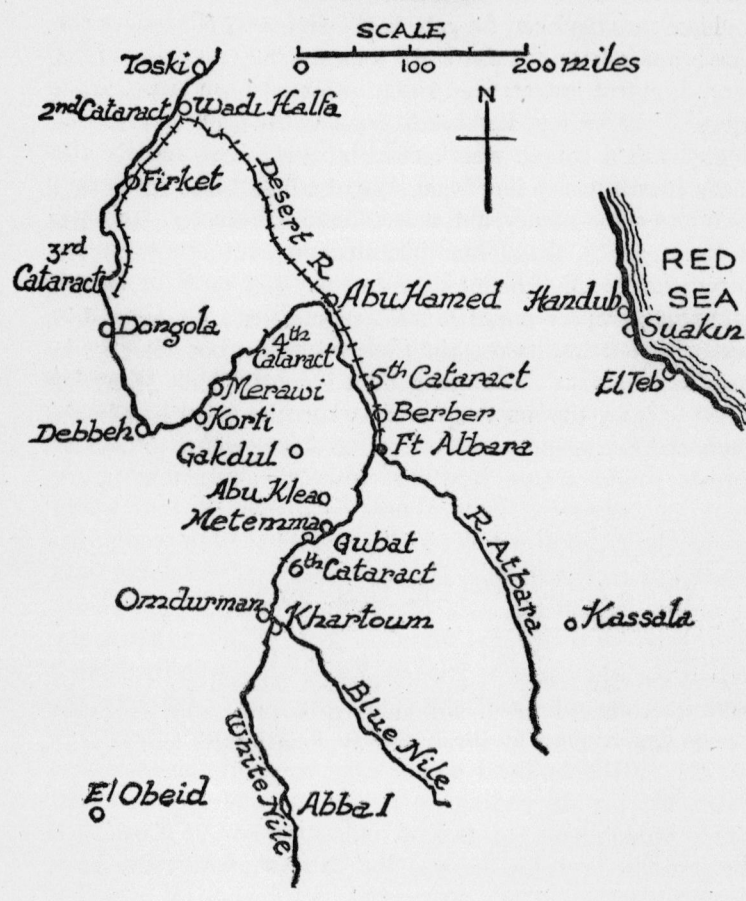

Kitchener had left Cairo before Gordon reached the Sudan. He can have known little of the attitude of Government or the strange proposals of their emissary. To him Gordon was a lonely brother officer in deadly peril, and if mortal man could have rescued him Kitchener would have done it. There could be no possibility of getting a relief force up before the Nile began to rise in July. Until then the only hope lay in the very doubtful assistance which might be obtained from tribes of the Valley. Kitchener grasped this fact and set out single-handed to see what could be done. Fortunately the authorities in Cairo had been impressed with his ability and gave him some money and a free hand. Character, training, and experience, fitted him magnificently for the task. He knew exactly the amount of deference that must be shown to the religious feeling of fanatical Dervishes; the allowance due to rooted traditions; the rank of each mudir and sheik, and the ceremony it demanded. At the same time he never failed to exact the respect due from them to a British officer. To keep the balance was no easy problem; harsh orders or threats would arouse hostility, while pleading might give them an impression of weakness; too many bribes would arouse the greed of worthless volunteers; too few would discourage useful partisans. He must approach them not as a humble suppliant but as a representative of a Great Power who asked for their loyal alliance. Above all it was necessary to find out who could be trusted. Emissaries from the Mahdi were busy on the other side. One false step might put the lonely Englishman at the mercy of a thousand rebels. For months Kitchener lived within easy reach of the assassin's spear, his life depending on his brains and moral power. There were plenty of British officers ready to face such dangers but probably he was the only one who could have survived them.

There were Egyptians in Cairo ready to give loyal co-operation had they felt assured that the British would remain in the country. But while Gladstone repeated his pledges about evacuation they feared to commit themselves—and they cannot be blamed. The same uncertainty was even more marked among the tribes who lived along the Valley. Though they knew nothing about the intention of the Cabinet in London they could see for themselves something of the situation. On the one side lay the Mahdi with a force which had overthrown Hicks Pasha; his troops could move across desert places impassable to white men; if he came as a conqueror there would be no mercy for those who had been in touch with the infidels and Turks. On the other side stood a single officer without even one regiment to enforce his wishes or to keep the Dervishes away. They had to weigh the threats of the Mahdi against the personality of Kitchener and English gold—after getting the gold they might be tempted or overawed into treachery.

While Gordon was reaching Khartoum, Kitchener began his first trek three hundred miles up the river, chiefly with the object of reporting on the road from Keneh to Kosseir on the Red Sea. He conceived the idea of enlisting a force of Bedouins. His own Egyptian cavalry were still too raw for work in the desert, but the Arabs knew no other home; they were mobile, carrying their own supplies and finding water for themselves. If only they could be trusted—

By the time Kitchener returned with his first report to Cairo the Sirdar was looking further forward. If a relief force were to start for Khartoum there were two lines by which it might advance: from Suakin over the desert to Berber, or up the river to Wadi Halfa and then thence across the loop to Abu Hamed, which would shorten the river route by 300 miles and avoid three bad cataracts. In either case Berber would be an important point and this was Kitchener's first objective when he started southwards for the second time in April. In company with Rundle he went as far as Assuan and then halted to form his troop of Bedouins. A thousand were collected, mounted on camels, and with these the two officers went on to Korosko in June. By this time news came in that Berber was already occupied by the

Mahdist forces; Khartoum was completely surrounded; tribes south of Korosko were in a state of terror.

Kitchener faced the situation without any illusions. He reported that the Mahdi's movement, far from being one of the usual disturbances, was on a big scale which would require 20,000 British troops for its suppression. In the meantime he was ordered to arrange messengers for keeping in touch with Gordon, and to examine the various routes towards Khartoum. Leaving Rundle and the main body of the new levies at Assuan he started off in Arab dress, with an escort of twenty trusted Bedouins, and reached Dongola on August 1.

Dongola was the headquarters of an important Mudir by name Mustafa Yawer, a Circassian. The Mahdi had sent messages offering to make him his Emir, but Mustafa protested his loyalty to Kitchener and at first made a favourable impression. In August definite news arrived that a British force would move up the river from Wadi. This declaration of course made a great deal of change in the work of the lonely Intelligence Officer. The coming of British forces had an effect on the tribes long before they were actually in sight. There was a definite object in making plans for the advance, and Kitchener with some of the Mudir's troops proceeded up the river. Forts were built or repaired to hold points along the Valley, providing safety against raids; the work was done by the Mudir's troops, who were found to be lazy, inefficient, and badly behaved. They were good enough, however, to repel a raid at Korti on September 10. After careful reconnaissance the road across the Bayuda Desert, from Korti to Metemma, was selected as the best for a further advance; by a march of 200 miles it avoids a big loop of 350 miles of river, including the dangerous Fourth and Fifth Cataracts.

Just at this time Gordon decided to send a steamer down the river with Colonel Stewart and European refugees. As soon as Kitchener had notice of this intention he sent a special messenger to catch Stewart at Berber, warning him that the tribes below that place were dangerous and advising that it would be better to leave the river and take the desert track to Korti. But this warning never reached the steamer and Stewart went on down the river to his death.

The first news of disaster reached Kitchener at Debbeh; he afterwards collected evidence and made out the report from which the following is an extract:

"Stewart's steamer came safely to the beginning of the Fourth Cataract—about 70 miles above Merawi—and there ran upon a rock below the island of Kanarett. The natives ran away at first, but were promised peace by Stewart and came back; they sent word to Suleiman Wad Gamr at Salamat, a village near. Unfortunately close to the spot where the steamer was wrecked a blind man named Etman lived: this man is a fanatical follower of the Mahdi and a principal adviser of Suleiman Wad Gamr. Suleiman came to his house at once on hearing the news and also collected his men together. He got hold of the rais, or pilot, of Stewart's steamer, a certain Mohammed (whom I know of and will catch), and found out that Stewart Pasha and the Consuls were on board. Suleiman and Etman promised the rais that if he would bring the white men unarmed to the house his life would be spared.

"Stewart spiked the gun on the steamer and threw some ammunition overboard; he then sent for camels to take him to Merawi. Camels were brought and the soldiers disembarked in a small boat with their luggage. Stewart then asked for the owner of the camels, Suleiman Wad Gamr, to come and be paid for them as far as Merawi; the camels were then being loaded. Suleiman sent back word that he was the chief of that district, and that if Stewart would come and take coffee with him he would be glad to receive him, and that he would then take half the price of the camels, the remainder to be paid on their safe arrival at Merawi.

"From the account of what occurred I believe the house of Etman was quite close to where the camels were being loaded, just across a small patch of cultivation and some trees. The durra was thick and high, so that any number of men could be hid. Stewart started with the Consuls to go to the house, the rais having recommended him to do so. As they were starting, Suleiman sent word that his family were afraid if they came armed and with soldiers; the soldiers were sent back and Stewart was the only one who had a small pistol or revolver. The Party consisted of four —Stewart, Power, the French Consul, and Hassan the interpreter, a telegraph clerk from Khartoum.

"They were well received by Suleiman and Etman, and had coffee and dates served. Suleiman then went out and his men almost immediately rushed in and filled the room, shouting "Surrender." Stewart said "What do you want? Is it my pistol? Take it. I surrender." When they had his pistol they began to cut down one of the Consuls. Stewart fought like a lion with his fists, trying to protect the Consuls. Hassan the interpreter caught hold of the blind man and used him as a shield; though severely wounded he escaped. The three Europeans were killed with swords in the small room at Etman's house.

"The party then sallied out and attacked the soldiers who were still loading the camels; they were surprised and attempted to get into the small boat, which was upset in the confusion; they were then killed as they came out of the water; only one or two Monasir were killed by the soldiers before the boat was upset."

Meanwhile our troops were making their way up the river. The Official Account says:

"Wolseley's expedition was a campaign less against men than against time. Had the British soldiers and Egyptian camels been able to subsist on sand and occasional water, or had the desert produced beef and biscuit, the Army might, in spite of its late start, have reached Khartoum in November." [1]

With the help of 350 Canadian voyageurs a fleet of river transports was hauled through the Cataracts and about

[1] Colvile, I, p. 61.

6,000 infantry made their way up to Korti; Headquarters were established at this place on December 16. Wolseley still intended to send the main body up the river, but information came in that the garrison of Khartoum was starving, so he decided to dispatch a mounted column across the desert to Metemma in hopes of effecting a quick relief. Colonel Herbert Stewart was appointed to the command and Kitchener went as Intelligence Officer.

From Korti to Metemma is 186 miles. The track lay through barren country; at Gakdul, half-way, were wells with a good supply of water; elsewhere there was nothing either to eat or drink. The chief difficulty, as often, lay in the matter of transport; Wolseley had a couple of thousand camels but, as there was practically no grazing, they were in poor condition.

On December 30 the Desert Column set out, about 1,500 strong, and Gakdul was reached on January 2. A halt was made while the transport camels were sent back to Korti for more supplies; Stewart and Kitchener went with them and the latter was ordered to remain at H.Q. when Stewart went back to resume the march. The Column reached Abu Klea on January 17 and fought a sharp action against 10,000 Dervishes before they could reach the wells at that place. On the 19th the Column approached the Nile at Gubat and had another fight in which Stewart was mortally wounded. Sir Charles Wilson then assumed command.

Gordon had sent four river steamers to meet the Column at this point, and in two of these Wilson embarked with a few men of the Sussex Regiment; they made their way to within sight of Khartoum at 11 A.M. on the 28th.[1] The steamers were fired on by forts at Omdurman. The flag on the Palace at Khartoum had been hauled down. Gordon was dead.

It was useless to press further forward, so Wilson turned back down the river; both his steamers were wrecked on the way but the troops were safely landed.

[1] Colvile, I, p. 35.

On receipt of the news of Stewart's death Wolseley decided to send up his Chief of Staff, Redvers Buller, to take command of the Desert Column, and Kitchener again went forward with him. As no more mounted troops were available the Royal Irish Regiment pluckily volunteered to make the march on foot. Leaving Korti on January 29 Buller reached Gubat on February 11 and found Wilson's column there. On the way news had been received that Khartoum had fallen.

Buller was anxious to maintain his position until the main body could arrive by the river route. But the information collected by Kitchener showed that the Mahdist forces were close at hand in overwhelming numbers. It was impossible to keep up communication with H.Q. and Buller had to act on the situation as he himself saw it. He could not afford to fight another battle because he would not have sufficient transport to move his wounded. He could not remain on the river for lack of supplies. With intense reluctance he issued orders for a retreat and the Desert Column started on the dangerous and tiring march back towards Korti. The enemy hung round and harassed the bivouac at Abu Klea. After that the chief difficulty was water along the stretch of 55 miles to Gakdul. When that point was reached the Dervishes had been shaken off and the Column made its way, unmolested but desperately weary, to the camp at Korti.

Meanwhile the River Column had worked its way through the difficult Fifth Cataract, fighting an action at Kirbekan in which General Earle was killed.

At first Wolseley hoped he would be able to continue the advance to Khartoum, and some contradictory orders were sent both to the Desert Column and to the main body on the river. But by February 24 it was evident that no further advance could be made until more transport was collected or until the river was rising. So all troops were ordered back to Korti.

Kitchener was detailed to examine such witnesses as could be found regarding the last days of Khartoum. His report, which was not completed till August, is given in full by Colvile: the following are the more important points in it:

"The last accurate information received about Khartoum is contained in General Gordon's Diary and dated December 14, 1884.

"The state of the town was then very critical, and General Gordon states 'the town may fall in ten days.'

"The town was then closely encircled by the rebels, who doubtless increased the intensity of their attack as they approached nearer and nearer to the works.

"The Mahdi was fully aware, from deserters, of the straits to which the garrison were reduced for want of food; and it was his intention that the town should fall into his hands without fighting, being obliged by famine to surrender.

"About January 6 General Gordon, seeing that the garrison were reduced to great want for food, and that existence for many of the inhabitants was almost impossible, issued a proclamation, offering to any of the inhabitants who liked, free permission to leave the town and go to the Mahdi. Great numbers availed themselves of this permission, and General Gordon wrote letters to the Mahdi requesting him to protect and feed these poor Muslim people as he had done for the last 9 months.

"It has been estimated that only about 14,000 remained in the town out of the total of 34,000 inhabitants, the number obtained by a census of the town in September.

"General Gordon kept heart in the garrison by proclamations announcing the near approach of the English relief expedition, and praising them for the resistance they had made, as well as by the example of his unshaken determination never to surrender the town to the rebels.

"About January 18, the rebel works having approached the south front, a sortie was made by the troops which led to desperate fighting; about 200 of the garrison were killed, and although large numbers of the rebels were said to have been slain, it does not appear that any great or permanent advantage was obtained by the besieged garrison. On the

GORDON

return of the troops to Khartoum, after this sortie, General Gordon personally addressed them, praising them for the splendid resistance they had made up to that time, and urging them still to do their utmost to hold out as relief was near; indeed that the English might arrive any day and all would then be well.

"The state of the garrison was then desperate from want of food, all the donkeys, dogs, cats, rats, &c., had been eaten; a small ration of rum was issued daily to the troops, and a sort of bread was made from pounded palm-tree fibres. Gordon held several councils of the leading inhabitants, and on one occasion had the town most rigorously searched for provisions—the result, however, was very poor, only yielding 4 ardebs of grain through the whole town; this was issued to the troops.

"Gordon continually visited the posts and personally encouraged the soldiers to stand firm; it was said during this period that he never slept. On January 20 the news of the defeat of the Mahdi's picked troops at Abu Klea created consternation in the Mahdi's camp. A council of the leaders was held, and it is said a considerable amount of resistance to the Mahdi's will, and want of discipline, was shown. On the 22nd the news of the arrival of the English on the Nile at Metemma, which was thought to have been taken, led the Mahdi to decide to make at once a desperate attack upon Khartoum, before reinforcements could enter the town. It is probable that next day the Mahdi sent letters to Farag Pasha, commanding the black troops, who had been previously in communication with him, offering terms for the surrender of the town and stating that the English had been defeated on the Nile. Rumours were also prevalent in Khartoum of the fighting at Abu Klea and the arrival of the English at Metemma.

"On the night of the 25th many of the famished troops left their posts on the fortifications in search of food in the town. Some of the troops were also too weak, from want of nourishment, to go to their posts. This state of things was known in the town and caused some alarm; many of the principal inhabitants armed themselves and their slaves, and went to the fortifications in place of the soldiers. This was not an unusual occurrence, only on this night more of the inhabitants went as volunteers than they had done on previous occasions.

"At about 3.30 a.m. on the morning of Monday the 26th a determined attack was made by the rebels on the south front.

"In my opinion, Khartoum fell from sudden assault when the garrison were too exhausted by privations to make proper resistance.

"Having entered the town, the rebels rushed through the streets, shouting and murdering everyone they met; thus increasing the panic and destroying any opposition.

"It is difficult, from the confused accounts, to make out exactly how General Gordon was killed. All the evidence tends to prove it happened at, or near, the palace, where his body was subsequently seen by several witnesses. It appears that there was one company of black troops in the palace when the rebels appeared, but I think this was after General Gordon had left the palace. The only account, by a person claiming to be an eye-witness, of the scene of General Gordon's death relates: 'On hearing the noise, I got my master's donkey and went with him to the palace; we met Gordon Pasha at the outer door of the palace. Mohammed Bey Mustafa, with my master, Ibrahim Bey Rushdi, and about 20 cavasses then went with Gordon towards the house of the Austrian Consul Hansell, near the church, when we met some rebels in an open place near the outer gate of the palace. Gordon Pasha was walking in front leading the party. The rebels fired a volley and Gordon was killed at once; nine of the cavasses, Ibrahim Bey Rushdi, and Mohammed Bey Mustafa were killed, the rest ran away.'

"A large number of witnesses state Gordon was killed near the gate of the palace, and various accounts have been related from hearsay of the exact manner in which he met his end. Several reliable witnesses saw, and recognized Gordon's body at the gate of the palace; one describes it as being dressed in light clothes.

"One apparently reliable witness relates that he saw the rebels cut off Gordon's head at the palace gate after the town was in their hands.

"The massacre in the town lasted some six hours and about 4,000 persons were killed.

"It has been stated that the Mahdi was angry when he heard of General Gordon's death; but though he may have simulated such a feeling on account of the black troops, there is very little doubt in my opinion that had he expressed the wish Gordon would not have been killed.

"The presence of Gordon as a prisoner in his camp would have been a source of great danger to the Mahdi, for the black troops from Kordofan and Khartoum all loved and venerated Gordon, and many other influential men knew him to be a wonderfully good man.

"The want of discipline in the Mahdi's camp made it dangerous for him to keep a man prisoner whom all the black troops liked better than himself, and in favour of whom, on a revulsion of feeling, a successful revolt might take place in his own camp. Moreover, if Gordon was dead, he calculated the English would retire and leave him in peace.

"The Mahdi had promised his followers as much gold and silver as they could carry when Khartoum fell, and immense disappointment was expressed at the failure to find the Government treasury.

"The memorable siege of Khartoum lasted 317 days and it is not too much to say that such a noble resistance was due to the indomitable resolution and resource of one Englishman.

"Never was a garrison so nearly rescued, never was a Commander so sincerely lamented."

The little detachment had sighted Khartoum about forty-eight hours after the tragedy. This led to an outcry in the Press, some of which was directed against Wilson. After the steamers had met him at Gubat he had waited four days before moving up-stream; even forty men of the Sussex Regiment would have been sufficient to put heart into the garrison; the dervishes would have recognized the smallest handful of white men as the vanguard of a big force. Surely something could have been done to save those fatal three days.

On the face of such meagre facts as were known the outcry was not unnatural. Those who are better informed have answered it by saying that the relief was too late not by two days but by two months. From the beginning of December the starving garrison had been at the mercy of the Mahdi. His men, who fought with real valour at Abu Klea, would not have been deterred from their prey even by the whole of the Desert Column. If the steamers had been able to move all the troops, nevertheless some must have been left at Gubat to guard the wounded and the transport; and even supposing that the whole of Wilson's force could have been transported to Khartoum it had no supplies, even for itself, much less for a large and starving garrison.

The blame must be cast not on the heroes of the Desert Column but on the indecision of Downing Street.

Though all troops had been brought back to Korti, Wolseley still hoped that he would be allowed to maintain them there and make an advance to Khartoum. It is significant to note that Kitchener was called on to draw up an appreciation of the situation—evidently he had been recognized as the best authority on all matters of intelligence.

His report is given in full by Colvile and is a model of clear thinking and sound deduction. Information tended to show that the Mahdi's power was on the wane, his troops were disappointed and insubordinate. If we retired from Dongola the possession of this rich province would add much to his prestige and resources. Buller, Wilson, and in fact all the officers, were of the same opinion. The British Government, however, insisted on retreat. The expedition had been sent out for one distinct object—to save Gordon and as many as possible of the Egyptian troops and foreigners. That object no longer existed, and the Government was not prepared to spend more life and money in recovering for the Khedive a province which had always been a source of trouble. Another reason for withdrawal was found in a scare of war with Russia; in such circumstances it would be distinctly inconvenient to have a large body of British troops locked up in the Sudan.

Definite orders were issued for a retreat as far as Wadi Halfa, and for twelve years the Sudan was abandoned to the Dervishes. On June 20, 1885, the Mahdi died suddenly of small-pox at Omdurman; a huge tomb was raised over him, which became the sacred shrine in the eyes of his followers. He bequeathed his power to Abdullah, one of his four Khalifas, whose unamiable personality will be discussed later.

Though Kitchener rarely gave vent to emotion, we can imagine him sad at heart as he made his way down the river in June to embark for England. He felt the loss of Herbert Stewart, one of his few friends, and the failure to relieve Gordon must have been a bitter blow. Apart from the tragic side of the story there had been a waste of effort and money—and he hated waste of any kind.

In one respect however there was no waste. The year of toil and danger on the banks of the Nile had left him with a store of knowledge and experience which bore fruit many years later.

CHAPTER IV

1886–1892

DURING the next six years Kitchener held various appointments; he was working hard—throughout his life there were no moments of relaxation—but it was work which looks insignificant beside the great achievements which have left a stamp on history. Therefore we can pass over this period quickly remembering only that he was always in a position of considerable independence, outside the routine of army work, and often outside the comforts of civilization.

On return home from Egypt a couple of months were spent on leave, after which he was appointed to a Joint Commission which dealt with the boundaries of Zanzibar. With one French and one German colleague he spent several months on the East Coast of Africa and wrote a long report which led to nothing.

On the way home he was stopped to take command as Governor of Suakin—and a glance must be thrown backwards at the situation which had been developing on the barren shores of the Red Sea.

The defeat of Hicks Pasha in 1883 aroused hopes throughout the Sudan that the Turks could be driven from the country. While the Mahdi raised his standard over the western Sudan and advanced towards Khartoum, Osman Digna headed the rebellion in the district which lies between the Nile and the Red Sea. He was a bold, crafty, and war-like slave dealer, whose troops could fight like wild-cats. Valentine Baker, formerly of the 10th Hussars, collected a mixed force of irregulars and gendarmerie, amounting to 3,500, and in February 1884 set out from Suakin. At El Teb, forty miles to the south, an inferior force of tribesmen appeared, and for some unknown reason panic seized the Egyptians, who fled in disorder, leaving a few guns and 3,000 rifles behind them. Baker and his Staff only escaped by charging through the enemy. As this district was within easy reach of the sea the difficulties of transport were very small in comparison with those of the Nile Valley, and the British Government had therefore no hesitation in sending troops to make good our hold on the coast.

General Sir Gerald Graham took command of one cavalry and one infantry brigade, with a strong landing-party of bluejackets and marines. At El Teb on February 29 there took place some of the most severe fighting that British troops ever saw in Egypt. Osman Digna had collected 12,000 warriors, very unlike the "Gyppies" who had run away from Tel-el-Kebir. For three hours they charged Graham's square and left 2,000 dead before they were defeated.

On March 13 Graham attacked Osman's camp at Tamai, 12 miles south-west of Suakin. Again the Arabs made a fierce onslaught and got into one corner of the square. But the steadiness of British troops saved the day. Osman Digna was so thoroughly defeated that the Red Sea Littoral might be considered safe for some time. All British troops were withdrawn, leaving native garrisons at Suakin and in a few forts outside.

This was the situation when the new Governor arrived towards the end of 1886. The Dervishes were not inclined to attack entrenchments and forts. Our Government insisted that nothing should be done which could in any way commit us to expensive operations. Kitchener made efforts, with some success, to enlist the friendship of neighbouring tribes, but the question of re-opening trade with the interior presented difficulty. At one time strings of caravans had been used to converge on Suakin; a prospect of trade would entice some of the sheiks into a benevolent attitude, which would be a distinct advantage. On the other hand, the return of caravans from Suakin, laden with supplies and possibly with ammunition, would facilitate the Arab advance if they contemplated raids. Kitchener thought that while the garrisons were kept at a low figure it would be too much of a temptation to Osman Digna if he found he could supply his followers with spoils from the enemy. It seems that this surmise was correct, for in 1887 several raids were carried out on friendly tribes, and in the autumn the old slave dealer advanced with considerable force.

Still clinging to the policy of "no commitments" the Government refused permission for the employment of troops, but Kitchener was allowed to collect a force of irregulars, police, and friendlies; a few of his Sudanese smuggled themselves in among this crowd. Osman was located near Handub, 20 miles up the coast, and on January 17, 1888, Kitchener led out his 450 scalliwags to round him up. The attempt failed; though 300 of the Arabs were killed they were too strong to be routed, and, after the friendlies had run away, Kitchener had some difficulty in holding his own with the trusted Blacks. He himself was hit by a bullet in the lower jaw, and Captain Hickman withdrew the little force back to Suakin.

The wound was serious, and for over a month Kitchener lay in hospital at Cairo. After returning to Suakin for a short visit in March he went home on leave. In September he returned to take up duty as A.-G. in Cairo, where Sir Francis Grenfell had succeeded Wood as Sirdar. Almost immediately Kitchener was to visit Suakin again. Osman Digna had pushed right up to the forts of the town. The Sirdar took a battalion of British and two battalions of Sudanese to deal with him. In December this force, together with the garrison, advanced and drove off the Dervishes, killing 500 of them. This was the end of activities in that district, and the A.-G returned to his office at Cairo.

From 1889 onwards his headquarters were in the Capital and for the first time in his life Kitchener found it necessary to

conform with the unwritten laws of a social centre. How far
he enjoyed himself is a matter of speculation, but he went
through official visits, levées, diplomatic receptions, dinners,
and even balls with stern determination. It was observed,
however, that office hours kept him away from the race
meetings and picnics which formed the lighter side of garrison life, and that inspection of outlying posts took the
A.-G. out of Cairo very frequently.

In another direction he was faced with new conditions in
the form of Army Regulations. While troops are more or less
on active service it is impossible to keep a strict watch on
all issues of rations, clothing, ammunition, and rough records are considered sufficient. On the Indian Frontier, at the
end of an expedition, the proverbial method of closing accounts was to have an accidental fire in the office. But once
peace is declared the official and officious clerk resumes his
spectacles; the issue of a ration or a button in excess of authorized allowance becomes the subject of correspondence. To
Kitchener both these methods were abhorrent. While on service he had generally made regulations for himself, based on
expediency, economy, and the local conditions; these regulations were strictly enforced. Irregulars were enlisted, paid,
clothed, and fed as opportunity offered and not by scale. But
accounts never got into arrears and were audited by his own
conscience. The same system was strictly enforced on those
under his orders; if money had been well spent no questions
were asked; if extravagance or wastefulness occurred there
was trouble for somebody. Measurements, however, were
made not by red tape but by Kitchener's own conception of
what the circumstances demanded. He was at first inclined to
set up the same standard in the office at Cairo. It distressed
him to find that a battalion had received a new set of boots, to
which they were entitled by regulations, when he knew from
personal inspection that the old ones were not worn out. On
the other hand, if some expenditure appeared obviously necessary he resented having to quote regulations in support of
it. Still more did he resent a demand for explanation once his

opinion had been recorded. This attitude was mellowed in after years by time and experience, but it never died out completely. He was self-opinionated, generally with good reason; what roused the antagonism of superiors, colleagues, and juniors was that even on minor subjects he would not launch into explanation of his conduct or views. "He-who-must-be-obeyed" was his name, and juniors soon found that it was not for them to reason why.

His objection to unnecessary correspondence became a subject of jest, and a list of maxims was drawn up for the benefit of newcomers:

1. Never write anything.
2. If you want something done, catch the A.-G.—he is sure to be here to-morrow.
3. If you want leave, catch the Sirdar.
4. If you get leave, go home at once and take care never to come back.

Legend, probably untrue, says that a copy of this document fell into the hands of Kitchener, who grimly put his initials at the bottom remarking that it was very sound.

Ever since the Khalifa had been established in power it was obviously his policy to follow up the Mahdi's success and make some sort of attempt on Egypt. After taking possession of Dongola, bands of Dervishes raided villages along the Nile, and though they were roughly handled in an action at Ginniss on December 30, 1885, they continued to follow up our retreat. In 1887 a chieftain called Wad-el-Nejumi collected some 4,000 men, with a huge following of women and children. He was a courageous and brilliant fighter, and is generally believed to have been a sincere fanatic. Some people think that the Khalifa was jealous of him as a dangerous rival, and gave him command of the attacking force for that reason. If he won success the Khalifa would benefit; if he happened to be defeated or killed it would remove him from dangerous rivalry.

In June 1889 Wad-el-Nejumi began a serious advance. On July 2 he attacked an Egyptian force under Colonel Wodehouse at Arguin near Wadi Halfa, where the Dervishes were defeated with a loss of 500 men. In spite of this they pushed forward another 50 miles. The Sirdar allowed them to advance while he collected troops; it was also important to draw them on into country where they would have difficulty in finding supplies for their huge numbers. On August 17, after frequent skirmishes, a pitched battle was fought at Toski, and though the Dervishes displayed much valour for seven hours they were utterly routed. Wad-el-Nejumi and half his fighting men were killed. In this engagement Kitchener commanded a mounted force, which consisted of one squadron of the 20th Hussars and the Egyptian cavalry.

Toski was an important success. The terror which had overhung Egypt since 1885 was removed. The Khalifa had quite enough to do in keeping his own turbulent tribes in subjection and could not muster any army that would threaten danger. Wadi Halfa was again established as our advanced post and the frontier remained comparatively peaceful. The British troops and Headquarters returned to Cairo.

The moral effect was of real value. At Toski the Dervishes had directed their furious attacks on Egyptian battalions on whom fell the brunt of the fighting. The much-despised fellahin had shown that when led by British officers they would not run away; this was a marked advance on their previous reputation. Kitchener must have rejoiced exceedingly in the promise of the future. He had never lost sight of the big object which lay 1,000 miles further south. Some day he would lead an Egyptian Army there, and already his soul was taken up with preparations.

At this stage it was disconcerting to be called to yet another appointment. Baring was set on reforming the police, and recognized in the Adjutant-General the one man who might be able to carry through re-organization. Kitchener demurred because he wanted and expected to be made Sirdar when Grenfell retired, and the police work had the appearance of being a side-track. Presumably Baring gave him some assurance. At any rate, the A.-G. took up the new appointment.

As Scott-Moncrieff said: "Happy is the reformer who finds things so bad that he cannot make a movement without making an improvement; and such was the state of Egypt." Such was certainly the state of the police. They numbered about 6,500, and were under the mudirs of each district. From the mudir's point of view the Force was a valuable institution. It provided lucrative jobs for all his relations; it enabled him to work off any scores against his enemies; sometimes, though more rarely, it assisted in suppressing crime. Valentine Baker had begun re-organization without much success; he alarmed the mudirs, who feared that they themselves would be the first victims of the inquisition. Between vengeful mudirs and stern British inspectors the policemen's lot was not a happy one.

The object of the new Inspector-General was to introduce the system which Baring had imposed on Government offices in Cairo. That is to say, the mudirs were to be re-assured; their power and dignity would be respected, and their legal emoluments would not be cut down. At the same time, British inspectors would give them "advice" which, for their own good, they had better accept. To begin with, the advice was not too harsh. Kitchener had lived long enough in the East to know that bribery is indigenous and cannot be uprooted by the mere issue of an order or even by hanging the more glaring offenders. The first thing was to suppress torture of prisoners or witnesses. Next, the principle was instilled that promotion depended on merit and not on relationship to higher authority. Another principle was that the Police should be defenders and not oppressors of the poor.

Statistics and reports were collected which showed a decrease of crime and provided the police with a much-needed coat of white-wash. How far the reforms penetrated below the surface is another question—on which I reserve my opinion because I was once a Chief of Police in Constantinople.

After a year of this effort there was a brief return to the A.-G.'s office in Cairo, until April 1892, when Sir Francis Grenfell resigned and Kitchener was appointed Sirdar.

CHAPTER V

THE SIRDAR

The Campaign which started in 1896 and ended at Omdurman on September 2, 1898, provides the best example of organization which has ever been seen in the British Army. Steadily but with remarkable foresight the successive steps were taken which led ever southwards to victory.

Without any intention to detract from the brilliance of Kitchener's achievement, it must be pointed out that he enjoyed several advantages which have rarely, in fact never, fallen to the lot of any other Commander.

In the first place his power was supreme. Knowledge of the people and their language, of the country and its resources, established him as the one authority whose decisions could not be questioned. His experience of the local troops was far deeper than that of any other officer. His record of service had won the confidence of those above and those below him. Baring gave him firm support. The War Office allowed a free hand, and the British public was solid behind him.

The object of the Campaign aroused general enthusiasm—though various people looked at it from different angles. Perhaps Kitchener himself shared the feelings of Scott-Moncrieff, who says:

"I could only look on this Sudan War as one that could be justified if it was entered into and carried through with the determination, not to revenge, in pagan fashion, Gordon's death, but to achieve what he would have died for: the abolition of that accursed slave trade, and in rescuing Egypt from the Mahdi."

Other people longed to re-establish our own self-respect which had been shamed by the disaster at Khartoum and the ignominious retreat. Others, more openly, admitted a desire for revenge. But however that may be, nothing less than the capture of Khartoum would satisfy anybody—and everybody agreed that Kitchener was the man to do it. Consequently the Campaign is always quoted as the perfect example of a "one-man show" where councils-of-war, or appeals to higher power, were unnecessary and unknown.

A second advantage was that the operations, though long and arduous, did not demand a large force. 10,000 would be too few; 30,000 would be difficult to move and supply; 25,000 was fixed as the desirable figure; it must include a stiffening of British troops for the decisive battle, and some light-moving natives to scour the country. A force of this size, scarcely more than one strong Division, can be controlled by a single hand. Kitchener could carry every detail in his own head.

Another, perhaps the greatest, advantage was that the problem before him dealt only with concrete facts. To look for the moment at military history, the palm for organization is always given to Moltke for the preparation which led to victory against the Austrians in 1866 and the French in 1870. The secret of his success lay in the fact that he studied a concrete plan and not an academic problem. Bismarck told him when and where the army was to go to war; Moltke got out his map of Austria and made out march tables according to the capacity of the roads which led towards his objective; the rest was comparatively easy. The British officer who struggles with strategy and tactics at the Staff College has a far more complicated task before him. British armies have fought on the plains of Flanders, across the barren stretches of the Spanish Peninsula, over the still more barren deserts of Africa, up in the mountain passes of the Indian Frontier. Having no idea where the next campaign will be, he vainly tries to frame a set of laws which, with small allowance for local conditions, will fit all circumstances. The result is beautiful, but not very practical.

Kitchener, like Moltke, began at the other end with a close

study of concrete facts, and on them he built his strategy and tactics. His information was practically complete. Intelligence lay in the capable hands of Wingate, who had more time than his Chief to devote to details, and therefore had deeper knowledge of the tribes and their leaders than even Kitchener himself. It was commonly said that Wingate knew more about the Khalifa's army than the Khalifa knew himself. He was one of the few who were admitted to confidence, the right-hand of the Sirdar, who knew what all the other hands were doing. Thus Kitchener could tell to within a few miles where the decisive battle would be fought, he knew every detail regarding the routes leading towards it and the natural obstacles to be overcome: more roughly, he knew the strength of the enemy and the state of his munitions. In the clear atmosphere of Egypt the fog of war did not exist.

The story is told of a certain General who gave thirteen good reasons for not bringing up his guns, and the first reason was that he had no guns. At first Kitchener had not 25,000 troops or anything like that number; in fact there were people who declared that the Egyptian Army contained no soldiers at all worthy of the name. The first obvious step was to collect some. By virtue of a treaty the number of the Khedive's troops was limited to 18,000, and the French deemed it their duty to watch carefully against any increase. But the new Sirdar was determined to see that his small force was efficient in every way. Of course he wanted to start as soon as possible, but there was no beleaguered garrison sending out signals of distress, no hurry to drag up boats when the river was at its worst, nor any necessity to fire off a forlorn hope on half-starved camels. This was the final, perhaps the crowning, advantage—he could choose his own time. Wolseley had rushed up to within sight of Khartoum in about four months—Kitchener spent four years in preparing his army and three more in the steady movement up the Nile.

During the years of preparation there was no assurance that he would be allowed to put into force the plans with

THE SIRDAR

which he was absorbed, but I think little doubt existed in his mind on this point. At all events he would be ready as far as lay in his power.

It is not necessary to go into details of the reconstruction of the Egyptian Army. Before the arrival of British officers the wretched conscripts had been dragged in chains from their homes to a life of torture in very insanitary quarters. Under Sir Evelyn Wood the first steps were taken along the path of reform. The recruit was well fed and housed; he was protected against ill treatment by native officers; faith was kept as regards length of service; pay, though small, was issued with regularity. It soon became apparent that the fellahin had many of the qualifications which go to make a soldier; they were of powerful physique, healthy, accustomed to hardship, obedient, and cleanly. Compared with the toil on the land the work in barracks was mere play which they found interesting and amusing; they drilled each other in spare hours. By degrees they acquired confidence which grew into military swagger. Leave was given which enabled them to visit their homes; they had tales to tell arousing incredulity, till proof was produced in the shape of real money, which turned disbelief into envy.

The question remained whether centuries of slavery had killed their fighting instinct. A few of them had gone up the river with Wolseley's Expedition, but were employed on the line of communications, where they fully earned their pay as fatigue parties. At Ginniss in December 1885 and again at Toski in July 1889 some battalions were engaged with creditable result.

In May 1884 the first Sudanese battalion was raised at Suakin. "Sambo" had nothing in common with the "fellah" of the Delta. He is a born fighter and perfectly fearless, mischievous and unruly, but devoted to his British officer, a bad shot but a good man at close quarters. Physically he was narrow and skinny, but he had immense powers of endurance. Nobody expected him to run away, but there was always a possibility that sheer excitement would overcome discipline and make him run at the enemy when steadiness required him to remain in the ranks. Constant drill seemed the only means of overcoming nature. The Sudanese quarrelled from time to time among themselves, but drunkenness and insubordination were unknown. Such men soon become soldiers.

There remained however one element in the Army which even British discipline could not reduce to order. Each battalion was accompanied by its "wives," who followed the Colours with a resolution that nothing could deter—up the river, across the desert, right on to the field of Omdurman. Threats and orders were met with sublime contempt and anybody who ventured to apply force might have had the worst of an encounter. Mrs. Sambo was the one person who defeated Kitchener. But she did her duty as housekeeper and cook with considerable skill and untiring patience.

In January 1892 Tewfik died, at the age of 40, and was succeeded by his son Abbas, aged 18. The new Khedive had gone through some education in Europe, chiefly at Vienna. Discontented Nationalists, sighing for the good old days, found it easy to gain his ear and excite jealousy against the obnoxious British who wanted to rule his country for him. Abbas dismissed his father's Cabinet without asking "advice" from the British Consul-General. Cromer had no desire to be harsh with the young man but was quite determined to show that interference could not be tolerated—strong steps must be taken. It is said that when he went to impress his views on Abbas a battalion of British infantry happened to be marching past the Palace. Perhaps they added weight to his advice; at all events the British Consul-General had his way.

The discontented Egyptians continued to stir up ill-feeling and their next attack was aimed at the Sirdar. In January 1894 the Khedive was making a tour of inspection along the Nile; the usual preparations had been arranged to do him honour, but without eliciting any words of satisfaction. At

Wadi Halfa the garrison paraded for a march past, and in the most pointed manner he made disparaging remarks about those battalions which were under British officers. When the review was over Kitchener said: "As Your Highness is evidently displeased with the efforts of myself and the British officers in training your Army, nothing remains for me but to place my own resignation and that of all the British officers in your hands."[1] Abbas, who had not expected so startling a result, made some effort to excuse himself, but Kitchener dismissed the troops and rode away. Within two days Cromer informed the Khedive that a General Order must be published, in English, French, and Arabic, expressing his complete satisfaction with the efficiency of his Army and his confidence in the officers to whose skill and labour that efficiency was due. The British Government expressed their confidence at the same time by conferring a K.C.M.G. on the Sirdar.

Abbas seems to have learnt his lesson, and perhaps he began to understand that Cromer and Kitchener were really his best friends. From this time he took pride in the troops, and gave such help as he could when the advance started southwards.

At the beginning of 1896 the Army consisted of 13 battalions of infantry, 8 squadrons of cavalry, 3 batteries of artillery, and a camel corps. Of the infantry five battalions were Sudanese. There were no engineers; the Departmental Staffs for supply, medical, and other services were cut down to an extent with has provoked criticism. Wingate managed the Intelligence, and this was the one branch which entailed a comparatively large outlay. Other staffs scarcely existed in the ordinary sense of the term, for Kitchener did the work himself, with some assistance from Rundle as A.-G. and a couple of devoted A.D.C.'s.

An enormous amount depended on the British officers; they were young captains and subalterns—Kitchener himself was

[1] Arthur, I, p. 182.

not 42 years of age when he took command—and no pains were spared in selecting suitable candidates. The subaltern on joining received local rank of Bimbashi (Major) and got £450 a year—about three times the amount of his pay in a British regiment. The Captain commanded a battalion as Kaimakam. Kitchener sternly rejected married men, on the grounds that the Sudan was no place for ladies and that he preferred to have officers whose thoughts were not too intent on leave. There was a saying that he showed great aversion to anyone who had been through the Divorce Court, on the ground that an officer who could not manage his private affairs would not be more successful in a public capacity; if this was really his reason I am afraid it points to a certain ignorance of military history.

The careers of those who served in this campaign proved that Kitchener was a first-rate judge of men. And he felt more at home with them than with any other body of officers in his whole career—they had common ground on which to meet. On the surface there appeared no immediate prospect of active operations, yet from the Sirdar downwards they all believed that the day would surely come, and thus they had a definite object for their work. Sooner or later they would lead these raw recruits into action, and their own lives, among other more important things, would hang on the result of the training. Like Kitchener's Army in the Great War they were preparing for the real thing. They could not rise to discussing the big plans—no one was ever allowed to do that—but the Sirdar could descend to their level, and even ask their opinion on such points as the promotion of a native officer or the clothing of the troops.

They earned their pay, for work never ceased, either on the frontier at Wadi Halfa or on the parade grounds near Cairo. Carrington Smith ("Smiler" of the Dublin Fusiliers) used to declare that in 24 hours he never did less than 25 hours' work, and generally spent the next day in undoing it again, because "He-who-must-be-obeyed" did not approve:

THE SIRDAR

he envied the Pharaohs, who had gone through plagues of their own but never suffered from Kitchener.

Economy was enforced to a pitch which aroused bitter complaints. It was, however, a stern necessity. Baring (who became Lord Cromer in 1892) and Grastin (who succeeded Scott-Moncrieff at this time) continued to extend the schemes for irrigation which absorbed capital. But I think that in addition to this there was a touch of guile in the zeal with which the young Sirdar cultivated a reputation for economy, not to say meanness. A time would come when he would go to Cromer with big demands for a big purpose: these demands were more likely to be met with sympathy and cash if no suspicion existed of wastefulness or extravagance.

In 1896 rumours began to reach London that Belgians from the Congo and French from the Atlantic were making their way towards the Southern Sudan. Either of these parties might establish a footing by promising the Khalifa that they would protect him against the British; very likely Abdullah would lend a ready ear. Then if ever we wanted to go back to Khartoum there would be international complications; and, as we did want to go back, it became necessary to go before anybody else could forestall us. This seems to have been a strong factor in deciding the Conservative Government of Lord Salisbury to sanction the expedition of 1896. For obvious reasons, however, the truth had to be discreetly veiled. A pretext was found elsewhere.

The Italians possessed a port on the Red Sea, Massowa, 300 miles south of Suakin; they had pushed their way up to Kassala, 200 miles inland; they were also engaged against Menelik of Abyssinia on the south; and on March 1, 1896, a force under General Barratieri suffered a terrible defeat at Adowa, 100 miles south of Massowa. The disaster was so complete that the Italians appeared to be in real danger, from Menelik on the south, from the Khalifa on the west.

This furnished Salisbury's Cabinet with a pretext for action which could be acknowledged without a blush. It only remained to stage-manage the production in such a manner that the curtain could be rung up before the French or other Powers had time to enter a protest and ask inconvenient questions. Mr. Curzon, Under-Secretary for Foreign Affairs, made an announcement to the House of Commons in his best style. It was understood that we were not going to war, but a demonstration would be made along the Nile Valley to "create a diversion" and relieve the pressure on our Italian friends. To prove the strict limitations of this benevolent move only such troops would be employed as were already in Egypt; no reinforcements would be sent from England; Dongola was the objective.

It must remain an official secret how far Kitchener had received any hints that the day to which he was looking forward was about to dawn. In any case both he and Cromer played their parts with every appearance of innocent surprise. The telegram announcing the Government's decision was handed to the Sirdar at 3 A. M. on March 13; he proceeded to wake up the Consul-General, and together they went to the Palace to wake up the Khedive with the news. Thus the Dongola expedition had begun its existence before the French Consul-General had drunk his morning coffee; he was quite as much surprised as anybody. That afternoon there was a sound of revelry at Shepheard's famous hotel when the rumour began to spread and turned out to be true. Certainly the surprise did not catch the Sirdar unprepared; without hesitation but without flurry troops were set in motion.

To relieve the garrison of Suakin a native brigade arrived from India. Three fresh battalions were formed from reservists. Thus Kitchener could assemble at Wadi Halfa the whole of the Egyptian Army and one battalion, the North Staffords, from the British garrison at Cairo.

Before this, on March 16, a small column had started to seize Akasha, 75 miles to the south, and form the first advanced post. A line of railway was rapidly constructed, chiefly out of derelict material, and by the end of May sufficient troops and stores had been accumulated to warrant a further advance, which was pushed up the east bank.

At Firket, 15 miles south of Akasha, about 3,000 Dervishes lay in wait. On June 7 Kitchener sent his cavalry under Colonel Burn Murdoch to sweep round behind the village and come in on the enemy's rear, while three brigades of infantry attacked from the front. The manœuvre succeeded; at small cost to ourselves the Dervishes were routed, leaving over 800 dead on the ground. In this fight Egyptian troops confirmed the hopes which their officers had been cherishing.

Further advance was steady but very slow, being dependent on the limitations of a very rickety line of rail. Various unforeseen accidents proved the truth of the old maxim that nothing is certain in war. In July cholera made its appearance and claimed 19 British and 260 native victims. The wind which was due to blow from the north and waft supply boats up the river gave way to violent sand-storms from the south —causing much delay and more discomfort. After a spell of calm and intense heat there followed in quick succession three tempests of rain, bringing the worst flood that had been known for 50 years, and washing away twelve miles of the precious railway. So serious was the situation that at one moment a retreat appeared to be necessary. But Kitchener, though sadly disturbed in his plans, refused to be defeated. With incredible energy men were rushed up to repair the damage, and he himself set to work like a foreman and taught every man his task. Early in September all seemed ready for a forward move when another disaster occurred. A fleet of eight armed steamers had been assembled on the river to keep pace with the advance. Of these the best and newest was the *Zafir*—brought out from England in sections and put together in time for the next move. The Sirdar and Staff had embarked in her on September 11, but she had scarcely gone twenty yards from the bank when a loud explosion rent the air: a cylinder had burst and the *Zafir* was useless for a fortnight.

In spite of all mishaps the advance was continued. The

Dervishes had learnt a lesson at Firket and, in order to avoid being surrounded, they crossed to the west bank at Hafir, where forts with a few guns had been built to command the river. On September 19 gunboats steamed up and peppered these forts with shell- and rifle-fire. The tribesmen held on pluckily to their entrenchments and then withdrew during the night. No further opposition was offered; after a little skirmishing with Dervish horsemen Dongola was occupied on September 23. During the next month advanced posts were established at Korti and Merawi.

By this time the fact that Dongola was our objective had faded from memory. We were going to Khartoum. But many preparations had to be made before starting on the next stage and a whole year went by before they were complete.

At one moment the question of finance threatened to cause trouble. The expedition was for the purpose of restoring a lost province to the Khedive, and therefore the Egyptian Treasury ought to defray the expense. There was £3,000,000 in hand, but this sum had been earmarked for the benefit of the bond-holders and could not be disbursed without consent of the Caisse de la Dette. Cromer wanted to take half a million, as a loan, for military purposes, but the French representative put in an objection which was upheld by the Mixed Tribunals at Cairo. By this time, however, the British Government was committed to action; a retreat would be a military error, an admission of weakness. Cromer was therefore instructed that the half-million would be guaranteed from British sources. As in the case of Arabi's rebellion, the refusal of the French to take part or approve really made things much easier for Cromer and the Sirdar. The expedition was now entirely in British hands, financed by the British, commanded by a British officer—and British troops could be sent to join them. This was what Kitchener wanted.

The whole of 1897 was spent in building the "desert railway." A glance at the map shows the enormous advantage of this line, which from Wadi-Halfa to Abu Hamed measures 230 miles, while the huge loop of the river measures 500 miles including the three worst cataracts. The construction was a triumph of engineering and still more of ingenuity and hard work. The Chief Engineer was a subaltern of Sappers, Girouard, an expert in railways and only second to Kitchener himself in energy and driving power. Progress was maintained at the rate of about one and a half miles a day. By the end of July railhead had been pushed up to within striking distance of Abu Hamed. It was not safe to go further until this point had been occupied. In August General Hunter with one brigade made a fine march from Merawi, 132 miles in eight days, and captured the place after a sharp skirmish. Friendlies were then sent ahead and reported that Berber had been evacuated; Hunter went on and took possession of this very important point. Meanwhile steamers had ascended the Fourth and Fifth Cataracts. An advanced post, Fort Atbara, was established in October.

Reconnaissances were sent some 80 miles against a force which Osman Digna commanded to the south-east, but could not bring him to bay. Steamers went up as far as Metemma, and did a little shelling, but no other fighting took place. On October 31 Girouard brought the first train to Abu Hamed amid cheers. The success was so obvious that Kitchener extracted another £200,000 for the extension of the line, and railhead was eventually established at Fort Atbara.

The year of toil and discomfort had left Kitchener in a strong position. Great work by Girouard and his men enabled an army to be maintained within 200 miles of the goal, even when the Nile was at its lowest. The final stage lay in sight. Up to this point nature had provided the worst obstacles and the Dervishes had done little. Further on, heavy fighting might be expected.

CHAPTER VI

THE ATBARA AND OMDURMAN

THOUGH the final act was about to be played, a little stage management became necessary before it opened.

An extra brigade of British troops was being assembled in Egypt, and Sir F. Grenfell returned to Cairo as G.O.C. of all British forces; since he was many years senior to Kitchener there was a danger that he might consider himself responsible for the operations and take over command. Fortunately, however, he had sufficient wisdom to see that the man who had worked out all the preliminary details would be the best man to finish the campaign, as well as too much generosity to rob his junior of the credit. The matter was settled with good feeling on both sides, and Kitchener retained the command.

The question of Kassala presented more serious difficulty. For five years the Italians had occupied this important point, with much discomfort and no profit to themselves. They proposed to hand it over to the Khedive, as it formed part of the Sudan and therefore might be considered as his property. But the Sirdar could spare no troops to take it over and, worse still, it would be an extra expense. Sir Edwin Palmer, now Director-General of Finance at Cairo, had taken alarm at the increase of the military budget; railways, supplies, and many items which arise from active service had mounted up in spite of the watchful eye of the economist. For the occupation of Kassala more transport, more everything, would be required. Palmer wanted to keep his accounts in order by handing over a definite sum, leaving the General to expend it as he pleased. This was the one form of official interference which annoyed Kitchener thoroughly; if the expedition was to be carried through it must be done

THE ATBARA AND OMDURMAN 63

properly, and he could judge what was proper better than a civilian sitting at an office desk a thousand miles away. Why should he spend hours in writing pages, which would not be understood, in justification of his expenditure? He sent off a telegram to Cromer which ended with an offer to resign:

"The reconnaissance of Mahmud's position proves that we have in front of us a force of Dervishes of better fighting qualities and far greater numerical strength than we have ever met before. In face of this the financial authorities appear to be unable to grant what I think necessary for military efficiency and to carry out the military programme. My estimate of the situation and military requirements may be wrong, but feeling, as I do, my inability to cope with the difficulties and the grave responsibilities of the position in which I find myself I beg to tender my resignation to your Lordship. I do not take this step without careful consideration and deeply regret that I should be forced thus to increase your Lordship's difficulties, but I feel that the position in which I am placed leaves me no alternative."

This telegram cannot have been entirely sincere. Of course Kitchener meant what he said, but he would have been a good deal surprised and still more disgusted if Cromer had accepted the resignation. For thirteen long years one thought and one ambition had filled his soul. The Army was his—those grinning black ranks had been conceived in his brain and nursed by his care till every man of them was a soldier; the railway was his—without looking at paper returns he could tell offhand how many sleepers had been laid and how many trucks had been running; the growing stacks of supplies and ammunition—all his. Like a young mother he had infinite pride in his offspring and yet was jealous of anyone coming too near.

If he resigned there was no one who could take up the burden. Wingate, Hunter, Rundle, Girouard were all good men, but their work was like the separate pieces of a delicate machine which can only be fitted together and set in motion by a master hand; they had never seen the big plans which lay hidden in Kitchener's mind. And even those officers who had groaned under his relentless discipline would have been dismayed to find themselves under any other commander.

Kitchener could not resign at this moment—and he knew it.

Cromer knew it equally well, and took the telegram for what it was worth—a strong hint to the Director-General to mind his own business.

The incident is worth noting because it foreshadowed others of the same type. Kitchener satisfied his own conscience that something was necessary and considered that this ought to satisfy everybody. He could not see the Director-General's point of view. Palmer very likely approved of the Sirdar's proposals and was willing to accept them all, but he would have to explain them to various colleagues, each of whom had some urgent demand for his own Department. For instance, irrigation would have to wait its turn; the Minister for Public Works would submit to the decision only if he received reasonable explanation. But Kitchener could not communicate all that was in his mind. For purely military reasons his plans must be kept secret; for diplomatic reasons the cosmopolitan world of Cairo must know as little as possible: for personal reasons he preferred to work out his own schemes in his own way.

I think that Cromer, who knew his colleagues well, must have suppressed a smile when he showed the Sirdar's telegram to the Director-General of Finance. In the end the solution presented no great difficulty. Kitchener was invited to Cairo, where he arrived on November 11; with Cromer and Grenfell supporting him all obstacles were smoothed away. The railway was to go on. Kassala was taken over from Italy by an Egyptian battalion from Suakin under Colonel Parsons. A brigade of British troops would be ready for the front as soon as they were wanted. And though His-

THE ATBARA AND OMDURMAN

tory does not relate what the Director-General said he was probably quite pleased.

Even the Mahdi, under the mantle of the Prophet, had found trouble in maintaining discipline among his unruly followers. When the loot of Khartoum proved disappointing the whole place was reduced to ruin and Omdurman, on the opposite bank of the White Nile, became the seat of Government. After the Mahdi's death his successor built a fine stone wall to enclose the tomb, the arsenal, a prison, and a comfortable harem for himself; this last building was well furnished in every respect. Outside the wall mud huts spread northwards for nearly three miles.

In an unfortunate moment Gladstone spoke of the Sudanese as a people "rightly struggling to be free." But when the yoke of Egypt had been thrown off they were further than ever from freedom. Jealousy among the emirs, feuds among the tribes, kept the country in a state of turbulence. The Baggara, fiercest and best of the warriors, were the only tribe upon whom perfect reliance could be placed; they came in thousands from their homes in the western Sudan to fill the new Capital and maintain the new power; by their strength Abdullah imposed his brutal will on the rest of the wretched inhabitants.

Trade with the outside world had ceased to exist. Whole towns and villages lay deserted as the result of starvation and raids, though it was scarcely worth while to capture slaves when the markets of Constantinople could not buy them. Calculations have been made that in the twelve years of freedom more than half the population perished.

The Khalifa gave himself up to debauchery, and some emirs followed his example. From time to time he had visions —of the capture and loot of Cairo—of vultures feasting on the bones of Turks. But the disaster at Toski put an end to offensive operations except on a small scale, and the Sirdar's advance to Dongola made it obvious that preparations must be made for defence.

The Khalifa's army numbered over 50,000, with perhaps 10,000 rifles of various patterns. The organization is said to have been wonderfully good; some of Gordon's clerks were installed at H.Q. to control the issue of ammunition and supplies; the emirs kept up muster rolls of their tribes. Parades were held and manœuvres were practised.

But as the troops of the Sirdar crept forward Abdullah made several mistakes in strategy. In 1885 the Desert Column had crossed from Korti to Metemma—they would surely follow the same road again. Kitchener took forward a mounted force as far as Gakdul to support this impression. The Khalifa sent 20,000 of his picked troops under a brave young emir called Mahmud to hold Metemma, and so intent was he on this point that the garrisons at Abu Hamed and Berber were reduced to very small numbers. This enabled Hunter to take possession of these two important points in August 1897.

By January Kitchener had established his position round Berber, and the Khalifa made another serious mistake. He ordered Mahmud either to return to Omdurman or to advance against the invaders. Mahmud chose the latter course and crossed the Nile from Metemma to the east bank in March, then cut across the desert to the Atbara, hoping that he would be able to swing right round the head of the British force and attack the rear behind Berber. The Sirdar watched the movement with joy, and did not allow his steamers to interfere with the crossing of the river, though they might have done so. Then, leaving a garrison at railhead and in Berber, he took his army about 15 miles up the Atbara. This forced Mahmud to make a wider sweep than he intended, and eventually he reached the Atbara at a point 35 miles above its junction with the Nile. During the dry season the river consisted of a string of pools without any current.

Mahmud now found himself in a bad way. To reach the Nile in rear of his enemy would entail a march of at least 50 or 60 miles across waterless desert; with his huge mass of followers this could not be thought of. A retreat would be al-

THE ATBARA AND OMDURMAN 67

most as difficult, and at the other end of it the Khalifa would have to be faced. He decided to sit still.

Nothing could have suited Kitchener better. The only danger had been in the enemy's numbers. A desperate onslaught by 50,000 fearless warriors is serious, even when met with modern fire-arms. If 20,000 of the best of them could be tackled as a first instalment more than half the danger would be removed; the Dervishes would be disheartened; the Egyption forces would be steadied; ammunition could be replenished and the wounded could be sent down the river before the second half of the Khalifa's army was encountered. In fact, Mahmud and his 20,000 men would provide a good rehearsal for the final act.

A British brigade under General Gatacre had begun to move up from Cairo in January, halting at various places on the way. Most of the long journey was done by rail and boat but it finished with a march of 134 miles in a week, which proved that the men had been kept in hard condition. The whole Force, 13,000 strong [1] was assembled at Ras-el-Hudi, 15 miles up the Atbara, about the same time that Mahmud reached the same river 20 miles higher up.

The Sirdar hoped and expected that the Dervishes would advance to attack in the open. An attempt was made to draw them out by cavalry reconnaissance. Mahmud, however, had decided to stand on the defensive; a strong zariba of thorn bushes was constructed, over two miles in circumference, surrounding a patch of scrub; inside this entrenchments were dug, palisades erected and guns placed.

By April 7 the Sirdar had moved up to within eight miles. That afternoon the whole force left camp and made a night march under a full moon which brought it to Mahmud's zariba at dawn on April 8 (Good Friday). Three brigades were drawn up in close formation, each on a front of five hundred yards; Gatacre on the left, Macdonald's Sudanese

---

[1] The Force consisted of Gatacre's Brigade of British Infantry, MacDonald's Brigade of Sudanese, Maxwell's Brigade of Sudanese, Lewis's Brigade of Egyptians, 8 squadrons under Broadwood, and 24 guns.

THE ATBARA
APRIL 8th 1898

0 — 500 — 1,000
Scale in Yards

Broadwood's Cavalry

OPEN PLAIN

Maxwell   Macdonald   Gatacre   Lewis

N

MAHMUD

THORN SCRUB

DENSE THORN SCRUB

Pool
Dry bed of R. ATBARA
Pool

THE ATBARA AND OMDURMAN 69

in the centre, Maxwell's Sudanese on the right. The zariba lay only six hundred yards in front of them. One brigade guarded the transport; cavalry spread out to the left.

That battle was a spectacular little affair in complete accordance with the principles of an Aldershot Field Day. Artillery preparation by 24 guns for an hour and a half; then bayonets were fixed and bugles sounded the advance; bands played and pipes skirled. Short halts were made for rifle fire. With much coolness the Dervishes held their fire until the attack was only 200 yards distant. Then a crash of musketry broke out and men began to drop. But the dense mass swept forward. Gatacre and his A.D.C. were the first two men to reach the zariba, followed closely by all three brigades in line. In less than a quarter of an hour after the general advance had been sounded the defences were torn aside and troops poured through the gaps. For twenty minutes there was fierce fighting, hand to hand, in the palisades and trenches. Then the "Cease Fire" sounded and all was over. The troops reformed in brigade squares and ate their breakfasts.

Our casualties were 568, including 125 of the British brigade. The Dervishes lost about 3,000 dead and over 2,000 prisoners. Mahmud himself was captured by the 10th Sudanese—much to their joy.

The Atbara was the first battle in which Kitchener held supreme command. The only fault which critics have found is that the artillery preparation ought to have been prolonged before the infantry advance. There was no manœuvre, but none was needed; the enemy sat still and allowed the brigades to form up as they pleased and in their own time. After that it was a soldiers' battle where the man in the ranks went straight ahead with the bayonet. The Sirdar could only look on.

All the same, I think the battle was a personal triumph for Kitchener. If the men won it for him, it was he who made the men and brought them up to the starting-post. The British brigade had only been under his orders for three months, but every day they marched and drilled and sweated till they were as hardy as natives of the soil. It was hard condition that won the battle, following good staff work. And the staff was Kitchener himself.

The next stage was plain sailing in more senses than one. Omdurman lay 150 miles up the river; there was no intention of bringing the railhead beyond the Atbara, and for the remainder of the journey all supplies must be moved by boat. Consequently a halt must be made until the Nile rose high enough to ensure safe navigation. The troops went into summer quarters along the east bank near Berber, and endured four months of heat, sand-flies, route marching, and boredom. Girouard's trains grunted painfully across the desert, bringing up supplies and ammunition. Streets of mud-huts sprang up at Fort Atbara, together with streets of boxes and bales. Bazaars and cafés were opened by enterprising Greeks, who did a roaring trade. Outside the town were long lines of horses, camels, and other beasts of burden.

The army already on the spot was sufficient to cope with the enemy if the Khalifa made another attack; he had not enough transport to bring up the whole of his strength. But if we had to move to Omdurman every man of the Dervishes would be waiting there for us. The Sirdar did not propose to take unnecessary risks; he demanded from the War Office another brigade of British troops, a regiment of cavalry, two batteries, with other details—and every demand was met with immediate compliance. He had no use for these troops, however, until the advance began; they would eat up supplies and entail further expense; so until the end of July they lay at Cairo and then began to entrain. The long journey took eight or ten days.

The Force now consisted of:

British Division. Maj.-General Gatacre.
    1st Bde., Brig.-General Wauchope.
    2nd Bde., Brig.-General Hon. N. Lyttleton.

THE ATBARA AND OMDURMAN 71

Egyptian Division. Maj.-General Sir A. Hunter.
    1st Bde., Colonel MacDonald.
    2nd Bde., Colonel Maxwell.
    3rd Bde., Colonel Lewis.
    4th Bde., Colonel Collinson.

Mounted Troops. 21st Lancers, 9 squadrons Egyptian Cavalry, 8 companies Camel Corps.

Artillery. 2 batteries R.F.A., 5 batteries Egyptian Artillery.

By August 18 the concentration round Atbara had been completed. Steamers, with one brigade of Egyptians, went ahead to establish a depot of supplies within 35 miles of Omdurman; after this they returned to ferry the army across the river and up it to Wad Hamed. From this point the remaining 60 miles were done on foot.

Even the Sirdar could not tell what tactics the Khalifa would use. He might swoop down in true Dervish fashion; like Mahmud at the Atbara he might await attack in Omdurman; some gloomy prophets said he would not fight at all. But every precaution was taken against surprise. From the starting-point at Wad Hamed the army moved forward in battle order—cavalry far in front and on the desert flank, infantry in mass of brigades, ten gun-boats on the left flank along the river, while on the far bank a crowd of Friendlies under Major Stuart Wortley kept pace with the main-body. Strong zaribas were built every night to protect the camp; troops slept in their clothes with rifles by their sides.

Except a few Dervish horsemen nothing was seen of the enemy during the seven days' march which brought the army on August 30 within six miles of Omdurman. On this day cavalry patrols saw the whole of the Khalifa's forces drawn up in five divisions on the open space north-west of the city. Their strength was estimated between 40,000 and 50,000. Extra precautions were taken at night.

On September 1 a short march brought the army across

OMDURMAN.
SEPT. 2nd 1898.

THE ATBARA AND OMDURMAN

a ridge, known as Kerreri, to a camp on the river bank five miles north of Omdurman. Gun-boats went forward to shell the forts and the Mahdi's tomb, and a battery of howitzers was landed on the far bank, under escort of the Friendlies, to join in the bombardment. The Dervishes again paraded in full force and seemed about to attack. But nothing happened. The Sirdar thought they might take advantage of the darkness to hurl themselves upon his camp. It would certainly have been their best chance of getting through the rifle and maxim fire. A stampede of horses and mules or the least unsteadiness in the ranks might start a panic—which is a thousand times more dangerous at night.

But the Khalifa missed his opportunity. Some local inhabitants had been caught near the camp. Kitchener bribed them to go forward and reconnoitre the enemy's position, giving them to understand that he intended to attack at once; he knew very well that they would disclose his plans to the Khalifa. Apparently they did their work well—the Dervishes sat still waiting for their enemy to leave the camp and come into the open. They waited till the night had passed, and then the Khalifa could wait no longer. He moved forward to attack.

Half an hour before day-break Kitchener's men were under arms. At 6 A. M. the long line of the enemy came into sight, 3,000 yards away; a mass of white garments and banners fluttering in the breeze, spears flashing in the sunlight, fanatical war-cries, emirs on horseback prancing in front of the array.

They were brave men. Right through the hail of bullets and shells they pressed on, regardless of the wide gaps which soon began to appear in the ranks. But even the bravest could not get within 300 yards of the zariba. In this first attack 3,000 Dervishes were killed and the remainder faded away to lick their wounds.

The Egyptian Cavalry, under Broadwood, had been sent out early in the morning on the right flank where they came into touch with the left of the Khalifa's line. Instead of retiring into the zariba Broadwood decided to move off to the northward, hoping to draw some of the enemy after him. The manœuvre was entirely successful; about 15,000 Dervishes, under Wad Helu, followed the cavalry for over three miles, and thus failed to take their share in the first assault on the camp. It is very doubtful whether their presence would have made any difference to the ultimate result, but their absence simplified the task of our infantry in repelling the onset.

The Sirdar now wanted to cut off the Khalifa's main-body from Omdurman; house-to-house fighting in the city would certainly entail casualties, and therefore risks must be taken to keep the enemy in the open. The 21st Lancers were sent ahead to reconnoitre, and the infantry, leaving the zariba, began to move towards the city, in echelon of brigades, the left in front.

When the cavalry had gone about a mile their scouts reported a force of a thousand Dervishes in a shallow *khor* (dry water-course) to the south-west. From column of troops the Lancers wheeled to the right into line and charged. Suddenly the *khor,* which was about four feet deep, became alive with a mass of Dervishes, not one thousand but nearly three thousand strong. The 400 Lancers were already in their stride a couple of hundred yards away—there was no time to change direction, nothing for it but to go straight ahead. The shock of impact was terrific; sheer momentum of galloping weight carried the horsemen through the mass and out again on the other side. Three hundred yards beyond the *khor* they reformed their broken ranks, dismounted and turned round to bring magazine fire on the figures which their charge had left sprawling on the ground. The Dervishes also reformed very steadily, but the magazine fire was too accurate for them and they made off northwards to re-join the Khalifa's main body. The whole affair had lasted about three minutes. The Lancers lost 70 killed and wounded, and 119 horses.

It was the first time this regiment had ever been in action. Probably it was the last cavalry charge in the History of War

—the last old-fashioned charge of horsemen against unbroken foot soldiers.

The Khalifa had not flung his whole strength into the first attack on the zariba; in fact more than half of the best warriors were still in reserve under the Black Flag which marked his H.Q. He was waiting for a chance when the British would be in the open. This chance came when the brigades were moving southwards with intervals of 600 yards between them. MacDonald was purposely left to bring up the rear, and he moved out westwards to cover the transport and hospitals which still lay in the zariba. As the other brigades were moving southward they left a wide gap between themselves and MacDonald. At this moment the Khalifa launched his second and main attack from the west. The time was well chosen, for all our troops were on the move and in bad formation to meet an onslaught. The result was that the Sirdar had to employ some pretty manœuvres in order to fill the gap and meet the new attack. The change of formation can best be seen by a glance at the map. Lyttleton and Maxwell had wheeled to the west, leaving a height called Surgham Hill on their right: next to them came Lewis, also facing west: then a wide gap of 1,200 yards: and finally MacDonald on the extreme right. It appeared that the full weight of the enemy would fall on this isolated brigade.

Quickly grasping the situation Kitchener ordered Wauchope to turn right about and close the gap. Before Wauchope's men had covered the mile which brought them up to the new line the Dervish attack had begun to slacken. At this moment, however, a new danger threatened MacDonald from the north. The 15,000 Dervishes under Wad Helu, who had followed Broadwood over the Kerreri Hills, were now returning and began to swarm down the slopes on MacDonald's right flank. With much coolness the Brigadier took battalions successively from his left and brought them to form a new front facing northward. One battalion, the Lincolns, of Wauchope's brigade, also doubled up to prolong the new line. The change of front under heavy fire was carried out with wonderful steadiness by all ranks; men moved as if on the barrack square, deployed into line, and opened independent fire. The waves of fierce Dervishes broke and fell before such rock-like steadiness.

If this third attack had been timed to fit in with the main attack MacDonald would have suffered much more heavily. It is said that the Khalifa was furious with Wad Helu for being late.

By 11:15 A. M. the brave Dervishes were utterly defeated. The Khalifa with scattered followers had taken to flight. The Black Flag hung over a heap of warriors faithful unto death.

The Sirdar's object had been successfully attained, for the enemy had been driven away clear of the city. The cavalry followed to keep up the pressure, but their horses were cooked and they only picked up some unimportant stragglers. After re-forming and resting his men till 2 P. M. Kitchener led the way into the city, followed by the Black Flag, which was carried by an Orderly.

Smith-Dorrien's 13th Sudanese were the first to reach the brick wall, and he relates the story of the occupation. It was reported that the Khalifa was still in his house. Smith-Dorrien with half a dozen men broke through the gate leading into the courtyard, and had a sharp struggle with some of the Baggara bodyguard. Unfortunately at this moment shells began to fall from some of our own guns who could not see that Smith-Dorrien had got so far forward. One of the shrapnel killed the Hon. Hubert Howard, who was acting as a Press Correspondent; another very nearly hit the Sirdar and his Staff. The 13th Sudanese soon got into the house but the Khalifa was not to be found. Some few shots were heard in the streets, but before nightfall all firing ceased, and about 10 P. M. the troops sank to rest, weary but happy.

The victory cost little. Three British officers were killed and 17 wounded. Of the other ranks 45 (25 British) were killed and just under 450 wounded, a total casualty list of 500. Among the enemy the slaughter had been terrible; over

THE ATBARA AND OMDURMAN

10,000 dead were counted; still more had been wounded; 5,000 prisoners remained in our hands. The power of the Khalifa was completely shattered.

While the troops, and especially the Sudanese, were intoxicated with success, Kitchener maintained unsmiling calm. A short telegram was drafted to announce the success, and then he slept. Only on September 4 did his composure give way for a moment in the old palace at Khartoum. There, where Gordon had fallen, the British and Egyptian flags were hoisted and saluted. The chaplains read a simple service ending with Gordon's favourite hymn "Abide with me." Kitchener was not ashamed of his tears.

The heavy fighting was over and the Commander was free to economize. British troops were no longer needed. They consumed many rations, and therefore the sooner they departed the better. Three days after the battle they began to embark on every available boat, and with the current now in their favour little time was lost on the journey down the river. A battalion of the Rifle Brigade fought at Omdurman on September 2; by the 23rd of the same month it had arrived in Crete; the Grenadier Guards were back in England ten days later. It was remarked that Kitchener held no farewell parade and said good-bye to nobody except the 21st Lancers. Nevertheless his dispatches prove that he had not failed to observe everything that had taken place, and a big batch of decorations followed.

Another reason for the rather curt dismissal of the troops may be found in the work entailed by the Fashoda incident, which will be discussed in the next chapter. Meanwhile the story of the Sudan can be dealt with briefly.

The Khalifa fled towards El Obeid, west of the Nile, and for over a year remained out of reach. The gunboats commanded all the navigable rivers, but waterless deserts provided refuge for bands of Dervishes in places where no white man could follow. Columns under Parsons and Lewis cleared up most of the country east of the Nile, and captured several thousands of prisoners. In January a force under Colonel Walter Kitchener, brother of the Sirdar, started from the Nile to hunt the Khalifa; but the dry season had set in and all water had to be carried on camels; this made the difficulties immense, for the Dervish camp lay 120 miles to the west. After a reconnaissance Colonel Kitchener decided that nothing could be done till the wet season came round, and he returned to Omdurman.

The Sirdar made preparations to start afresh as soon as conditions became more favourable. In November, Wingate, who commanded in Kitchener's temporary absence, suddenly heard a rumour that the Khalifa had changed his tactics and was advancing to attack. Two battalions of Sudanese were sent at once to land on the west bank near Abba Island. The rumour turned out to be true. On November 22, Wingate had a preliminary skirmish and on the 24th he came upon the Dervish camp. Abdullah placed himself at the head of his Baggara tribesmen and led a furious charge. Once again the maxim guns mowed down the devoted fanatics. The Khalifa was hit in three places and fell dead 300 yards from our line. His son was taken prisoner and all the chief emirs lay dead or wounded. Mahdism existed no more. Wingate and his men returned to Omdurman by November 29.

CHAPTER VII

FASHODA

Rumours had reached London in 1896 that a French expedition was making its way from the Atlantic coast towards the upper waters of the Nile Valley. Marchand's little band consisted of 8 French officers and 120 Senegalese men; they made their way across the great continent of Africa—surely one of the finest achievements on record—and arrived at Fashoda on July 10, 1898. The news reached London in October and gave rise to an excitement which seems rather ridiculous, when we remember the attitude of the British Government during the previous twelve years. The Liberal Cabinet had given pledges to evacuate Egypt, and, though this had not been done, the evacuation of the Sudan was completed in 1885; Gladstone's reference to the Sudanese as a people rightly struggling to be free was a clear declaration that we intended to wash our hands of further responsibility with regard to the country. Even hard-headed statesmen like Cromer agreed that this was the only possible solution. Cromer had no illusions about a "freedom" which meant the worst form of tyranny, the revival of the slave trade in all its horrors, and the extinction of peaceful commerce; but neither Egypt nor England could afford the men and money to carry out a crusade of reform. And this had been our policy for twelve years. Yet we reserved to ourselves the rights of the dog in the manger—no other Power would be allowed to enter the Sudan either for purposes of conquest or humanity. If the French had made their appearance at Fashoda while the Liberals were in office a delicate situation would have resulted, for Gladstone could hardly have claimed the rights of a protector after leaving the country derelict for so long. Salisbury, who came to power at the end of 1895, apparently recognized that our position was a false one. When reports came to hand about the French Mission he determined that the British and Egyptian flags must be hoisted at Khartoum in order to show the world that we held ourselves responsible for the future of the Sudan. The first steps were taken with caution to avoid awkward questions in Parliament or elsewhere. The demonstration to Dongola, the advance to Khartoum, were perfectly in order, and established our rights. Instructions had been issued to the Sirdar for his guidance in case he found intruders.

On September 7 one of the Khalifa's steamers came lumbering down the river to Khartoum. The Captain had heard nothing about the defeat of the Dervishes; he surrendered at once, and told a story of strange white men whom he had seen at Fashoda. This was the first definite news of Marchand. On the 10th the Sirdar set off with five steamers, in which were a company of Cameron Highlanders, the 11th and 13th Sudanese, and a Mountain Battery. Smith-Dorrien, who commanded the troops, has given an account of the proceedings. Kitchener did not explain to anybody the object of his mission, but issued careful orders for the landing of troops and the hoisting of the Egyptian flag. A message was sent ahead to warn the French of the approach of the British, and as soon as the flotilla came abreast of the fort, on September 19, Marchand came on board for an interview.

After an exchange of civilities Kitchener informed the Commandant that he had instructions to occupy Fashoda in the name of its lawful owner, the Khedive; he offered to place a steamer at the disposal of the French to take them away. Marchand, as in duty bound, replied that he was there under the orders of his Government, and could not haul down the French flag without instructions from Paris. Kitchener had sufficient troops to enforce his intentions but was not so foolish as to use them; he contented himself with planting the Egyptian flag at a distance of 500 yards from the fort; leaving a garrison there, and another 50 miles further south, he returned to Khartoum. A fortnight later he went on to London and made his report, after which "L'affaire Marchand" was dealt with by the Foreign Office.

Salisbury insisted that the whole of the Sudan belonged to the Khedive; the British had helped him to recover it from the rebel tribes and would undertake to administer it; Marchand must therefore be withdrawn. After the Quai d'Orsay had made a few ineffectual protests it was agreed that Marchand had been a heroic explorer whose achievements reflected honour on his nation, but there had been no intention of interfering with British rights. The London Press gave vent to an outburst of satisfaction. Marchand received instructions to return to France, and Egyptian bands played the "Marseillaise" as he passed through Khartoum at the end of November.

Throughout the affair Kitchener had acted under instructions from Downing Street, and his share consisted in a courteous and correct demeanour towards the unfortunate French officer. But as Salisbury had declared his desire for a peaceful solution the "climb down" might have been made easier both for the French Government and the gallant Commandant. By an agreement of 1895 the French had acknowledged the Khedive as sovereign of the White Nile. We could therefore have assumed that Marchand had no official status. A diplomatic note might have been presented in Paris giving the French Government news of the explorer's arrival at Fashoda and offering help to get him out of a dangerous situation. If this offer had been accepted the Sirdar could have gone as a deliverer with a note of instructions from Paris to Marchand; the meeting would have been cordial, and an exchange of honest congratulations would have cemented the friendship. Marchand was running short of ammunition and supplies, and there can be little doubt that he would have welcomed the offer of relief, provided that he could do so without leaving a stain on the uniform of France. On the other hand, if the Quai d'Orsay refused the offer there still remained time to adopt the firmer tone of insistance.

Precipitate action gave the Press on both sides of the Channel an opportunity for noisy sabre-rattling which did nobody any good and left echoes which did us much harm. The least mistake on the part of either Kitchener or Marchand might have led to something worse.

A great reception awaited the hero of Omdurman on his return home. The Queen conferred on him a peerage; the cities of Great Britain vied with each other in their efforts to do him honour; the whole nation accepted him as a leader who could be trusted. Gordon had been avenged—the shame had been lifted from our hearts—and one man alone had done it. That was the feeling which made us turn to Kitchener in the hour of need sixteen years later.

Two months were spent in a round of festivities, at the end of which "Baron Kitchener of Khartoum in Africa and of Aspall in the County of Suffolk" was a freeman of London and held degrees at Oxford and Cambridge. He accepted the honours, and made an appeal for money which was to be devoted to a college at Khartoum in memory of Gordon. Queen Victoria became Patron of the Fund, and the Sirdar left England with £80,000 in his pocket.

The next year was spent as Governor-General of the Sudan, and I think Kitchener found more congenial work in that appointment than in any other period of his career. The administration of the Province lay entirely in his own hands; finance and justice, education and public works, everything depended on his will. His enthusiasm was not hampered by the trammels of divided authority. He could speak to the people in their own language, he understood their history and religion, their ignorance and vices. His technical training as an engineer could be constantly applied. Above all he had the self-confidence of a born ruler of men. The Sudan was a glorious field for his skill and energy. But in December 1899 there came the call to South Africa.

PART II
SOUTH AFRICA

CHAPTER VIII

THE TANGLED MESS

FAR BACK in 1652 a handful of emigrants from Holland settled in South Africa, and later in the same century they were joined by Huguenots who fled from France after the Revocation of the Edict of Nantes. From this sturdy Puritan stock there sprang and multiplied a race of yeoman farmers, the Boers. Like the pioneers of America who crossed the Alleghenies to thrust out the Indians, they spread gradually to the north and east, driving the savage tribes before them. At first the government was in the hands of a company of Amsterdam merchants, who had found at Capetown a useful port of call for ships trading with the East. Then the colony was recognized as belonging to Holland until after the Napoleonic Wars, when it passed into the possession of England. The population, however, remained Dutch in blood and tradition, and the Boers resented what they considered the harsh jurisdiction of British governors. Hoping to escape to places where they would be allowed to govern themselves they started the Great Trek northwards in 1836 and founded the Orange River Free State and South African Republic of the Transvaal. In the long train of wagons which toiled painfully across the veldt was a lad called Paul Kruger.

The Government in London claimed that the trekkers were still British subjects and therefore the new States were part of the British Empire. In 1848 a rebellion broke out which was crushed by Sir Harry Smith at Boomplatz. After that the Government grew tired of trying to rule a possession which was apparently worthless, and in 1852 the independence both of the Free State and of the Transvaal was acknowledged. The re-annexation of the Transvaal in 1877 was followed by the rebellion of 1880 and the disaster of Majuba

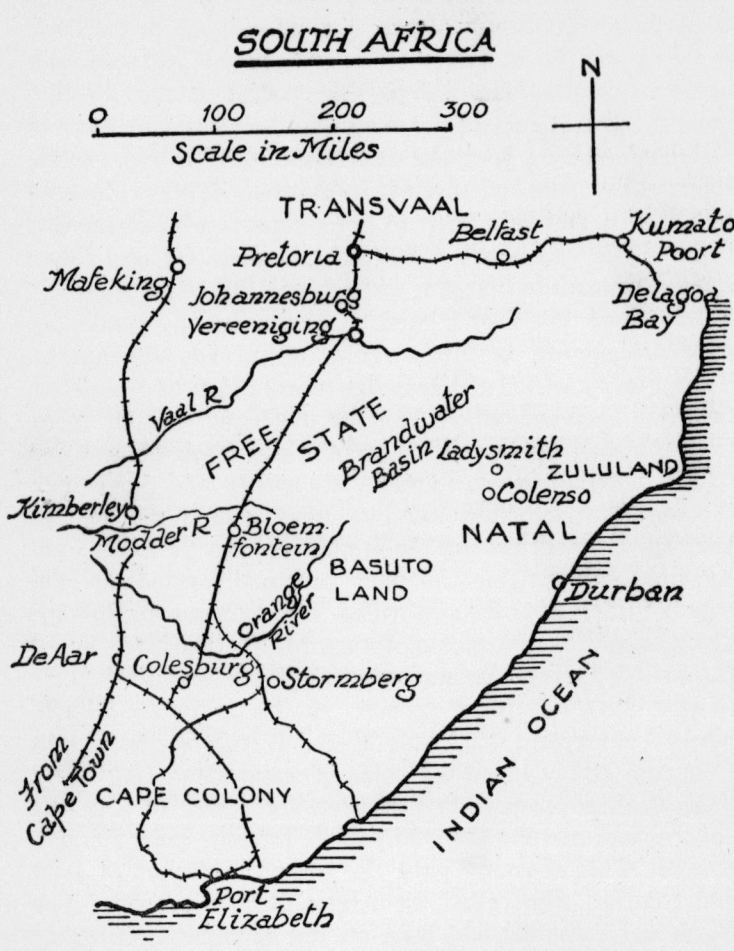

THE TANGLED MESS

in 1881, and the recognition by the Gladstone administration of the substantial independence of the Transvaal Republic. Meanwhile, in 1862 an event occurred which altered the whole history of South Africa. A child playing on the bank of the Orange River picked up a pretty pebble and carried it home to his father's farm. A passing guest, by name O'Reilly, noticed the brilliancy of the stone and took it to Colesberg to be examined by a Jew; the first experts said it was a white topaz of no value and threw it in the road. It was recovered by O'Reilly and submitted to other experts who declared it to be a diamond worth £500. Another diamond was found soon afterwards in the same district—and the rush began.

In a short time over a hundred companies and syndicates were prospecting, besides a crowd of private adventurers. The majority settled at Kimberley where the most productive field had been located. In 1871 an undergraduate, by name Cecil Rhodes, left Oxford on account of ill-health and came to the diamond fields. Through his energy and persistence the various conflicting interests were bought out and in 1888 the industry became the property of the De Beers Consolidated Mines. This Company practically ruled the diamond fields, and Rhodes ruled the Company. But his ambition was ever stretching forward to further extension of the British Empire; he persuaded the Directors of De Beers to provide funds for a pioneer movement to the North, where a settlement was made by the British South African Company and received the name of Rhodesia.

Meanwhile prospectors had been spreading all over the country and in 1886 the gold reef at Johannesburg was discovered. This of course gave rise to another influx of Jews and Gentiles who called themselves British subjects. The Transvaal Republic had been on the verge of bankruptcy and consequently the "Uitlanders" who brought money with them were at first received with some favour. Farmers could sell plots of barren land at high prices; by a system of monopolies the treasury was refilled. But when the gold-seekers found that they were paying practically all the taxes and financing the country they began to demand a share in the Government. This demand was fiercely opposed by President Kruger, and the result was a crop of grievances which divided the country into two groups bitterly hostile to each other. On one side were the Dutch burghers, spread out over the Veldt, jealous of their liberty and opposed to any measure which would give the British Government an excuse for interference in their affairs. On the other side a cosmopolitan crowd, closely concentrated on the Rand; heavily taxed but without any voice in the government of the country; striving by every means in their power to persuade the authorities in Downing Street to take up their quarrel.

The grievances of the Uitlanders went on accumulating until in January 1896 the financiers of Johannesburg made a futile effort to obtain redress by force of arms. This was the celebrated "Jameson Raid." It was absurdly mismanaged, and the 700 raiders made abject surrender to an inferior force of Boers. The attitude of British Ministers, who looked on calmly, was regarded by Kruger as a sign of weakness, and he became still more assertive. Increasing friction led to war in 1899.

The information which reached the London Press was coloured at its source by the views of Johannesburg; British subjects were under the tyranny of uncivilized and vindictive foreigners who refused to listen to the voice of reason and justice. It is not to be supposed that the Cabinet of Lord Salisbury accepted all these views without reservation, but none the less they cannot be acquitted of extraordinary ignorance. Up to the last moment they had no idea that their action would plunge the country into a long and expensive war. The belief seems to have been that the quarrel between Boer and Uitlander arose from faults on both sides. The grievances of the British might be exaggerated, but they were not without foundation. Since President Kruger refused to accept any suggestions from Downing Street he must be taught that he could not domineer over the subjects of the Empire; as soon as he realized that we were in earnest he would use a milder tone. After that, the High Commissioner at Capetown, Sir Alfred Milner, would adjust the differences—and that would be the end of a troublesome business. To avoid any possibility of resistance it was decided to send out an overwhelming force of three Divisions. Sir Redvers Buller, who had served in Zululand twenty years previously, was appointed to the Command, and orders for mobilization were issued on September 22.

If the Colonial Office, which had been dealing with the matter, is convicted of ignorance, still more profound was the ignorance of the War Office. As late as September 14 the Under-Secretary, George Wyndham, wrote to his father: "You must not believe the papers as to the chances of war; I am almost certain that the Transvaalers will give in." While such views were held by those in authority the rest of the army took only a luke-warm interest in the prospects of active service.

Another cause of ignorance arose from our study of military history. For nearly a century our campaigns had been on the small scale against uncivilized armies; it was therefore natural that we had based our training on the experience of the Prussians, who had carried out two big wars under the latest conditions of military science and modern invention. British military studies were concentrated on Moltke's campaigns of 1866 and 1870. But the American War of Independence might have taught us a good deal. There, too, a sturdy race of independent farmers had fought for liberty. Their methods were unconventional, their training was not that of the parade ground and rifle range; but they knew their ground and experience had taught them the use of their weapons. Everybody admitted that the Boers could shoot; they had smashed up a little British detachment of 530 men at Majuba in 1881; still more easily they had captured Jameson's raiders in 1896. But Moltke's campaigns had proved that success could only be won by infantry, artillery, and cavalry working together. The Boers had few guns and no cavalry in the correct meaning of the term; their infantry carried no bayonets; their leaders had never studied the campaigns of Napoleon—what could they know of strategy or tactics?

It was not to be imagined that three Divisions of British infantry would find any difficulty in overcoming a mob of undisciplined farmers. A few officers who knew something about the Boers ventured to suggest that their resistance would be serious, but none of them had sufficient authority to carry any weight. No General of established reputation had lately been serving at the Cape, which, from the point of view of ambitious officers, was regarded as a backwater. It was a comfortable station, outside the range of obnoxious inspecting officers, but there were few troops and therefore nobody of exalted rank. Those who hoped for active service worked their way to Egypt or the North-West Frontier; other roads to promotion ran through the War Office, the Staff College, or Aldershot. The garrisons in Cape Colony and Natal had been warned to avoid any activity which might look provocative—in other words, they were not encouraged to study the local conditions from a military point of view. If Fate or the War Office had sent Kitchener to South Africa ten years earlier he might have had a chance of planning a campaign based on knowledge of the enemy and of the ground. But Kitchener was still at Khartoum.

The Regular Forces in Great Britain cannot be mobilized at a moment's notice. A Battalion is complete in officers and non-commissioned officers but has only about half its complement of trained men; before it can embark, reservists must be called up and equipped. Consequently the first troop-ship did not leave England till October 20, just four weeks after the order for mobilization had been issued. Regiments in India, however, are maintained at the full strength of all ranks, and are therefore ready to embark at shorter notice. The Viceroy, Lord Curzon, was asked to send a contingent of 8,000 men to Natal as quickly as possible. In a week they were at sea, and they began to disembark at Durban on Oc-

THE TANGLED MESS 91

tober 7. Sir George White was hurried out to take command of this force; he had lately been Commander-in-Chief in India and had just been appointed Governor of Gibraltar. He reached Durban on October 6.

As soon as Kruger learned about these movements he issued an ultimatum on October 9, demanding the withdrawal of the troops recently landed and the diversion of those on their way to South Africa. This was practically a declaration of war, and without waiting for further argument the Boers decided to strike before the full strength of their enemy could be developed. 15,000 Transvaalers from the north and 6,000 Free Staters from the west converged on Ladysmith, where Sir George White was collecting the British forces as quickly as they arrived.

The first two engagements were fought by detachments at Talana Hill on October 20, and Elandslaagte on October 21. In both of these the British infantry drove their opponents out of their positions and claimed victory. The successes, however, were unreal, for in each case the ground had to be given up immediately afterwards, and the detachments made the best of their way to join White's main body at Ladysmith. On October 30 another attempt was made to drive back the advancing commandos at Nicholson's Nek and Lombard's Kop, a few miles outside Ladysmith, but in both cases the results were disastrous. By November 2 White, with 13,000 men, was surrounded in Ladysmith by about 23,000 Boers. Kimberley and Mafeking were besieged at the same time.

Severe comments have been directed against the British authorities for allowing these garrisons to be locked up in forward positions; but the great American writer, Captain Mahan, has pointed out that the Boers neglected big opportunities in the hope of capturing these three towns. By September 22 they knew that three Divisions were under orders in England, but that several weeks must elapse before the first transports could reach Capetown. During this period the British must be in very inferior force. The Boers could mobilize about 50,000 men and could move quickly; a resolute movement by such a force might have led to great results. But instead of adopting such a plan they contented themselves with surrounding three widely separated points and then sat down until the balance of numbers, far from being on their side, was very much against them. Captain Mahan suggests that if the baits at Ladysmith, Kimberley, and Mafeking had not attracted them, they could have done much better elsewhere, and even Capetown might have been in danger.

However that may be, the events of October entirely upset Buller's plans. He had originally intended to advance with his whole force through the Free State to Pretoria; now his object must be to relieve the beleaguered towns. The first transports were directed to Durban, and General Clery with four brigades was ordered to advance on Ladysmith. Then Lord Methuen, with about 10,000 men, was sent towards Kimberley. Between these two a central force under General Gatacre held Sterkstrom. Buller was still confident that as soon as Ladysmith and Kimberley had been relieved the opposition would collapse, and up to the end of November no alarm was felt.

Methuen moved steadily along the railway towards Kimberley. At Belmont and Graspan he turned the Boers out of strong positions. On November 28 he attacked them at Modder River and though they were not defeated they retired next day. He was now within 25 miles of Kimberley, and halted to get up supplies and reinforcements for his final move.

Buller himself went to Natal. He collected 19,000 men on the south bank of the Tugela, and was reconnoitring the river with a view to crossing, preferably by a wide movement to his left.

Then followed three disasters in quick succession during the "Black Week" of December 10–15.

On December 9 Gatacre made a night march towards Stormberg. He lost his way, and wandered about until the dawn; while the troops were still marching in fours the Boers opened fire and threw the whole column into confusion. This was made worse by another commando which appeared on the left flank. Gatacre ordered a retreat, but by some neglect the order never reached many of the troops, and 600 were left behind to fall into the hands of the enemy. The casualties on both sides were small but the moral result was considerable.

On the following day came Methuen's attack at Magersfontein. To avoid casualties at long range he had made a night march, but the Highland Brigade stumbled on the Boer trenches while still in quarter-column and suffered very heavily; the flanking troops were easily held up and the whole attempt ended in a repulse with the loss of 860 men.

Apparently the news of these two events goaded Buller into precipitate action. Instead of attempting a turning movement he flung his men on December 15 into a frontal attack by daylight—the battle of Colenso. Various mistakes were made, but even without them there was small chance for a frontal attack on so good a position as that which the Boers held on the north bank of the river. Our men never got within close range; we lost several guns and nearly 900 killed and wounded. The Boer loss is said to have been about a score.

The result was a bitter disappointment, and Buller came to the conclusion that he could not relieve Ladysmith; he heliographed a message to White in which he hinted that the garrison might have to surrender. This was meant as a generous offer to relieve White of painful responsibility, but the necessity for surrender did not arise. White replied that Ladysmith would hold out at all costs.

These humiliating reverses aroused the British Empire. The whole of the Army Reserve was called out and the Colonies volunteered to send contingents. It was announced that, as the campaign in Natal would require the undivided attention of General Buller, Lord Roberts had been appointed Commander-in-Chief with Kitchener as his Chief-of-Staff.

Leaving Khartoum on December 18 the new Chief-of-Staff hastened to Alexandria and embarked on a fast cruiser, H.M.S. *Isis*. An officer of that ship says that Kitchener suffered badly from sea-sickness and scarcely appeared before they arrived at Gibraltar on the 27th. There he was transferred to join Roberts on the *Dunnottar Castle*. During the fortnight's voyage to Capetown there was time for careful consideration of the problem before them.

Reports which had come to hand up to this time showed that the Boers made full use of their superior mobility, which, in a country of wide spaces, gave them an enormous advantage. They could refuse battle when the odds were against them; they could threaten a flank or rear; they could concentrate quickly at a decisive point. Secondly, the battles at Talana, Belmont and Graspan showed that frontal attacks had proved expensive even when successful, and that small movements by infantry were of little use because they gave the Boers time to swing round and face them, so that they became "frontal attacks from another direction." Therefore the first problem was to improve our mobility; the enemy must be pinned down to battle and the turning movements must make a quick and wide circle. Lack of transport had tied Buller and Methuen to the railway and lack of mounted men had made the turning movements slow. The natural deduction was that our army must be improved in these two respects, and it was useless to throw infantry masses against prepared positions until the improvement had been effected. The chief question was whether the besieged towns could hold out until mobility had been increased so far as to give the army liberty of movement. This vital question must remain unanswered until Roberts arrived in Capetown and the latest reports had been received.

Throughout the Sudan campaign Kitchener had kept on excellent terms with the War Office because he had established a reputation as an expert on the local situation; he

THE TANGLED MESS

knew what he wanted and his demands had been moderate. But of South Africa he had no personal experience and apparently the War Office preferred its own opinion to his. Sir George Arthur quotes a letter written by Kitchener on the *Dunnottar Castle* which gives us a good clue to his frame of mind.

"I hope we shall manage it all right out at the Cape, but it is a big business badly begun, and the difficulty of unravelling the tangled mess will be very great. No transport seems to have been organized, and all the troops are mixed up. Our Artillery has turned out useless, as I expected. When you think, all our field guns were originally 12-pr.; they were then bored out to make them 15-pr., which naturally only allows of their being fired at reduced charges! We are hopelessly behind the age, owing to our Artillery Officers' dislike of anything new. I wired from Cairo what guns we ought to have, but of course the official reply was against doing anything. My God! I can scarcely credit their taking the fearful responsibility of sending us into the field practically unarmed with artillery. Roberts, I am glad to say, is wiring again." [1]

This letter shows that even on the scanty information then in hand Kitchener had made up his mind on two of the factors which afterwards turned out to be of vital importance. Also we can see in it the first signs of irritation at the mentality of the War Office—an irritation which was not healed by time. The *Dunnottar Castle* reached Capetown on January 10, and the latest news was eagerly studied, after which Roberts and Kitchener proceeded to take stock of the "tangled mess." Nothing of real importance had developed while they had been at sea. Buller had collected more troops after Colenso, and a turning movement by Spion Kop had again failed. Methuen stood on the Modder, Gatacre remained unmolested about Sterkstrom, and French kept up a more aggressive attitude near Colesberg.

[1] Arthur, I, p. 267.

Whatever other sins the War Office had committed, real energy had been shown in the dispatch of troops, for which the Admiralty must receive a big share of praise. The first three Divisions had begun to embark on October 20, and 28,000 men were on the voyage before the end of that month; in November 29,000 followed; in December 20,000. Then, after the "Black Week" there was a spurt of 27,000 in January, 33,000 in February, 27,000 in March. These were in addition to 9,000 troops from the distant colonies of Canada, Australia, New Zealand. Altogether over 166,000 were landed in less than six months. Considering that the distance was 6,000 miles and the voyage took twenty-two days, this was a fine performance. In January Roberts found himself in command of the largest army that the British Empire had ever placed in the field, spread over a front of 500 miles. The "tangled mess" required careful sorting and on the whole the results were good, but this was chiefly due to the energy and capacity of Kitchener and other individual officers. The Staff as a properly constituted machine with well-defined duties did not exist, because up to this date no British army had been large enough to require a staff machine. Consequently there was overlapping at some points and gaps at others.

From the first an urgent necessity for haste had broken up the original units. Odds and ends had been flung into Natal; Gatacre's Division had been so scattered that he never saw a complete brigade. Colonial units of varying strength were bunched together with a battalion of British infantry and half a battery to form a column for some particular job. And each of these bunches of very indefinite size had to be fed and supplied.

It has been said that Kitchener did everybody's work except his own as Chief-of-Staff, but in the circumstances this seems to have been unavoidable. Roberts could take care of the strategy provided that he had the means to carry it out. Kitchener set himself to tackle the transport question, to collect wagons of local pattern which would not jolt to

THE TANGLED MESS 97

pieces on the tracks and drifts of the veldt; animals which could stand the work and keep up with the march. He then studied how to use them in the most economical way, so that each unit should have just sufficient wagons for the number of men who were actually present in the ranks and not for the number who ought to have been there. Thus a battalion which had lost half its strength from any cause was deprived of half its wagons—a simple plan in theory, but difficult to put into practice. When a battalion finds half its transport taken away it attempts to solve the difficulty by overloading the remaining half, which kills the mules; "and then there is none." The Transport Officer blames the Quartermaster who blames the Mess Sergeant, and so on. Kitchener was clever enough to see that no system of allotting transport would be of any use unless the officers in charge of it had sufficient authority to enforce their orders. A scale laid down the load for each wagon, which must never be exceeded—that was simple enough; but when mules are underfed and in poor condition, when the march is long and the road bad, the load must be reduced—then the trouble begins. A wise Quartermaster will jettison certain unauthorized stores which have very innocent labels on them, and so get the really necessary articles to the next camp. The foolish Quartermaster insists on loading up everything, and the wagons break down. Kitchener's plan was to appoint transport officers who could neither be bullied nor bluffed, and this was a real revolution. A non-combatant branch of the Service fails to attract ambitious officers, who naturally look for jobs either in the front line or among the higher circles; a transport man who did his duty would probably quarrel with everybody and get reported for his pains. This did not happen after Kitchener had appointed the new transport staff, which included several very well-known men, a royal prince, some guardsmen, and several "Egyptian pets." Instead of being slaves they were soon masters, and it speedily became known that the surest road to promotion was through the despised ranks of oxen and mules. Without doubt, this was the factor which enabled Roberts to leave the railway line and plan operations on a wider scale.

Hopes had been cherished that Buller's fresh attempt to relieve Ladysmith might be more successful, but on January 11 news came in of another set-back at Vaalkrantz on the Tugela. White's garrison was now reduced to very short rations, but Roberts wisely resisted the temptation to rush matters, and spent three weeks in Capetown before leaving for the Front. He believed that a big movement on Bloemfontein, by calling the commandos in that direction, would automatically relieve both Kimberley and Ladysmith. It was commonly understood that the advance would be direct, up the main line into the Free State, and everything was done to encourage this belief. So strong was the impression that it reached the ears of Cecil Rhodes in Kimberley and caused an outcry. Rhodes had thrown himself into the diamond city shortly before it was besieged, and expected to find that his power was still as autocratic as it had always been. He was not pleased to find that the commandmant of the garrison, Colonel Kekewich, took precedence in military affairs, and there was much friction. The Colonel worked hard and well to organize and improve the defences; like White at Ladysmith he would starve before surrendering, and starvation was still a long way off. He saw that by detaining the Boers round the place he could lighten the task of Roberts, and therefore he kept on worrying the besiegers by sallies. But he saw nothing else which raised Kimberley above the status of any other town that happened to be besieged. The diamond magnates saw a great deal more. To them Kimberley was the sacred city. The Boers looked on Rhodes as the chief villain of the Uitlanders, whose wealth and power had always been opposed to Kruger. Frantic messages were sent to Capetown implying that the whole British Army ought to march as one man to prevent such a disaster as the fall of Kimberley and the fall of Rhodes. As early as October the directors of De Beers demanded information regarding the plans of the military authorities "so as to enable us to take our own steps in case relief is refused"; when Buller refused to divulge his plans to civilians their annoyance was extreme. Later on, in February, Rhodes threatened to call a public meeting to "consider the situation" unless he was informed of the plans for relief; but Kekewich received authority from Headquarters to forbid the meeting and even to arrest Rhodes if necessary.

These drastic steps do not imply that Roberts paid no attention to the political situation. The garrison of Kimberley was small, only 600 regulars and some Colonial troops, and the town was not a strategic point or a railway centre—yet its capture would certainly raise the morale of the Boers perhaps even more than the surrender of White in Ladysmith. How far Roberts allowed this political factor to influence his strategy must remain a matter of conjecture. But it so happened that the relief of Kimberley did not lead him far out of his way. It is said that two years earlier he had drawn up a scheme which was based on an advance along the western line of railway, followed by a move across country eastwards; and, though he could not push along the railway as far as he would have liked, this plan was still the main idea of his opening move.

CHAPTER IX

PAARDEBERG

THE BIG concentration was completed at Modder River by February 10. To ensure secrecy some of the troops had been brought down at the last moment and a demonstration had been thrown out westwards to give the impression that the movement would take that direction.

In addition to Methuen's original force, which was to remain at Modder, Roberts now had the following troops:

The Cavalry Division of 3 Brigades and some Colonial units, under Lieutenant-General J. French.
Colonel Hannay's Brigade of Mounted Infantry.
VI Division. Lieut.-General Sir T. Kelly Kenny.
VII Division. Lieut.-General Sir C. Tucker.
IX Division. Lieut.-General Sir H. Colville.
98 guns.
700 wagons.
The fighting troops amounted to 34,000 men.

On February 11 French set out from Modder River Camp, marching southwards away from the enemy; he started in the night and left the tents standing deceitfully empty. He reached Ramdam, 17 miles, and next day went on to Watervaal Drift; finding this held by a handful of Boers he pushed on quickly to De Kiel's Drift and, after securing a crossing, halted. Kitchener came up during the night with the leading infantry who had marched from Graspan station.

On the 13th the Cavalry had to do 25 miles to reach the Modder at Klip Drift. The heat was terrific and many horses broke down. There were signs of the enemy near the river, but French, despite the general exhaustion, pressed on and occupied some high ground on the far bank. Next day a halt was made to allow the infantry to close up. Kitchener arrived during the night and at dawn on the 15th the VI Division staggered in. This made the crossing of the river secure and French was at liberty to move on.

The Cavalry, spread out in wide formation, started northwards. Some scattered detachments of the enemy held various kopjes on the road, hoping to delay the advance. French refused to be deterred; he had no idea what strength lay in front of him, but without waiting to ask questions about this, and without dismounting to open fire, he spurred his weary animals into something like a gallop, and the sheer weight of those 6,000 horsemen brushed aside the opposition, which was really very thin. By sunset Kimberley was relieved.

Cronje, who commanded the Boers at Magersfontein, had been thoroughly deceived. It was late on the 11th before he found out that the Cavalry had left the camp facing him; their direction, due south, was puzzling, but he sent a commando of about 1,000 strong under Christian De Wet along the east bank of the Riet River to keep a look-out.

De Wet thought that French would continue in a southerly direction and therefore went on past De Kiel's Drift with the intention of hindering such a move. When the Cavalry suddenly turned round northwards and was followed by infantry, De Wet saw that he had been mistaken; it was too late, however, to get in front of the big column, nor could he dash through it to rejoin Cronje. For two days he sat still—and then brought off the first of the many brilliant exploits which made him famous. The supply wagons took a long time in crossing De Kiel's Drift; Kitchener would not keep the VI Division halted until they were all over; consequently 170 wagons under a small escort were still at the Drift on February 15 when Kitchener marched away. At 8 A. M. De Wet swooped down on them. The escort offered a stout resistance. Roberts, who was then near Jacobsdaal, 12 miles to the north, sent back a battalion and afterwards a brigade to save his precious supplies. But by that time De Wet had taken up a

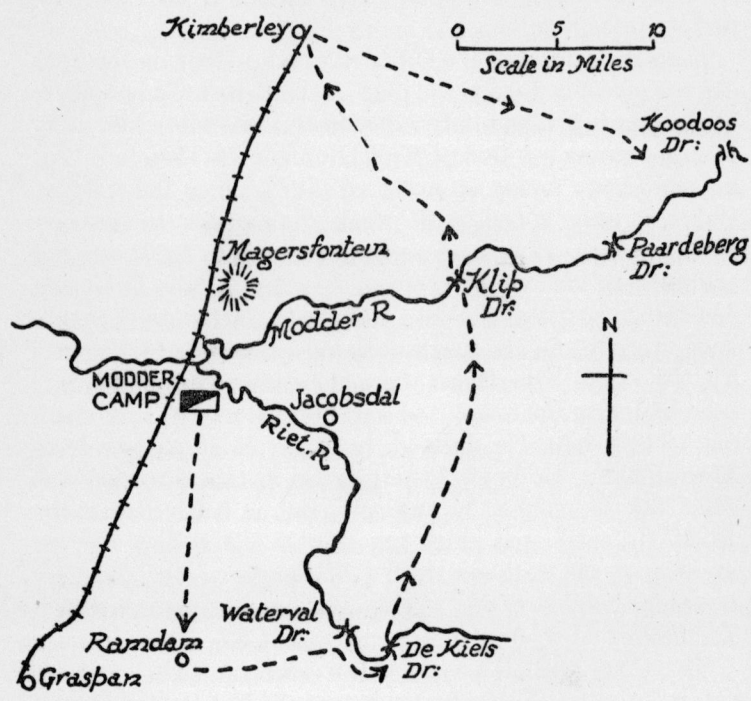

very strong position and appeared to be in considerable strength. Roberts decided to abandon the convoy sooner than delay the bigger operation; he therefore ordered all the troops to resume the march northwards. As a consequence of this loss the army had to go on half rations for the next month. The sacrifice must have cost the Commander-in-Chief an unhappy moment, but he could console himself afterwards with the thought that if he had turned back to save those wagons he would have missed a far more important prize.

Even the arrival of the Cavalry at Klip Drift on the 13th did not reveal to Cronje the plan of the British Commander; he thought that it was only a demonstration to lure him away from his strong position at Magersfontein. He therefore kept his main-body facing an expected attack along the railway, and sent only a couple of weak commandos to obstruct French, which, as we have seen, they failed to do. It was not till the 15th that the presence of infantry at Klip Drift and Jacobsdaal startled him into movement. He could probably have made his escape northwards on either side of Kimberley; he would have found there the commandos which had been besieging the town; and French's cavalry was too worn out to hold him. He decided, however, to go eastwards to Bloemfontein. He knew that the road in that direction was clear, for the moment at any rate, and he believed that the British infantry was much too slow to catch him. On the evening of the 15th he started his long convoy, and next morning the dust of his wagons was seen by patrols which Kitchener had sent out northwards from Klip Drift.

The Chief-of-Staff recognized at once the significance of this information. Since the big movement had started he had undertaken a roving commission to supply driving force wherever it might be needed, and he was now at a spot where it was very much needed. The VI Division which had been under orders to march on Kimberley was switched on to Cronje's tail. Hannay's Brigade of Mounted Infantry was turned in the same direction. An urgent message was sent to French ordering him to get in front of Cronje by moving to Koodoo's Drift, 30 miles east of Kimberley.

The Cavalry Division had spent the 16th wandering round on the north side of Kimberley. A Colonial officer belonging to the town believed he could locate the big gun, Long Tom, which had been shelling the defences, and French was induced to send out all his troops in hopes of capturing either the gun or some of the laagers which had been lying round the town. But the result was almost disastrous. The big gun had disappeared. A few Boers were seen, but they put up a rear-guard fight and could not be surrounded; the long day, terribly hot and with no opportunities for watering, took the last gasp out of more than half the horses. On returning to camp late in the evening French found Kitchener's message calling for another march of 30 miles next day. Out of the fine Division which had left Modder a week before, only enough horses could be mustered to mount about 1,200 men. With these French set out at 4:30 A. M. on the 17th; in six hours he had reached the Kopjes north of Vendutie's Drift, and this happened to be the exact spot where he was wanted.

During the 16th Cronje had plodded along with Kitchener close on his tail; he intended to cross to the south bank of the Modder, where De Wet and some other commandos might be expected to join him. It was a surprise to find that British troops "who could not march" were still maintaining touch, but a rear-guard kept them from doing any serious harm. Early on the 17th he halted on the north side of Vendutie's Drift, where he intended to cross the river later the same day. Suddenly from the Kopje two miles north some shells began to drop among his wagons; the oxen, which were grazing in the open, stampeded, and the whole convoy was seized with panic. The shells came from French's Horse Artillery.

In fact the little handful of British cavalry, tired, hungry, and unsupported, was in a more dangerous position than Cronje himself. Fortunately the fog of war concealed the truth from the enemy. Further north a commando under

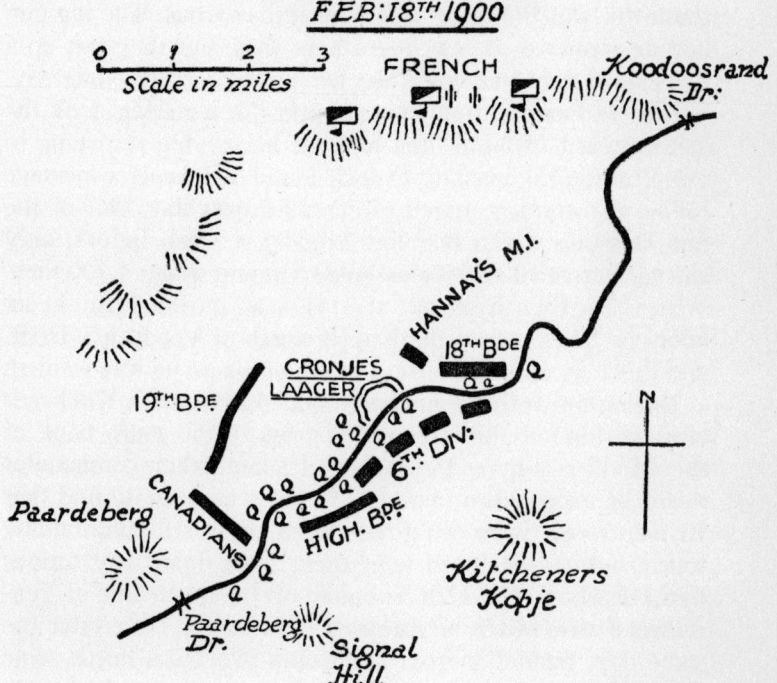

Ferreira, about 2,000 strong, was groping its way to join Cronje; but when Ferreira found a force of unknown strength blocking his road, he rather feebly gave up his intention and sheered off. On the south at Vendutie's Drift were 5,000 Boers, whose horses were still in good condition. Between these two forces the British cavalry had been spread out very thinly along three miles of broken ground. The Official Account says that French had 1,200 men when he left Kimberley that morning; perhaps 800 of them had reached the spot when Cronje's laager was located and the Horse Artillery opened fire; others straggled in later on, many of them on foot. If Ferreira and Cronje could have combined, in an attack from both sides, the handful of cavalry would have been in serious danger. If Cronje was afraid to commit himself to an attack against a force of unknown strength, he could have escaped any time during that afternoon without fighting, provided that he resigned himself to the loss of his wagons. He was urged to take this course by many of his followers. There was nobody to the south of him. But instead of making an effort to save himself he seems to have relied on help from outside; he knew that De Wet and Ferreira were hovering round. During the night several hundred of his men deserted, and escaped without difficulty, but the main-body was still at Vendutie's Drift next morning—and this led to what is known as the Battle of Paardeberg.

On the 18th Kitchener reached Paardeberg Drift at dawn with Hannay's Mounted Infantry. He immediately had a complete view of the situation. To the north-east lay a big oval of flat ground surrounded by broken kopjes. Down the centre of this the Modder River flowed swiftly in a winding bed about fifty yards broad with steep banks over twenty feet high; thin scrub and a few trees close to the stream gave cover from view, but elsewhere the veldt was bare. The distance from Paardeberg Drift to Koodoo's Drift at the far end of the oval was about 8 miles, and near the centre lay a huddled mass of wagons, on the north bank, which were made very conspicuous by their white covers. Puffs of smoke from the heights on the north showed that the cavalry had reached the appointed spot. Communication was soon established with French, who reported that he could hold his position but had not sufficient strength to do more—he could not attack. Kitchener was satisfied to know that Cronje could not escape northwards. The other exits could be blocked by troops who were arriving along the south bank.

Kitchener looked at his watch and said: "It is now seven o'clock; we shall be in that laager by half-past ten; I'll then load up French and send him on to Bloemfontein at once."

Hannay was ordered to swing round by the south and cross the river bend on the far side of the laager; one brigade, Stephenson's, of the VI Division, was to follow and remain on the south bank. These two could block the exit eastward. Another brigade of the VI Division—Knox's—was to deploy facing the laager from the south. Two brigades of the IX Division, which came up later, were to advance eastward up the river, one on each bank. When all were in position they would make a simultaneous attack towards the laager, supported by artillery fire.

The decision to attack has been severely criticized on the ground that it was unnecessary to expose men in the open to deadly rifle fire in order to capture a force which in any case could not escape. The casualties on this day amounted to 85 officers and 1,185 other ranks, a heavier total than on any other day of the whole war. The critics maintain that this loss could have been avoided.

But Kitchener had to make his decision on the situation as it appeared to him at the moment. Though it seemed simple enough as far as the immediate facts were concerned, there was a disturbing element in the unknown facts outside his range of view. De Wet's commando was at large somewhere to the south; a considerable force which had been besieging Kimberley must be still in the neighbourhood on the north side; quite possibly other commandos might be hastening from Bloemfontein on the east. The extraordinary position had therefore come about that Cronje lay in the centre like the bull's-eye of a target; round him was an inner circle of British troops, drawing gradually closer; outside these came a fringe of commandos, not continuous and of unknown strength, but still sufficient to cause anxiety. It might be necessary to turn and face them. Better therefore to deal as quickly as possible with the one lot which had been pinned down within reach. Such were the considerations which decided Kitchener to press home an attack at once.

It was nevertheless a difficult matter. In the first place the question of supreme command remained indefinite. Roberts himself had been detained at Jacobsdal by a sudden indisposition. Kelly Kenny, Colville, and French, though junior to Kitchener as Major-Generals, had been given local rank as Lieut.-Generals, and were therefore senior to him on the field of battle. Roberts had written to Kelly Kenny telling him to accept orders from Kitchener as if they came from Headquarters, but the other Generals had not been informed of this. Worse still, though Roberts certainly intended to give Kitchener authority he had not provided him with a staff to assist in issuing orders. The proper procedure would have been to establish Headquarters in some prominent spot, out of the enemy's range, and easily found by wandering messengers; from this centre communication should have been arranged with French, Hannay, and the two Divisional Commanders, by helio, flag, or mounted orderlies. Kitchener could then have controlled the battle; units would have known where to send reports and where to ask for instructions if they were at a loss.

Instead of this, Kitchener had only one staff officer with him and a couple of A.D.C.'s; a few signallers, who were of little use because the day was cloudy and the helio could only be worked during occasional glimpses of sunshine. He could not keep touch with units who were scattered over a circle twenty-five miles round. The Official History says: "It was a gallant attempt to substitute his own vigorous personality for the missing agency of command." Kitchener and his A.D.C.'s were seen galloping from place to place, issuing verbal orders, in some cases to battalions without informing the Brigadiers or Divisional Generals, who at the same time were ordering something else. And the three attacks from west, south, and east, which, to have any chance of success, should have been simultaneous, were quite disjointed.

A good example of the resulting confusion is given by Smith-Dorrien. His brigade, the 19th, had been ordered to the north bank. The river at Paardeberg Drift was in flood and over waist-deep, so that the men had difficulty in fording it; but before midday Smith-Dorrien was in position and his front line lay extended half a mile from the nearest trenches. He says:

"I was in a complete fog as to what was happening, and knew nothing of the situation, either of our own troops or of the Boers, beyond what I could see and infer myself. It was not until next day that I learnt that the guns about Kameelfontein belonged to our cavalry. The only order I had received was the one to establish my Brigade on the north side of the river, and I could get neither instructions nor information from anyone. At 5.15 p.m. I was horrified at seeing our troops on the right of my line rise and charge forward with a ringing cheer. I, at that time, believed that only Canadians were there; but it appeared that Lieutenant-Colonel Aldworth, D.S.O., with three and a half companies of my baggage guard, the Cornwalls, and some Seaforth Highlanders, on the far side of the river, had been sent over by a higher authority to charge the Boer position, and that the Canadians, who would not be left behind, had joined in. Of course it was quite irregular that my troops should have been ordered to execute such an important movement, except through me, as any possibility of my supporting the charge with the rest of the Brigade was effectually prevented, for by the time I realized what was happening, the attack was over, since it only occupied a minute or two." [1]

On the other side of the battle further confusion arose. Hannay crossed the river by a drift two miles east of the

[1] Smith-Dorrien, p. 152.

laager, and formed up; after reconnoitring towards the Boer trenches he sent a message to Kitchener saying he was too weak to make a successful attack. Shortly afterwards shells began to drop on him from the outside; these came from a commando which had hastened up from Natal, and had reached a kopje at the east end of the oval. Naturally Hannay faced about to meet this unexpected enemy. His change of front upset Stephenson's Brigade, which was following him. This Brigade of the VI Division had originally been ordered by Kelly Kenny to cross to the north bank at Paardeberg Drift; it was then recalled by Kitchener, who sent it to follow the Mounted Infantry; two battalions were dropped on the way, so that only half a brigade was left by the time it approached the river. Seeing that Hannay was facing eastwards, away from the laager, Stephenson also turned in that direction. Thus, when Kitchener was trying to attack from three sides he saw a third of his force facing the wrong way. Irritated at this miscarriage of his plan he sent a peremptory message to Hannay, ordering him to rush the laager at all costs and at once. Hannay, having already reported that he was too weak, regarded this order as a reflection on his personal courage. He collected three officers and about fifty men, ordered them to fix bayonets and mount, and then led a charge across the open; when his horse was killed under him he advanced on foot to meet his death. The rest of his Brigade made an effort to follow but none of them got to within three hundred yards of the Boer line.[1]

When it was seen that Hannay had thrown himself away, Stephenson was ordered to renew the attack with his infantry. He took the two battalions to the north bank and got within five hundred yards of the Boer line. At this point he

---

[1] Captain Cramer-Roberts, Norfolk Regiment, took part in this charge. He was wounded in the thigh and lost control of his horse, which carried him into the laager, where he lay for nine days. He told me afterwards that he had received kind treatment, and his wound was carefully dressed. The Boers did not seem to have many casualties, and our shell fire was quite harmless; though he could not understand what was being said, people about him appeared to be quite calm.

PAARDEBERG

was held up, and the two battalions entrenched themselves for the night.

Meanwhile Knox's Brigade, immediately south of the laager, had fared no better. It deployed for attack on a very wide front but did not get within half a mile of the river-bed. In fact, the attempted assaults had all failed.

In the afternoon an event occurred which justified Kitchener's anxiety about interference from the outside. A couple of miles south of the laager stood a hill about three hundred feet high which was afterwards known as Kitchener's Kopje. Early in the day Kelly Kenny sent a detachment of infantry to hold it; without his knowledge some wandering staff officer removed this party, replacing it with Kitchener's Horse, a newly raised regiment of South African Colonials. About 4 P. M. De Wet arrived from the south and made for this kopje. The defenders were watching the infantry attack and apparently nobody thought of keeping a look-out in the other direction. De Wet captured all of them, seized the hill, and opened fire with two guns on the artillery of the VI Division. This caused further dislocation of the main attack because troops had to be diverted to deal with the new threat from the rear. It was fortunate that De Wet had not brought the whole of his men with him; the presence of British infantry at Jacobsdal, forty miles to the west, deceived him into leaving half his commando on that side; with another five hundred men he might have effected the relief of Cronje.

At sunset the laager still held out. Round it a circle of infantry had been completed on the west, south, and east, at a distance varying between five hundred and a thousand yards from the Boer trenches. On the north French had got up some more cavalry from Kimberley, and he was now securely established, though at long range. De Wet held Kitchener's Kopje, where he hung on for two more days in spite of attempts to eject him. Another Boer force under Commandant Steyn was further east.

Though our assaults had all been repulsed, one important

gain resulted from the heavy shell and rifle fire which had been continuous during the day. The Boers themselves suffered little in their deep trenches, but all their oxen and most of their horses had been killed. A sudden dash for freedom was no longer possible, and only a few succeeded in trickling out of the laager by night. If Cronje had been able to mount his men he might have made a rush to join De Wet when the latter was holding Kitchener's Kopje.

On the morning of the 19th Roberts arrived and collected several Generals to hear their reports and consider further plans. Smith-Dorrien gives an account of what followed:

"During this morning I was sent for by Lord Roberts and asked, in the presence of Lord Kitchener, Generals French and Colvile, whether I thought I could at once carry the laager by direct assault. Kitchener and Colvile seemed to be in favour of such action, but I deprecated it most strongly, saying that the losses would be great and our chances of success small. I urged a bombardment for a few days with our fine force of artillery, and constant harassing on all sides, whilst I pushed my trenches nearer every night, until I was satisfied that an assault must succeed. My views were accepted, and, as I mounted to ride back, Lord Kitchener came up to me, saying that if I would attack them at once I should be a made man. To which I, with a smile, replied 'You heard my views, and I shall only attack now if ordered to." [1]

The events of these two days throw a strong light on Kitchener. During the battle of the 18th his action had been irregular but excusable. In the absence of the Commander-in-Chief he had assumed command over three senior officers who were on the spot. This was excusable because Roberts evidently intended to give him authority, though his intention had been vaguely expressed, and because the Chief-of-Staff knew more about the situation as a whole than Generals

[1] Smith-Dorrien, p. 155.

whose attention had been concentrated on their own troops. He had issued orders to battalions without informing the Brigadiers. This also was excusable on the ground that the Brigadiers were on the move, and much time might have been wasted in sending orders through the proper channels. In the course of a battle time may be the most important of all factors.

But on the 19th the conditions were entirely different and there was no necessity for hasty action. Before issuing his orders Roberts called a meeting of Generals, and Kitchener had full opportunity to state his views—which apparently he did. After some argument Roberts made his decision—to abandon the immediate assault and to rely on siege methods. The decision of the Commander-in-Chief, right or wrong, is final, and of all people who ought to support it loyally the Chief-of-Staff is the first. Yet on leaving the meeting Kitchener went to a Brigadier and tempted him to make an immediate assault. In anybody else such conduct would have been rank insubordination.

Of course Kitchener was quite unconscious of any wilful disloyalty. He had nothing to gain for himself by putting pressure on Smith-Dorrien; and he would gladly have given to others any credit which a success might have brought. But he had got it into his mind that it was necessary to assault the laager at once, and that it was his duty to his country to bring such an assault about. The incident shows how one fixed idea could blind him to every other consideration. For some years he had exercised supreme authority, where his decisions were law. The habit of command had become stronger than his sense of discipline.

The decision of the Commander-in-Chief was based on the fact that Cronje's main-body could not escape. The investment was practically complete and the arrival of the VII Division under Tucker would make it safe from any interference by De Wet or other commandos. The loss of the convoy at Watervaal Drift had reduced the transport; already there were 800 wounded to be removed, and another batch would have strained the medical services to breaking-point.

Sir George Arthur argues that the investment, as opposed to assault, did not prove in the long run an economy of life:

"For ten days the British forces lay round the laager drinking the waters of the Modder fouled by the rotting carcases of Cronje's slaughtered horses and oxen. The stench in the laager at the time of Cronje's surrender was so overpowering as to overcome the curiosity of all save the most hardy of the victors, and the rain which followed the battle of the 18th washed its filth into the river. So, when Bloemfontein was reached, the poison in the blood of the troops, who were weakened by long marches and short rations, broke out in an epidemic of enteric which accounted for many more lives than were lost in the assaults upon Cronje's lines. Kitchener—as was his wont—was taking the long view both when he determined to attack on the 18th and when he sought to renew the attempt on the following morning; and if his methods in the battle were inevitably incorrect, his broad grasp of the situation—more especially in its relation to the future—was correct in itself and stands vindicated in the light of the later story of the campaign." [1]

This is a fair argument only if it is conceded that the assault would have been a success. But what if it had failed again? The casualties would have amounted to another thousand or more, and the epidemic would not have been avoided. The question therefore is, what were the chances of a general assault? I pin my faith to Smith-Dorrien. His Brigade had put up a gallant effort on the previous day; he had examined the ground and the Boer position. Smith-Dorrien was what Wellington would have called "a glutton for fighting," but though he was ready to face casualties he was not the man to sacrifice his men uselessly. His opinion was, "Our chances of success would be small." I may add that after all

[1] Arthur, I, p. 287.

was over I discussed the question with many infantry officers who had been in the firing-line opposite the Boer trenches, and they were unanimously of the same opinion. The effect of fire against troops in the open in the Great War points to the same conclusion; though the Boers had neither guns nor maxims their rifles were steady and sure. Finally there is the opinion of Lord Roberts himself—no hasty inspiration but the calm decision of a responsible and experienced soldier.

Three days later, on the 22nd, Kitchener went off to Nauwport to urge forward the troops who had remained on that side under Gatacre and Clements. There he had ample scope for his organizing powers in preparing the line of communications which would be wanted as soon as Roberts reached the Bloemfontein railway. He also had to send flying columns to deal with risings in Cape Colony westwards from De Aar. As he took no further share in the proceedings round Paardeberg they can be dealt with briefly.

From the moment that Roberts arrived, the situation was well in hand, and sufficient troops were present to deal with it, though they suffered a good deal from hunger and exposure. On the 26th howitzers bombarded the laager heavily, and Smith-Dorrien's Brigade, led by the Royal Canadians, crept gallantly closer and closer till they entrenched themselves within 100 yards of the Boer line. Soon after sunrise on February 27, Majuba Day, the White Flag was raised in the laager and Cronje with 4,000 men surrendered unconditionally.

It was then learned that the Boers had lost only 70 killed and 200 wounded, a very small casualty list in the circumstances. For nine days fire had been maintained from every side, by 90 guns and over 10,000 rifles, on the narrow space two miles long and roughly a hundred yards wide, in which 5,000 men and many women had been crowded. Fortunately for them the ground was well adapted for spade work, not too hard for digging and yet firm enough to stand vertically without revetment. Smith-Dorrien, who was the first to enter the laager at the head of the Canadians, says:

"The Boer trenches round the laager were extremely strong, well traced, and well constructed, and were evidence that a frontal attack by day a week previously would only have succeeded with heavy casualties; they appeared to have an immense supply of ammunition."

Next day news arrived that Buller had at last fought his way into Ladysmith. Undoubtedly the movements of Roberts had made the road easier for him by diverting several commandos away from Natal.

A week elapsed before the troops at Paardeberg could resume their advance. Cavalry and artillery horses had been on shorter rations even than the men, and it was necessary to await full supplies, which had to come from the Kimberley railway in wagons. The halt gave the Boers time to pull themselves together. De Wet refused to be dismayed by the disheartening results of Paardeberg; the two Presidents, Steyn of the Free State and Kruger of the Transvaal, came to exhort their burghers; strong positions were prepared at Poplar Grove, 12 miles east of Paardeberg, and at Driefontein, 14 miles further on; these were held by Boer forces estimated at 14,000 men. But Roberts had sufficient troops to spread out on a wide front, and the enemy was manœuvred out of both these places without much fighting. At Poplar Grove an attempt to surround the Boers failed badly through a misunderstanding of the scheme by the Cavalry Commander.

On March 12 the vanguard reached the railway south of Bloemfontein and next day the municipality and leading citizens of the town came out to tender their submission.

The news of Paardeberg and Bloemfontein was received with rapturous joy in England, where the impression gained ground that the Boer opposition would now collapse. Since leaving the Kimberley line there had been a month of operations which owed a good deal of success to luck and something more to the stupidity of Cronje. At the same time real credit must be given to the British Generals. The result showed that Roberts had exercised wisdom in refusing to be diverted from the main operation by De Wet's raid on the convoy at Watervaal. French gained much in reputation by the dash on Kimberley and the march to head off Cronje. It is a question whether the condition of his horses was entirely due to accidents beyond his control. They were certainly called upon for hard work on short forage and often in terrible heat, but some critics have pointed out that the watering arrangements were very bad, and that this was the chief cause of breakdown. Measured by the map the marches were nothing out of the way in length. Kitchener has also been criticized for the first day of Paardeberg. Certainly his methods were irregular: the policy of hustle led to disjointed attacks and entailed some casualties which perhaps might have been avoided. Nevertheless the hustle produced a paralysing effect on Cronje, and surely this was a big factor in the victory.

CHAPTER X

PRETORIA

THE CAPTURE of Bloemfontein marks a distinct stage in the war. During the next six weeks Headquarters remained in that town and a Proclamation was issued calling on the burghers to submit. Those who brought in their rifles and took an oath of neutrality were then allowed to return to their farms. Many took advantage of this, and hopes were raised that the Free Staters had accepted the occupation of their Capital as decisive. This, however, was far from being the case, and though there were no more general engagements on a big scale the war dragged on for another two years in a way which was infinitely more irritating.

Hitherto the Boers had been working in bodies of considerable size, with only a few flying detachments like those of De Wet; the big masses could not live without a train of wagons and therefore were slow. Assisted by Kitchener's reorganization of transport Roberts had given his troops a power of movement which thoroughly surprised Cronje and led to his surrender. The Boers therefore found it necessary to revise their ideas, and a "krijgsraad" was held at Kronstad, 130 miles to the north of Bloemfontein, to consider the situation. De la Rey, one of the most brilliant of the Transvaal leaders, maintained that the commandos were too large; they should be divided up into smaller bodies and spread out widely; this would force the British to spread out also in order to guard their long lines of railways and the depots of supplies; then the small commandos, having superior mobility, could concentrate to attack the weakest point. This was the system which was carried out with much success by leaders like De Wet and Botha. Before the British had time to realize the new conditions with which they were confronted De Wet brought off two very daring raids.

A mounted force under Broadwood had been sent about 30 miles eastwards, chiefly in order to hold the pumping station on the Modder which supplied Bloemfontein with water. At dawn on March 31 this force was unexpectedly shelled from the north, and Broadwood decided to move back to a strong position at Boesman's Kopje, ten miles nearer Bloemfontein. Confident that the enemy lay to the north and east he set his wagons in motion and followed with the troops as a rearguard. During the night De Wet had taken up a position in the Korn Spruit, near Sannah's Post, where his men were perfectly concealed from view. When the wagons reached the spruit De Wet allowed some of them to cross without showing himself, and this led the troops behind to assume that the road was clear. U Battery R.H.A. with an escort of Roberts' Horse marched calmly into the trap, and were within 50 yards of the spruit when the bank was suddenly lined by the burghers, who poured a rapid fire on the congested mass. Before Broadwood could extricate himself and work round by the south to Boesman's Kopje he had lost seven guns and three hundred men. Though Colvile, with an infantry Division and a brigade of Mounted Infantry, reached Boesman's Kopje in the morning, De Wet was able to carry off his trophies.

On April 4 the same leader carried out another venture. Gatacre and Clements had advanced from the Colesberg direction on each side of the main line towards Bloemfontein. As it had been assumed that the Free State was submitting, detachments were spread out in order to receive the surrender of the farmers and inhabitants; several small towns were peacefully occupied. De Wet had protested violently against those who had given up their rifles, and he now determined to lead his commandos southwards and revive the spirit of opposition; it is said that in one day he persuaded 100 burghers to break their oath of neutrality and join him. At the same time he saw a possibility of snatching up some of the detached columns.

The disaster at Sannah's Post on March 31 opened the

eyes of Roberts, and orders were issued for all the wandering detachments to concentrate. One of them was on the march towards Bloemfontein when, on April 2, it was surprised near Reddersburg by De Wet, who had with him two thousand men and four guns. The column consisted of 550 men without any artillery; a position was taken up on a ridge and held throughout the day; next morning after the last drop of water had been served out, and De Wet had gained one end of the ridge, the white flag was hoisted and the whole force surrendered. Another hour of resistance might have saved it, as reliefs were hurrying up. As in the case of Sannah's Post, De Wet escaped with his booty. Gatacre was held responsible for having sent out a weak column without guns, and he received orders to hand over his command and return to England.

Not contented with these two successes De Wet went on in search of other detached forces. Wepener, 60 miles southeast of Bloemfontein, had been occupied by Colonel Dalgety with 1,900 men and 7 guns. De Wet collected 6,000 burghers and with these he besieged the town on April 9. An attempt to storm one of the outlying posts by night was repulsed with loss, after which the besiegers relied on the blockade and bombardment. For sixteen days the garrison held out; then two columns which had been organized by Kitchener came to the relief, and De Wet found himself compelled to trek off northwards without further fighting.

Though in this case De Wet had no success, there can be little doubt that his daring activity revived the drooping spirit of the Boers, who might have accepted the terms of Roberts' Proclamation, might even have allowed the war to come to an end unless he had persuaded and forced them to resist.

During the same period attempts had been made to stir the Dutch population of Cape Colony into rebellion, especially in the district west of Kimberley. General Warren, who had previous experience in this part of the country, was sent to deal with it, and by the end of June the risings were quelled.

In considering his further strategy Roberts had two courses open to him. First, to take no step forward until his rear and flanks were absolutely and finally safe from local risings or from raids like those of De Wet. Sir Alfred Milner was strongly in favour of this course; he felt the insecurity of our position in Cape Colony and the Free State, and believed that Roberts would be taking an unjustifiable risk in leaving any elements of rebellion behind him. It is generally believed that Kitchener also favoured this plan, which had features in common with his steady and methodical progress up the Nile; but to occupy such a wide stretch of country would have been a big undertaking and raids could only have been prevented by some system of blockhouse lines such as were introduced later.

The second course was to advance boldly into the Transvaal, taking ordinary precautions to guard the lines of communication. Roberts adopted this as the basis of his strategy. Though De Wet's raids at Sannah's Post and Reddersburg had come as a shock, the belief was that they were the last flicker of forlorn hope. Many Free Staters were still coming in; to escape from the stigma of cowardice and desertion they maintained that the whole country was at heart sick of the war and ready for peace at almost any price; they said that their friends who broke the oath of neutrality had done so under pressure, sometimes under violence, from the few extremists like De Wet and Steyn. Such assurances were, of course, very welcome at Headquarters as they proved that the occupation of Bloemfontein had exercised a real moral effect. Therefore it might be assumed that an advance to the big towns of Johannesburg and Pretoria would have a further and final effect. If the Boer leaders made a determined stand to defend the Transvaal, Roberts had sufficient force for a decisive attack which would destroy the last of the fighting commandos. If, on the other hand, the Boers refused to accept battle and allowed the British to take Pretoria, then the moral effect would be of equal value. A few die-hards might remain at large, but a vast majority of the burghers would accept the inevitable. The argument seemed perfectly sound, especially when many hundreds of Boers gave it their support. The flaw was that nobody then knew the extraordinary powers of De Wet and Steyn, and the extraordinary ignorance of the Boer farmers, who were ready to accept any story about intervention by European nations in their favour. At the krijgsraad in Kronstad they were told that Russia was about to invade India and that consequently all British troops must soon be withdrawn. Of course the hope of foreign intervention was a tremendously powerful inducement to hold out; those who were still in the field when the British troops went away would be able to pose for ever more as heroes, while those who surrendered could not escape ignominy as faint-hearted deserters.

Another flaw in the argument was that the Boers did not depend on their towns; their homes were spread over the wide veldt; they could supply themselves with food and horses; they had hidden stores of ammunition; they needed little else.

These two flaws were not seen at the time, and in any case they would probably have failed to outweigh the big advantage which could accrue from the capture of Pretoria. So, as soon as Roberts had satisfied himself about the railways and supplies, he resumed his advance.

Kitchener seems to have taken little part in the strategy and tactics of the main-body; he was still intent on organization, which never ceased to distress him. The invaluable Girouard had come out to attend to the railways, and he was one of the very few to whom Kitchener could delegate work without giving it personal supervision. Repairs were already required in many places; more would certainly be required on the long stretch between Bloemfontein and Pretoria; but they would be done well and quickly by Girouard. On this point Kitchener felt secure. In every other direction, however, the necessity for organization demanded his own personal attention. The breakdown of the Cavalry had provided lessons which were painful but instructive. To cover the wide spaces men must be mounted; this meant that the horses must be fed, and as the animals from England, the Argentine and elsewhere, could not subsist on the meagre grazing of the veldt, forage must be carried on wagons; this would impair mobility because the wagons must be slow. The result was a vicious circle. Either the mounted men went off, far and fast, and killed their horses, or they remained, well fed and fit, but tied down to a slow-moving convoy. A perfect solution could not be devised and improvement could only be effected by cutting down in every conceivable way the loads of the horses and of the wagons. This meant going into the most minute details of equipment. Units were ordered to return to store spare boots, blankets, sheets, and practically everything they possessed except what a man had on him. Supplies were pushed forward as far as possible; sickly animals were taken out and shot; every wagon was overhauled and greased. A stern example was made of one or two officers who tried to evade orders by carrying unauthorized luxuries.

By the end of April the preparations were complete and the British Army began its advance on May 3 in four big columns. On the left Methuen and Hunter, each with about 10,000 men, started from Kimberley. From Bloemfontein Roberts himself led the main-body of 43,000 along the railway. Ian Hamilton kept a parallel line about 40 miles to the right, with two Brigades of Infantry, Broadwood's Cavalry, and a strong force of Mounted Infantry. Far away in Natal, Buller was to form the extreme right, working up along the railway into the Transvaal.

Everybody hoped that the Boers would make a stand. But it seems that they had taken the lesson of Paardeberg to heart, and they fell back in every direction. They even abandoned the siege of Mafeking, which under the resourceful

Baden-Powell had resisted them for 213 days. Steadily the big columns plodded along, halting for only a few days to let the railway be repaired. On May 24 the Vaal was crossed, on the 29th Johannesburg was occupied after Ian Hamilton had driven the Boers out of a position on the west of the town. A couple of days' rest was given to the troops and then the advance was continued; on June 5 the British Army marched into Pretoria. President Kruger with his Government and with all the money he could collect had already escaped in the direction of Delagoa Bay.

The occupation of Pretoria, like the occupation of Bloemfontein, had an undoubted effect on the spirit of the Boers. Leaders complained that the President had deserted them; farmers wanted to get back to their homes; the big array of British forces struck them with dismay. Louis Botha, who had been acting commandant of all the Transvaal forces since the death of Joubert in April, went as far as to arrange a meeting with Roberts. Nearly two years of destructive warfare might have been saved, had not De Wet again intervened.

The crafty free-lance had not been caught by the advancing lines of the British. There were big meshes in the net through which anyone could slip back southward. As Roberts moved towards Pretoria the long line of communications was being drawn out, the garrisons were spread more thinly. De Wet did not fail to take advantage of this fact. He first succeeded in surrounding and capturing 500 Imperial Yeomanry near Lindley on May 30. On June 7 he appeared on the railway and took Roodeval station, 150 miles north of Bloemfontein; an accumulation of stores was lying at this place waiting till a bridge over a river was ready for traffic. For a week De Wet interrupted communication between Bloemfontein and Pretoria, and the loss of stores caused anxious moments at Headquarters. Once more Kitchener was deputed to deal with the trouble; he hurried southward from Pretoria to the scene of this last disaster.

Practically all the mounted forces were with Roberts in

Pretoria, except a few very raw squadrons of Yeomanry, but Kitchener was able to collect by train a considerable force of infantry. De Wet destroyed most of the stores, buried some ammunition for future use, and then left the railway, moving westwards. After making a short circle he doubled back and on June 12 hit the line again a few miles further north. On this occasion he very nearly had the honour of capturing Kitchener himself, who happened to be in bivouac just outside the small station. The Chief-of-Staff only escaped by making a dash to his horse and galloping to a yeomanry camp a few miles off. De Wet picked up another fifty prisoners on the spot which Kitchener had left in a hurry. The capture of a Chief-of-Staff would have been a real triumph, though De Wet might have been puzzled to know what to do with so exalted a prisoner.

Fresh columns were then set in motion from various directions. De Wet was hunted eastwards, and an attempt was made with some success to pen the Free Staters into the Brandwater Basin, up against the border of Basutoland. There were only four wagon-roads leading through the circle of hills which encloses the Basin, and strong columns were directed to block each of them. De Wet, however, was determined not to be caught, and it seems that he spread false information which led Rundle's Column to leave one gate open. Through this De Wet's own commando crept out. The other commandos had announced their intention of following him; but perhaps they were half-hearted and failed to seize the opportunity. Rundle, after seeing that he had made a mistake, was quick to shut the open gate. On July 30 the main-body in the Basin, to the number of 4,000, laid down their arms. This was the most important success since Paardeberg, compensating for the previous mishaps and again raising false hopes that the opposition would collapse.

While these events had been filling the Free State with alarms Roberts was slowly pushing along the railway towards Delagoa Bay. This line was the only remaining means of communication with the outside world which still lay open to the Boers. It was therefore an obvious step in strategy to close it. Botha had first postponed and finally refused the proposed meeting with Roberts. With the main body of the Transvaalers he retired slowly eastwards and took up a position astride the railway about twenty miles from Pretoria. The Commander-in-Chief gave his troops two days' rest round the Capital, and made it safe against surprise attacks. On June 10 he set out. On the 12th he found himself up against Botha's position and spread his force out wide in hopes of making a capture. The most severe fighting took place at Diamond Hill, which has given its name to the engagement. The results were not decisive but the Boers retired.

It had been hoped that Buller would have forced his way up from Natal in time to strike the Delagoa railway before Roberts arrived at Pretoria; this would have blocked the eastern exit from the Capital. But Buller advanced very slowly; while Roberts was fighting near Pretoria and Kitchener was escaping from De Wet, the British forces from Natal had only just passed into the Transvaal. From this point Roberts wanted Buller to turn due north across country to hit the Delagoa railway. But two months went by in sluggish movement before Buller joined hands with Roberts' main-body near Belfast on August 25. Though the combined forces from Natal and Pretoria were too strong for Botha, progress was still slow and it was not before the end of September that British troops got into Kumati Poort. The Boers had been hanging on to the precious railway as long as they could, but when they found themselves in danger of being hemmed in against the Portuguese frontier they were obliged to disperse. Kruger fled to Holland. A large amount of rolling stock and supplies were abandoned. But Botha, with President Steyn and his followers, had little difficulty in escaping into the hilly and broken country which forms the northern Transvaal. Shortly after this Buller went home.

As the whole country had now been overrun, Roberts considered that his work was practically finished. One day in September I lunched at the Headquarters mess in Pretoria. An officer at table said he believed the war might drag on for another three months. Kitchener was not present, and I did not hear whether Roberts himself made any comment, but there was no doubt that the Headquarters staff regarded the speaker as a pessimist and expected that the Army would be on its way home before the end of the year. All the railways were in our hands; all the towns of importance had been occupied; 16,000 Boers had surrendered—what could they gain by maintaining a hopeless resistance? It was true that unexpected commandos had a way of springing suddenly into irritating existence; a sort of police force might be required to mop up outlying die-hards. But the Transvaal and Free State had been conquered; and on September 1 a Proclamation had been issued declaring the annexation of the Transvaal to the British Empire.

In November Lord Roberts handed over the command to Kitchener and left for England to take his seat in the War Office as Commander-in-Chief of the British Army. He was the last to hold this appointment, which was superseded in 1904 by the Army Council.

CHAPTER XI

COMMANDER-IN-CHIEF

As everybody knows, the forecast about the end of the war was wrong; from first to last of the Boer War we seem to have been quite incapable of seeing anything in its true light. The new Commander-in-Chief in South Africa had before him a task of extreme difficulty which was not made any easier by the cheerful prophecies of those who went home.

Kitchener must have looked back with regret at the Sudan. There he had had a nice little army of 25,000 first-rate troops, on a single line, with no danger to the flanks or rear, no complicated questions of civil administration, and a concentrated enemy awaiting his approach at a well-known point. His only problem was how to get to Omdurman—there was nothing else to think about, and he could take action without referring to anybody. In South Africa these conditions were almost exactly reversed. The Army was numerous but unwieldy; the long lines of communication lay open to raids; nobody knew where the enemy would be found. Over thirty columns were wandering about, and before orders could be issued the latest information must be studied. This meant a lot of work, but it only represented a fraction of what Kitchener had to do. There were scandals about Army contracts to be cleared up, and Courts-Martial to be confirmed; Uitlanders wanted to see him about re-opening mines; Boers who had surrendered wanted to suggest schemes for getting their friends to surrender; Press Correspondents wanted to talk and argue—in fact everybody wanted to see the Chief. Every proposal for action immediately raised some point which often demanded reference to the High Commissioner at Capetown or to the authorities in London.

The Secretary of State at the War Office, Mr. Brodrick,

was so convinced that the war was over that he wrote suggesting a reduction of the army—while Kitchener was writing at the same time to ask for an increase. It cannot be said that Brodrick, Roberts, or the British Public failed to give Kitchener generous support, and the Dominions were magnificent in their readiness to share the burden. At the same time Kitchener must have felt that he was expected to do more than he was doing—to bring off some startling coup, another Omdurman.

The Boers had about 70,000 still in the field, broken up into small commandos which infested the Transvaal, the Free State, and made raids into Cape Colony. Against these the British Army had a strength which on paper seemed to be overwhelming—a total of 240,000, including 80,000 mounted men. This force, however, had to be spread over a huge area, seven hundred miles from north to south, and nearly as much from east to west. The railways covered over two thousand miles and of these about half lay in the dangerous area; every bridge and station must have its guard, and the larger towns with supply depots must have strong garrisons. Moreover, Sir Alfred Milner was constantly insisting that Cape Colony might be a source of danger.

Kitchener had from the first seen the necessity for increasing the mobility of the British troops. In spite of the improvements that had been made, experience showed that we were still a long way behind the Boers, indeed that we could never catch them up. It began to dawn upon Headquarters that, if there was no possibility of screwing our mobility any higher, steps might be taken to screw the Boers' mobility down to ours. This could be done, first by stripping the country of supplies, and secondly by dividing up the country by means of blockhouse lines into smaller sections; if once a commando could be effectively penned into a section its fate would be sealed.

The first method had been started by Roberts soon after reaching Pretoria, and on paper it seemed likely to give good results. Herds of sheep and cattle were collected, farms were burnt, supplies of every kind were removed or destroyed. Then the trouble began. Women and children were living on those farms and could not be left to starve. Concentration camps were established, and by October 1901 over 80,000 refugees had been collected. Some of them settled down, contented to be housed and fed at the expense of their enemy; others gave as much trouble as they could, which was saying a good deal. In addition to this, humanitarians in England began to intervene. The concentration camps were seized upon as awful examples of the horrors of war—they were dirty, insanitary, full of germs—in short, regular deathtraps. A Committee of ladies came out from London to investigate the facts, and on the whole they were satisfied that the Camp Officials had done their best. They went back, after giving some good advice, and making some regulations regarding washing, which to some of the older women was quite a novelty and caused more discontent.

Between complaints from England about dirt and complaints from the refugees about enforced cleanliness the Medical Officers and others in authority had an uneasy time. And in the end it turned out that the removal of women from the veldt, far from reducing the mobility of the Boers, really increased it. The farmer had no longer any inducement to remain at home. His family was provided for; the house was burnt and the cattle had gone; having nothing else to lose he joined De Wet or De la Rey. Supplies were certainly scanty, but he need have no qualms about seizing anything that the British columns had overlooked; when starvation threatened, there was generally a convoy, a train, or a small post which could be captured.

The policy of stripping the country was anything but a success. It caused infinite trouble to ourselves and discontent among the Boers, it sent many men back to the commandos who would otherwise have remained quiet at home, and it inspired the leaders to some very daring raids. In the end it ran up a big bill, not only for the maintenance of camps, but also for reparation of buildings and stock.

The institution of blockhouse lines was more effective, though much time was spent and many failures reported before success could be attained. The first lines were constructed to protect the railway; when these were reasonably secure the system was extended across country in various directions, gradually cutting it up into pens. A strong fence of barbed wire was planted, with blockhouses at intervals of a mile and a half; intermediate houses were then built, reducing the intervals till in the end they rarely exceeded four hundred yards. The garrisons consisted of a corporal and half-a-dozen privates, sometimes more.

The infantry soldier found life in a blockhouse a delightful change from the wearisome trek. He was kept in hard condition by constant patrolling, and yet had time to devote to various occupations. Commanding officers reported that the best results were obtained by keeping each squad permanently in the same blockhouse, which then became a home. Knowing that their own safety depended on their work the men applied themselves with zeal to the defences. Walls were strengthened until most of them were safe against anything but heavy artillery; dummy figures were arranged to draw the enemy's fire;[1] trip wires were laid with alarm signals; watchdogs were taught to go on double sentry with their owners. In addition to defence work there were lighter forms of occupation. By the end of the war vegetable gardens were flourishing and nearly every house had a farmyard of some kind, containing chickens, pigeons, and a goat. Only the garrison knew where these all came from. The art of interior decoration was also highly developed; passing trains dropped bundles of magazines and newspapers, the illustrations from which were used to paper the walls.

[1] One dummy, a disappearing figure, was so successful in deluding the Boers that he got three bullets through him; he was then awarded a row of medal ribbons on his breast.

From the first these lines were of value in guarding the railways, but so long as the intervals between blockhouses were over a mile the Boers often succeeded in cutting their way through. Later on the system was improved till only the most daring of the raiders ventured to face the line. The mobility of the Boers was definitely cramped, and the slow-moving British columns had now a chance to corner their slippery opponents. Big "drives" were instituted. Half-a-dozen columns were drawn up along some convenient starting-line and advanced abreast. It sounds extraordinary that five thousand troops, sometimes more, should have been necessary in order to corner a few dozen burghers—but such was the case. Many drives failed altogether. The captures rarely exceeded a couple of hundred; the most successful and biggest ended up near Harrismith, where 706 Boers laid down their arms.

The establishment of the drive and blockhouse system demanded much organization. The wastage of horseflesh had been terrible, expensive, cruel; it may have been one of the unavoidable horrors of war while strategy demanded long and immediate marches. Now, however, the necessity for sacrificing horses did not exist. Occasional rests and full forage improved the condition of the mounted troops to a wonderful extent. Though they were scarcely ever quick enough to gallop down the flying Dutchmen they did some record marches and surprised several commandos in laager. During the last year of the war the wastage was quite low except for the fatal horse-sickness of the veldt.

Besides the condition of the horses, Kitchener found much to perturb him in the condition of the troops. Drafts and fresh units from overseas were raw, and time was required to teach them the new conditions of warfare. At the same time those men who had been on the veldt were stale; their morale had suffered from the fact that they had marched continuously for a year or more without bringing the enemy to bay. The joyful effects of Paardeberg, Bloemfontein, Pretoria, soon wore off when the hope of a quick peace was seen to be false. There was another consideration which to many people gave the war a sort of unreality—we had no ill-feeling against the Boers. In the Sudan there had been the desire to avenge Gordon and to break down a barbaric despotism; in the Great War the stakes were too heavy to permit of any slackening in the will to conquer. But in South Africa the war seemed more like a football match. We wanted to win, of course, but nothing very vital depended on the result. It was not a struggle to save our country and our homes. In fact we thought the Boers were rather good fellows. From a humanitarian point of view this is an admirable feeling, but it does not conduce to desperate fighting. There is no doubt that some troops laid down their arms tamely; they knew their lives would be spared and that they would soon be released. They carried out a few Aldershot manœuvres but when the Boers seemed to have the best of the game, they put up their hands and hoped for better luck at the next meeting. This slackness caused Kitchener infinite embarrassment. Just when a complicated drive seemed to promise a big bag, news would come in of a surrender which threw the whole machine out of gear, and very often re-stocked the enemy with supplies and ammunition.

Another cause of slackness was that the tangled mess had never been unravelled: in fact as time went on units became more and more broken up. Every British regiment has its own traditions, and every individual who joins it is taught that he is an heir and guardian of those traditions; if he surrenders the shame falls on all ranks. For such a sentiment men will fight and die. Certainly there were difficulties in keeping a regiment together. Sick were left behind in hospital; detachments were taken for various duties; officers went off to the staff—yet while men come and go the *esprit de corps* remains as long as the regiment preserves its identity.

A mounted column was a very different thing—a scratch team, without past or future, consisting of a few hundred men collected almost at haphazard from many units.[1] A capable commander might inspire a spirit of emulation, to rival the achievements of other columns, but this is a poor substitute for *esprit de corps*. Officers had no hesitation in leaving the ranks for Staff appointments; the friends of Lord Roberts had gone home, and therefore humbler people might be excused if they wanted to follow that example; there was evidently no necessity to remain in the field and little honour to be won.

Moreover the war had a peculiarly disagreeable side to it. Burning houses, driving cattle, and herding women into camps was repulsive work. The Dutch loved their farms, and the distress of the women was piteous when the homesteads on which they had expended so much love and labour went up in flames. But half-measures were worse than useless. The Commander-in-Chief had to harden his heart in the hope that stern measures against slack officers on the one side and the Boers on the other would put an earlier end to the suffering.

No doubt the task was all the more painful because Kitchener felt sympathy for the Boers and understood their cause. These burghers were far removed from savages. When Gladstone spoke of the Sudanese as "people rightly struggling to be free" his words provoked amusement in those who knew the truth. Had he applied them to the Boers they would have been less open to criticism. These men had lived in a state of liberty, and imperfect as their government was they were content with it. So far as they knew, they had done nothing to forfeit that liberty. Their idea of the British was derived from the specimens they had met in Johannesburg, men who had made money out of South Africa and hurried off to spend it elsewhere. Their proud and liberty-loving spirit felt it a degradation to be ruled by such men, and bred in them a wonderful fighting spirit.

---

[1] Rawlinson's column (to which I was detached for eighteen months) consisted of Mounted Infantry drawn from thirty-four regular units; the eleven guns came from seven different batteries.

The order for annexation came from London and Kitchener never faltered in imposing it. He could look forward, however, to the time when the Boers would be members of the British Empire. If their loyalty could be enlisted on our side they would be valuable fellow-subjects; but if bitterness and rebellion remained in their hearts there could be no real peace; a truce perhaps for a few years, a sullen submission till the British Army went away, and then revenge. Kitchener wanted a real peace. We had shown our power and could afford to be generous; the first condition must be complete amnesty for all who had been in arms against us. As far as the Boers from the Transvaal and Free State were concerned there was no difficulty. They had been recognized as open enemies and had not been convicted of any crime. But unfortunately they had been joined by some Boers from Natal and Cape Colony, who had been living under the British Flag and were therefore technically guilty of rebellion. A number of these had already been sentenced to six years' imprisonment for high treason. The big question was whether they could be included in the amnesty.

Whatever Kitchener may have thought about the real rights and wrongs of the matter, he certainly believed that as a practical measure it would be advisable to extend a pardon to all, first because it would remove bitterness, and secondly because it would be unprofitable to prolong the war on account of three hundred men. He knew that Botha and other responsible leaders wanted peace. They would accept annexation because they could not avoid it; but they would not and could not desert the cause of their brothers-in-arms. Botha himself said that if he allowed the rebels to be punished, his authority would be gone and his own followers would repudiate the treachery.

Milner opposed any pardon for inhabitants of Cape Colony who had been caught red-handed. He thought they would accept it not as an act of grace but as a confession of weakness, which would prune rebellion for the moment to give it fresh strength later on. Perhaps he misjudged the military situation; his final interview with Roberts may have left him under the impression that Kitchener would soon finish off the outstanding commandos and then there would be no need to discuss conditions. We would simply impose our own terms.

Kitchener's first meeting with Botha took place on February 28, 1901. The Boer leader impressed the Commander-in-Chief very favourably as a man of authority, reason, and high honour. They talked over the war without bitterness, and discussed peace terms. On most points agreement was easy. Kitchener realized that the legal debts of the Republic must be acknowledged, and that money must be found to set the farmers on their feet again; otherwise the new Colony could not revive from the devastation. He recommended a grant not exceeding two million sterling, which, as he pointed out, was less than the cost of one month of the war. He also recommended an amnesty for all. The proposals were submitted to London through the High Commissioner, who objected to the final condition, and he was supported by the Government, who refused pardon for the rebels and added other minor amendments. A letter was sent to Botha announcing this decision, with the result that all negotiations were broken off. This was a real disappointment to Kitchener, who did not conceal his opinion. He wrote to the Secretary of State for War:

"I was afraid Botha could hardly accept the terms offered. The Boers have a good deal of sentiment of honour amongst them—particularly the leaders—and leaving those that had helped them to go to prison for six years, as has been done in Natal, would, I felt sure, make it almost impossible for them to accept. I therefore insisted on my views being sent home in Milner's telegram to the Colonial Secretary. I hardly expected, however, after Milner's strongly worded objection to my proposition, that the Government would decide differently to what they did.

"I did all in my power to urge Milner to change his

views, which on this subject seem to me very narrow. I feel certain, and have good grounds for knowing, that an amnesty or King's pardon for the two or three hundred rebels in question (carrying with it disenfranchisement, which Botha willingly accepted) would be extremely popular amongst the majority of the British and all the Dutch in South Africa; but there no doubt exists a small section in both Colonies who are opposed to any conciliatory measures being taken to end the war, and I fear their influence is paramount; they want extermination, and I suppose will get it.

"My views were that once the Boers gave up their independence and laid down their arms, the main object of the Government was attained, and that the future Civil Administration would soon heal old sores and bring the people together again. After the lesson they have had, they are not likely to break out again. Milner's views may be strictly just, but they are to my mind vindictive, and I do not know of a case in history when, under similar circumstances, an amnesty has not been granted.

"We are now carrying the war on to put two or three hundred Dutchmen in prison at the end of it. It seems to me absurd and wrong, and I wonder the Chancellor of the Exchequer did not have a fit."

Unfortunately Milner's view was accepted in Downing Street. Brodrick wrote:

"We are all very much opposed to a complete amnesty to Cape and Natal rebels. The feeling is that it will be a surviving reproach on us. The loyalists at least have surely a right to see the very moderate Cape punishments inflicted on rebels. . . . Is it not likely that with one more turn of the military screw, they will be ready for submission? We shall be glad in any case when the time arrives." [1]

The time to which Brodrick was looking forward did not arrive till fourteen months later, and then the terms of peace

[1] Arthur, II, p. 26.

were practically those which Kitchener recommended in March 1901. In the meanwhile many lives were lost, much country was devastated, and our National Debt rose by something like a hundred million pounds.

Kitchener felt so strongly on the subject that it would not have been surprising if he had repeated the manœuvre that had succeeded in Egypt—an offer to resign. But on the former occasion there had been no principle at stake—it was merely a matter of money, and Cromer could be relied on for support. At the present time Milner was on the other side, and therefore the resignation might be accepted, in which case there was no hope for any policy of conciliation. The fact that Kitchener did not attempt to throw up his very thankless task is a real proof of his sense of duty. One important point in the controversy deserves notice—though the soldier and civilian differed strongly on the vital question of policy, they continued on the best of terms with each other. This has an important bearing on another controversy which arose later between Kitchener and Curzon in India.

In spite of disappointing instructions from London and constant bad news from several directions Kitchener bore the strain well. No doubt he felt that while so many were feeling infected with staleness it was necessary for the staff to avoid any symptoms of that disease. The Headquarters mess was hospitable and cheery; between treks I had several glimpses of it through my close acquaintance with one of the A.D.C.'s, Frank Maxwell. "The Brat" had been my fag at the United Service College, Westward Ho,[1] and we served together for a year in Roberts's Horse. He won the V.C. for helping to save the guns at Sannah's Post. Afterwards he

---

[1] The mention of Frank Maxwell reminds me that Rudyard Kipling and Lionel Dunsterville were in the same house at school, but before Maxwell's time. In a bundle of old papers I lately found a letter which I wrote home describing a dormitory rag: "Gigger Kipling" is described as "a fellow who thinks a good deal of himself because he is in the Fifth Form and sub-editor of the School Chronicle." It is amusing to remember that we called him "Gigger" because he was the only boy out of 200 who wore spectacles.

joined Kitchener's personal staff, and though Kitchener and he had never met before, Frank soon became the most intimate of all with his Chief. Sixteen years later he was killed in France.

At school Frank had gained a reputation as a fine gymnast and a plucky half-back at football. He was notorious for irrepressible cheek; it was noticeable, however, that his sallies were generally directed against the people he liked best. In Pretoria he held a position something like that of a court jester of the olden days, privileged to say outrageous things without respect for rank or dignity, and not even sparing the Commander-in-Chief. But there was method in this fooling. Frank worshipped the ground his Chief trod on—I believe he would have murdered anybody who doubted Kitchener's wisdom—and he wanted to let the world know that the great man was not such a tyrant as he appeared to some people. Also he knew, perhaps better than anybody, how deeply Kitchener felt the annoyances and disappointments of those days; the schoolboy cheek was intended in its own way as an expression of sympathy and understanding. Kitchener certainly took it in this sense and encouraged it. The result was that Maxwell rose to fame as the hero of many stories, some of which he told himself. The following is his own version of the story of the starling which became so well known in Pretoria.

One night the Chief was awakened by a noise in his chimney followed by a dishevelled mass of blood and feathers which on examination turned out to be something like a starling. Kitchener, who was very fond of birds, roused the household, and the Principal Veterinary Officer was called in to perform an operation while the whole of the army staff looked on and pretended to be interested. The "Bloody Bird" survived, and under that name became a prominent member of the Headquarters mess. Maxwell would get up from table —"Excuse me while I see whether the Bloody Bird has had its dinner; if the beast can be kept alive I have been promised a C.B. in the next Gazette—and I shall deserve it."

After one of the last big Drives, which happened to be very successful, the Chief paid a flying visit to Rawlinson's column; on this occasion Maxwell was left in Pretoria. Kitchener dined in mess and during the meal a telegram was brought to him; he read it in silence and passed it round the table. Everybody expected to see one of the usual messages of congratulation from Lord Roberts, but it was signed by Maxwell—"Your Bloody Bird ill. Staff in tears. Return at once."

As "the Brat" used to say, what with birds and one thing and another life was very hard. At Headquarters it was especially hard because of the close system of centralization. However much we admire Kitchener's devotion to duty, it must be admitted that he attempted too much. While the commandos were appearing and disappearing in unexpected places it was of course imperative to have all the latest intelligence collected at one central point where it could be fitted together; consequently each of the thirty columns sent a daily report direct to Headquarters. So far so good. But the further consequence was that Headquarters issued a daily order direct to each column, and this led to several mistakes. In the mounted troops there were no Brigades or Divisions and the only unit was the column, which term might mean anything from 400 to 3,000 men; worse still, the columns were often broken up and re-formed. One rough example is sufficient to explain the confusion which very often arose.

French had been sent to deal with Cape Colony, and he was given a free hand to use all the troops in that district. Smuts took a commando of Transvaalers into the Colony and created a big stir. Thereupon Rawlinson's column was sent by train from the Western Transvaal across the Free State down to the Orange River; but sufficient rolling stock could not be collected to carry all his transport. This was therefore left behind, and he received a fresh lot, collected in haste from anywhere. By direct order from Kitchener the supplies were sent to Burghersdorp, but French ordered

Rawlinson to disentrain at Bethulie, thirty miles away. By the time these matters had been adjusted Smuts had a couple of days' start. Rawlinson then did double marches to catch up, needless to say, without catching up. After references to French and Pretoria a few days were spent aimlessly and then the column went back by train to the Western Transvaal. French blamed Rawlinson, who blamed the transport. Similar circumstances were not unusual. A General suddenly found himself commanding a bunch of troops whom he had never seen before; the troops found themselves in company quite unknown to them. This put a heavy handicap on all ranks.

It is true that the emergency measures sometimes had good results, but much waste of material, and of temper, might have been avoided if there had been a permanent organization of the mounted troops. This had been created for the infantry. Tucker commanded at Bloemfontein, with full authority over all garrisons and blockhouse lines in the Free State; he knew his officers and his units, and made the best use of them. With troops on the move the problem was of course more difficult. But a permanent commander in each district with a number of permanent troops would have had a better chance; he and his men would have soon known the ground; he would have known his officers; by personal inspection he could have seen which units required a rest and which were fit for hard work. Each column could still have reported daily to Headquarters; but orders should then have been sent to the District General. Such a method would have avoided disjointed movements, and enabled the General on the spot to repair mistakes.

In theory all great commanders have accepted the principle that subordinates should be allowed to exercise initiative. Napoleon constantly affirmed this as one of his maxims, but in practice he demanded blind obedience and little else. Even the Marshals were so afraid of the Emperor that they hesitated to take responsibility; Davoust at Auerstaat dared to fight a battle and win a victory, but got little credit for it;

Bernadotte failed for this reason at Jena, Ney at Quatre Bras, Grouchy after Ligny. Fearless before the enemy, they feared their own Chief.

Kitchener urged his subordinates to exercise initiative, and honestly believed that he allowed them a free hand, but the system of close supervision cramped their style. If a column commander issued an order, it might be cancelled by something which arrived from Pretoria next day. This happened so often that commanders naturally got into the habit of waiting to see what Headquarters wanted before they made a start. A completely free hand is incompatible with combined movement—and Kitchener insisted on combining the movements.

The system was unfair on the commanders and on the troops and most of all on Kitchener himself. Let us admit that in order to combine the moving columns it was necessary to control them from Headquarters; still, it does not follow that the Commander-in-Chief need have gone into all the details himself. Though the staff machine in the modern sense of the word did not yet exist, there were Officers who could have saved Kitchener three-quarters of the work had they been allowed to do so. The Chief-of-Staff collects and digests information; he plots out the position of each column and of each commando as far as is known; orders are drafted and submitted to the Commander-in-Chief for approval. The latter only looks at the important intelligence on which he must base a decision; after a short discussion the Chief-of-Staff goes back to his own room and issues the orders to various units, also to the Directors of Railways, Supplies, Transports, and other Departments. At a moment of crisis the Commander-in-Chief will have plenty to do, but on ordinary occasions he should be relieved of all routine work. Of course there were officers who assisted Kitchener, but there was no Chief-of-Staff. When Kitchener vacated that post no one was appointed in his place. A year later, Roberts offered to send out Ian Hamilton, and the offer was gladly accepted, but when Ian Hamilton arrived he never had time to settle down. Just as Kitchener himself had been used as "emergency man" by Lord Roberts, so the new Chief-of-Staff was sent off in every direction. Was De Wet reported to have passed into the Transvaal? Ian Hamilton collected columns from all directions and led the hunt. He supplied a driving power which sometimes was badly needed; but he would have had a better chance if he had been permanently in command of a district where he knew the ground and the troops.

A Chief-of-Staff who could devote all his attention to the office would have saved Kitchener an enormous amount of time and would also have relieved him of strain. When he took on his own shoulders the responsibility for each of those thirty columns they naturally absorbed all his thoughts, and other matters scarcely received the attention they deserved. While thinking out a dispatch to the War Office he was waiting for news from French or wondering where De la Rey would next be found. The one man method which had brought such good results in Egypt was incapable of making the best of South Africa.

The weary months of 1901 dragged their slow length along. Any attempt to follow the various columns on their erratic course would be equally wearisome. It is enough to say that by degrees the blockhouse lines were fulfilling their object. One great advantage was that the Boers could not get remounts—and a Boer on his own feet is no longer a fighting man. But as the commandos dwindled in numbers they became all the more difficult to catch; only the best and bravest men remained in the ranks to follow the best and bravest commandants. Even among these a feeling began to gain ground that the war was lost. No hope could be cherished now of European intervention; it was clear that the British would not abandon the struggle when victory had come in sight. Tired as our troops might be of the war, the Boers were far more tired.

After Kruger left the country Schalk Burgher was acting President. He wanted peace; Botha supported him, and most of the Transvaalers were quite ready to follow their lead. But the Free State men, Steyn and De Wet, nailed the Flag of Liberty to the staff. De Wet in particular was irreconcilable. He threatened to shoot his own brother for meeting Methuen in a conference; he is said to have shot deserters; he certainly flogged some of his men who refused to follow him; he loaded with abuse anybody who talked of surrender. Many burghers knew that their cause was hopeless, and wanted to save their country from further devastation; they believed the British Government would be just and even generous. But the thought of being called a "hands upper" was compelling them to sacrifice what they knew to be the good of their country to their personal pride. Kitchener's Intelligence was good, and at the end of 1901 there were hopes that negotiations might be resumed. Then a fresh crop of disasters came to postpone the end. On Christmas Eve De Wet made a surprise attack on a yeomanry camp and scuppered it. A little later a very mixed column under Methuen was attacked from the rear by De la Rey; panic led to a stampede of the mules and the whole force was thrown into confusion; the surrenders were many and very humiliating. Another big convoy fell into Boer hands at Wolmaranstad.

In spite of these set-backs the movement towards peace began to take shape in March 1902. Schalk Burgher was allowed to arrange a meeting with Steyn and several other leaders; they agreed to go in a body to meet the Commander-in-Chief at Pretoria on April 12.

The discussions which followed were spread out over six weeks, taxing Kitchener's powers of diplomacy to the utmost, but his wisdom and patience never failed. At first a gracious reception of the burghers won their confidence; then Steyn and De Wet stood out against annexation. Though it was necessary to be firm on this point Kitchener agreed to refer it to London. This was a clever move; the great thing was to let the idea of peace sink deep into their minds; the longer they thought about it the more attractive would it appear. Further time was then granted in order to allow the election of sixty representatives, thirty from each State, who were to assemble at Vereeniging for a general discussion. This again was a good move, letting the idea of peace permeate to all the commandos.

The first meeting of representatives was stormy. With great moral courage Schalk Burgher took the lead and announced that the British Government would decline to listen to any terms which implied independence for their States. Steyn was too ill to attend, but De Wet spoke fiercely against peace without liberty. The debate lasted two days. Then Commissioners were sent to Pretoria with fresh proposals.

By this time Kitchener saw with unerring intuition that most of them wanted peace if only it could be put in a form that would save their self-respect. Except De Wet they were reasonable enough to see that the terms were generous and resistance was hopeless, but sentiment remained the decisive factor. An aggressive attitude, even a tactless word, might inflame their pride and send them back to fight in desperation. That would mean a few more months of the drive and blockhouse struggle, followed by years of smouldering hate and rebellion. With infinite patience he listened to their proposals and soothed their feelings. No stress was laid on the fact that the two States had already been formally annexed by the British Government; nor were the delegates reminded that they had been proclaimed as outlaws. In order to sweeten the bitterness of surrender a promise was held out of self-government, to be introduced at a date which was purposely left vague. Another concession was made when the new draft provided not for a declaration of submission but for a joint treaty. The former difficulty about the rebels of Cape Colony and Natal was shelved by leaving their fate in the hands of the Colonial Governments—which meant they would soon be pardoned. In matters of finance Kitchener was determined to be liberal, for the good reason that it was better to give three millions for restoring the farms than to spend that sum, and much more, on doing further damage.

On May 28 the Commissioners went back to the conference at Vereeniging with a copy of the new draft. Steyn resigned his office as President of the Free State and denounced the Treaty. Another stormy discussion lasted for two days. Then De Wet suddenly and unexpectedly changed his mind, for some reason which has not been explained. After that the opposition fell to the ground and the Treaty was approved by 54 votes to 6. The Commissioners hastened back to Pretoria and the Peace received its final signature at 10:30 P. M. on May 31.

At last Kitchener was free to lay down the burden which for eighteen months he had carried on his own shoulders. He could afford to disregard the criticism which hinted at weakness in the terms of peace, because he knew that there had been no weakness on his side; he abandoned no principle, no territory, no dignity; from the first his aim had been reconstruction in the new Colonies, and every step was deliberately intended to lay the foundations of goodwill. The negotiations were a real triumph of common sense, clever management, and firmness. The only weakness had been in the Government which would not allow the same terms to be offered fourteen months sooner.

Three weeks later Kitchener was on his way to England where another great reception awaited him. King Edward was recovering from the operation which had thrown a gloom over his people, but he received the victorious General in his sick-room and conferred on him the Order of Merit. On August 9 Kitchener commanded the troops in London at the Coronation. There followed two months of public dinners and receptions, at which the speeches of the honoured guest set a fine example of brevity.

The question of his future employment had given rise to some discussion. The Cabinet, and especially Brodrick, wanted him to succeed Roberts as Commander-in-Chief, but Kitchener would have nothing to do with the War Office. Though he was ready to accept responsibility he would only do so on the condition that authority went with it. As Commander-in-Chief he would be responsible for the military forces of the Empire, but as the servant of a political party his power would be small. Perhaps if he had taken the burden on his shoulders he would have been better prepared to face the big problems of August 1914. There would have been opportunities to study the situation in Europe, to draw up schemes for the expansion of the army, for the supply of munitions, for the employment of our resources. He could have learnt something about the leaders of men with whom he would afterwards be working. But on the other hand perhaps it was as well that he stood aloof, reserving his strength for the great occasion. The Liberals came to power in 1906 and were pledged to measures which clashed with his ideas of duty. Years of fractious argument with politicians, who cried peace when there was no peace, would have weakened his powers. Some of the glamour and mystery which surrounded him would have been dispelled. He would have made more enemies than friends.

Unless he returned to civil administration in Egypt or went as Ambassador to Constantinople there was only one appointment which could be given to him—the Command in India. He knew what it meant, and his readiness to accept it after the long strain of work in Egypt and South Africa affords a proof of marvellous energy.

He left England in October and broke the journey in Egypt, to open the Gordon College at Khartoum and inspect the new dam at Assuan. Then, leaving these familiar scenes behind him, he entered upon the third stage of his career.

PART III
INDIA

CHAPTER XII

REFORMS

During the six years that Kitchener spent in India as Commander-in-Chief there were no military operations, and the story of that period is therefore comparatively unexciting. An attempt to discuss in detail the many reforms which he introduced would require a big volume to itself, and even then it would convey little except to those who have served in the country and know something of its geography, its peoples, its institutions. Nevertheless an endeavour must be made to sketch the outstanding problems with which he was confronted, if only for the reason that an occasional clue may be found to the working of his mind.

In Egypt Kitchener's role had been that of a builder who starts from the foundation. In South Africa his work had been that of an opportunist who has to do the best he can, at top speed, with very rough materials. In India the building had been completed many years before his arrival; a fine old edifice in its way, but badly in need of an overhaul. From time to time a coat of paint had been laid on to improve its appearance, but Kitchener was determined to take structural repairs in hand. Some elderly inhabitants shook their heads and predicted trouble. Kitchener had no experience of India and was known to be very self-willed; if he dug too deep he might injure the time-honoured foundations.

On the whole the prophets of disaster were agreeably disappointed. The "Kitchener Reforms" did not introduce anything of a very revolutionary nature. Some of them had been suggested, discussed, approved, and then laid aside, generally for reasons of finance. Big questions had to go through many offices before they were finally answered. A

Commander-in-Chief might want new guns for the artillery. He must first secure the support of senior Generals. Then he must forward a long "note" to the Military Member of Council, who would add his remarks and submit it to the Viceroy. The note would then be passed to the Finance Member for his comments. After that the full Council would have a turn at it. If it survived these ordeals the Viceroy would send it home for approval by the Secretary of State, who would have to consult another Council at the India Office, and might apply to the War Office for advice. By that time the Commander-in-Chief had probably handed over his command to a successor who took no interest in guns but wanted new barracks. So the guns would go into a pigeon-hole and stay there.

Two special reasons had contributed to the holding up of reform during the last three years. In 1900 Sir William Lockhart, the Commander-in-Chief, died after long ill-health. The Viceroy, Lord Curzon, wanted Kitchener to succeed him, and at that time it was generally supposed that the Boer War would soon be finished and the new Commander-in-Chief would be free to come to India. Pending his arrival General Sir Power Palmer acted for him. Though Palmer had ideas on the subject of reform, some of which were afterwards carried out, he did not feel justified in pressing them very strongly while he was acting as a stop-gap.

A more serious obstacle to military reform was the attitude of the Viceroy. Lord Ronaldshay has given us a life of the "Young Man in a Hurry." Coming from the pen of one who has himself held office as a Governor in India it bears the stamp of authority. In summing-up the Viceroyalty of Curzon he says: "It was great in the manner of its discharge, greater still in the measure of its fruitfulness, greatest of all in the high conception of duty by which it was inspired." [1] We have a full-length portrait of the statesman, an indefatigable worker, a brilliant writer and speaker, with a passion for justice; but the portrait of the man, which his biographer

[1] Ronaldshay, II, p. 416.

does not shirk the duty of painting, has some less agreeable characteristics. Curzon was self-opinionated, petulant, with "frayed nerves"; though constantly analysing his own feelings he had very little consideration for the feelings of other people, and his sarcastic humour generally left a sting; he was apt to regard any criticism of his own measures as an imputation on his wisdom or his justice, to be taken as an attack on himself. Consequently a difference of opinion on a matter of policy often developed into a personal quarrel. He quarrelled with a Lieutenant-Governor of the Punjab (Sir Mackworth Young), with two Commanders-in-Chief (Power Palmer and Kitchener), with a Secretary of State (St. John Brodrick, who had been an intimate friend): In every case he was honestly convinced of his own righteousness.

His quarrel with the Army as a whole became the subject of much talk. He took no trouble to conceal his opinion, which seems to have been based on two particular incidents.

During the first year of his reign an outrage was committed by some British soldiers at Rangoon. The officers made no attempt to palliate the crime, which they regarded with horror, but the prosecution broke down on a point of law, and there was no conviction. Curzon determined to make an example of what he considered culpable laxity on the part of those concerned. The Colonel and Sergeant-major were compulsorily retired, the Adjutant was forced to resign his appointment; the regiment was banished for two years to Aden, where all leave and indulgences were stopped. How far these sentences were just is a matter of opinion—what the Army resented was that an isolated case should be considered sufficient to tar the whole Service. In any body of 70,000 men there will always be a few bad characters; it would be absurd to deny the fact, but it was more absurd to assume that all officers were lax and incapable over the administration of justice. Curzon made no secret of his opinion that the Army was an inferior profession, the officers were of low intellect, the rank and file brutal and licentious. The troops could not reply directly to his strictures, but they lost no opportunity of letting the world know what they thought of Curzon's sense of justice and of himself. The barrack-room wag addressed the native cook with exaggerated politeness as Mister George Nathaniel.

Though Power Palmer accepted the Viceroy's decision he did not support the policy of collective punishment with enthusiasm, and consequently he was regarded by the Viceroy as a bad disciplinarian and a useless administrator. When Kitchener's arrival was expected, Curzon wrote: "I have been waiting for a Commander-in-Chief who is worthy of the post." This was tantamount to saying that Power Palmer was unworthy of it; and in fact any reforms which he recommended were criticized or snubbed till he naturally became shy about suggesting them.

The other incident took place at Sialkot in the spring of 1902. The 9th Lancers, who had lately arrived from South Africa, were entertaining another regiment, and a somewhat jovial evening resulted. Smith-Dorrien was then Adjutant-General in India, and as the whole of the subsequent correspondence passed through his hands his account is authoritative. He says:

"In the course of the festivities a certain Indian cook named Ata died under suspicious circumstances. The local military authorities naturally took steps to trace how this man had met his death, and the General commanding the Punjab, as well as the C.-in-C. were doing their utmost to trace the cause, and, should it prove a case of murder or culpable manslaughter, to bring someone to justice. A court of inquiry was assembled, and their opinion eagerly awaited. The Viceroy, who was credited with always being ready to champion a native where British soldiers were concerned, was much excited over the case, and, not content to await the verdict of the court of inquiry, day after day bombarded Army Headquarters with demands, couched in terms none too pleasantly worded, that the verdict should be hurried up, accompanied with disparaging insinuations on the army methods generally. It was most unpleasant for the C.-in-C., for it was no fault of his that evidence took time to collect, and he was doing all he could to push things on.

"At the time when I read the summing up, which I did before sending the dossier on to the Viceroy, I remarked, 'General——has fallen into the jaws of the lion.' Little did I think, though, how headlong he had done so, for next day, or certainly within two days, back came the dossier with a nice little minute covering some sides of foolscap, in the Viceroy's own handwriting, simply rending the General in question, and tearing him limb from limb. As an example of powerful expression in perfect language, of hard hitting and savage invective, of laborious scrutiny and of biting metaphor, I cannot imagine a more perfect model; but as the summing up of a ruler who could not be answered back, it did not commend itself to me.

"In spite of there being no direct evidence and that circumstantial evidence was only sufficient to point with the hand of suspicion, the Viceroy insisted that one of the regiments concerned should be made to suffer and that their leave should be stopped. It was this decision which rankled in the mind of the Army."[1]

Curzon had no illusion as to the view which would be taken in military circles of his interference in the case. He wrote to a friend: "As you know, anyone who dares to touch a crack regiment of the British Army—even though it contains two murderers—is looked upon as though he laid hands on the Ark of the Covenant." These words show in one sentence both that he had no hesitation in assuming a guilt which had not been proved, and that he was incapable of understanding the feelings of British soldiers. To the soldier the regiment is a sacred thing; he resents nothing so bitterly as sneers at its expense. The British community took the side of the Army, and at the big Coronation Durbar gave vent to an outburst of feeling which could not be misunderstood. Though

[1] Smith-Dorrien, pp. 317–18.

Curzon wrapped himself up in a mantle of righteousness it was not quite thick enough to comfort him. He wrote to the Secretary of State:

"One interesting event happened. The 9th Lancers rode by amid a storm of cheering; I say nothing of the bad taste of the demonstration. On such an occasion and before such a crowd (for of course every European in India is on the side of the Army in the matter) nothing better could be expected. But as I sat alone and unmoved on my horse, conscious of the implication of the cheers, I could not help being struck by the irony of the situation. . . . I do not suppose that anybody in that vast crowd was less disturbed by the demonstration than myself. On the contrary I felt a certain gloomy pride in having dared to do the right. But I also felt that if it could truthfully be claimed for me that I have (in these cases) loved righteousness and hated iniquity—no one could add that in return I have been anointed with the oil of gladness above my fellows." [1]

The reproach against him is not that he hated iniquity, but that he allotted to himself the office of judging iniquity. He was the only St. George, and anybody who failed to accept his ruling must be on the side of the Dragon. This attitude was of course inspired by his passion for justice; but it was certainly a very foolish attitude, because the fierce demand for justice defeated its own end. Though the native had died it did not follow that he had been deliberately murdered. There was, in fact, no ground for assuming a preconceived intention to kill him. Manslaughter might have resulted from brutality or merely stupidity; cases have been known where death has followed a silly practical joke. A British judge and jury would have administered justice, but the common (and not unfounded) belief was that the Viceroy had already declared that murder had been committed and intended to have the culprit or culprits hanged.

---

[1] Ronaldshay, II, pp. 246–47.

There is in everybody a natural reluctance to give evidence which will send a man to the gallows, and this is intensified if the accused is a comrade. When a recruit joins his regiment he is taught to stand by his comrades at all times and in all circumstances. Among men who are not highly educated this tends to a certain confusion of ideas; yet, as every Commanding Officer knows, in a good regiment there is a keen sense of justice, and a culprit will not be shielded by his friends as long as they feel he will get fair play. On the other hand, any suspicion of unfairness will throw every man in the ranks on the side of the offender, even when they know him to be guilty. Perhaps in this case there was no evidence to produce, but certainly the attitude of the Viceroy did not help the investigation. Though the Commander-in-Chief was "doing his utmost" to trace the cause, a court of inquiry was unable to fix the responsibility for the death of Ata on anyone.

It was fortunate that these two unpleasant incidents had taken place before the new Commander-in-Chief arrived in India on November 28, 1902. He was not forced to give an opinion, nor was he dragged into the personal quarrel between Curzon and the Army. But he knew that the atmosphere had been thundery, and, though he was eager to begin work at once, he had sufficient wisdom to move with caution. His first proposals did not attack any vested interests, and they were approved by every officer in the Service. If Kitchener had failed to impose organization on the troops in South Africa, he had brought away with him valuable lessons which he was now in a position to apply.

The first of these lessons was that, for purposes of command and administration, an army must be organized in standard units of recognized strength; for infantry the Division, and for cavalry the Brigade, had been accepted as the standard units in the British Army. Secondly, the Division or Brigade which had been moulded together during peace should not be broken up or altered when it is sent on active service. Technical training is of great value, but still greater is the value of the personal factor. If a Commander and his subordinates know each other, a very few words will be sufficient to convey his orders and his wishes; if they have never met before, long explanations will be necessary, and even then the Commander wonders whether the subordinate has grasped his meaning. The Division should therefore go to war under the officers who administered and trained it in peace.

Kitchener's views on this subject contained nothing new. For many years permanent organization had been established in the big armies of Europe, and the principle is so obvious that no objection could be raised against it. But various obstacles stood in the way before it could be applied in practice.

The original function of British troops in India had been to assist the Civil Power. The three hundred millions of natives contain a greater number of races and languages and religions than the whole continent of Europe. About 90 per cent are agricultural workers spread out in small villages; a peaceful industrious population, very primitive and quite harmless. In big towns, however, there will always be a mass of the lower classes, too ignorant to understand any appeal to reason, and easily stirred by sedition-mongers. The only hope of preventing disorder lies in overawing them by a parade of power, in other words by showing them a British garrison. Therefore the British troops, instead of being collected for training at big centres like Aldershot, were distributed, generally in single battalions, all over the country; and even in time of war the Indian Government would insist that a certain number should be left on garrison duty. The first thing was to reduce the compulsory garrisons to the lowest number compatible with safety. This involved discussion with the Civil authorities, but they were very reasonable in their demands, and agreement was soon reached.

After the question of internal defence had thus been settled, the surplus troops became available to form a field

REFORMS

army. It was found that there were sufficient for nine complete Divisions, each of which was to be self-contained with all equipment necessary for immediate mobilization.

This also seems an obvious step in the preparation for war, but again there were difficulties in grouping units together. For purposes of fighting, everybody agreed that each Division should have a stiffening of British troops; therefore for purposes of training the same organization should be adopted. There was some difference of opinion about the composition of brigades. Some officers of experience maintained that mixed brigades, containing both British and Native battalions, would give the best fighting formation; others, while admitting this, pointed out the difficulties which would arise in distributing rations, which of course are on a different scale for the two services. In peace the trouble could easily be overcome, but on active service a great deal depends on a simple system of issuing supplies, so much so that any complications must be avoided at all costs. Finally it was decided that each Division should consist of one British and two Indian brigades.

The nine Divisions were divided into two groups. Five were spread in a line facing the northern frontier, from Peshawur through Rawal Pindi, Lahore, Meerut to Lucknow. Of the other four one was on the frontier at Quetta, the remainder further south in Mhow, Poona, and Secunderabad. This was the "Redistribution Scheme" at which Kitchener aimed. There were many details to be arranged before it could be complete; some of them involved much labour, some demanded time, others were held up for considerations of expense. But before he left India Kitchener had the satisfaction of knowing that preparedness for war had been advanced by many stages.

So far the Commander-in-Chief had found himself in agreement with officers who could claim experience in Indian affairs, but his next reform, which affected the native regiments, gave rise to some jealousy and heartburning. Origi-

INDIAN DISTRIBUTION SCHEME

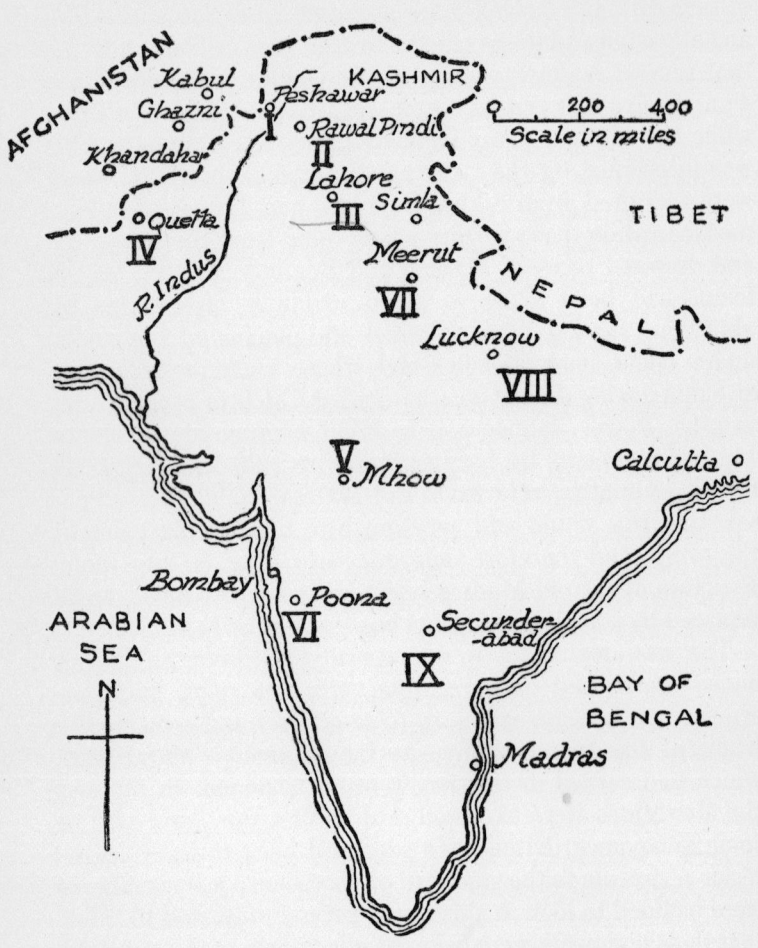

nally the three Presidencies of Bengal, Bombay, and Madras had each a separate army, recruited from its own native races and with its own Commander-in-Chief. As the best chances of active service were on the North-West Frontier the troops in that district received more attention from the authorities and attracted ambitious officers to their ranks. The result was that several regiments, such as the Guides and units of the Punjab Frontier Force, were regarded as *Corps d'Elite*, while the Madras Army sank to a very low standard. This was intensified by the fact that the regiments of the north were recruited from Sikhs, Gurkhas, and Punjabi Mahommedans, while those further south came from the unwarlike and despised races of Madras and Bombay. In 1895 an attempt had been made to avoid invidious distinctions by abolishing the Presidency Armies and placing all the troops under one Commander-in-Chief whose Headquarters were at Simla during the hot weather and at Calcutta in the winter months. Power Palmer had in mind a proposal to replace Madras regiments by hardier troops recruited in the north, but like his other reforms it did not materialize. Kitchener saw that this would add very much to the fighting value of the army, and therefore determined to bring it into force. Fourteen of the old Madras regiments were disbanded, to be replaced by Punjabis and Gurkhas.

The new regiments were naturally unwilling to inherit names which had been regarded with contempt, and consequently it became necessary to re-number and re-name the whole of the Indian Army; as far as possible those titles which had earned distinction were not changed. In the end the alterations were accepted, but at first they gave rise to some annoyance. Kitchener's idea had been to level up inferior regiments to the standard of good ones; jealous officers were inclined to look at this in the reverse way, and to think that their regiments were being levelled down to the standard of those which they had always regarded with scorn.

In addition to giving new names and new recruiting areas

an attempt was made to give all regiments an equal chance of training on the Frontier. In those stations which lay close to the border the troops lived in a state of readiness which almost amounted to active service conditions. At any moment they might be turned out to chase some Ghazi fanatic or a party of rifle thieves; it was unsafe for individuals to leave the cantonments unless they were armed; in some places the outpost duty was serious business. The Punjab Frontier Force had been permanently stationed along the borderline and had learnt a good deal about the tribesmen and their tricks. Kitchener thought that by giving the south country regiments a tour of duty under those conditions their training would be much improved. In the end, however, he was forced to admit that this was a mistake. The tribesmen are the cleverest and most daring thieves in the world. They regarded the newcomers as a god-send, and helped themselves without hesitation to rifles, transport, or anything else that caught their fancy. The veterans of the Frontier Force listened to stories of raids with thinly disguised satisfaction. Kitchener had to acknowledge that duty on the Frontier is a science in itself, demanding highly specialized training and the study of a lifetime. The old Punjab regiments were brought back.

CHAPTER XIII

THE NORTH-WEST FRONTIER

UP TO THIS point Kitchener had a very clear object before him—to increase the fighting value of the troops, and to organize them so as to be ready for war. Over internal defence he had no anxiety, but plans for active operations brought up many questions of a much more difficult nature. The problem of the North-West Frontier depends on so many hypothetical factors that the men who have most experience in those parts are generally the least inclined to lay down the law on the subject. It was commonly believed that the great Empire of Russia had designs on India; much activity had certainly been shown in pushing strategic railways towards Afghanistan. But the Russian bogey, if taken by itself, held no terrors. Between our frontier and the nearest Russian post there lie 500 miles of mountains; the roads are impassable for wheeled transport; it is doubtful whether a line of railway could ever be laid—at all events the construction would take years to complete. Therefore the idea of a Russian host pouring suddenly into the plains of India was as impossible as anything can be in war. Whether the conquest of the air will alter the problem is a question which did not arise in Kitchener's time and may be left to a future generation.

But though the Russians could not bring their own troops to India they might incite the Afghans and frontier tribes to give trouble unless we took steps to prevent such action. And the trouble might be very serious. The Amir had a regular army of 100,000 men and 500 guns, besides irregulars who might amount to another 50,000 or more.

It was our obvious policy to establish friendly relations with the Amir, but how far that friendship ought to go was a matter which has perplexed generations of Indian statesmen. The Government had guaranteed the integrity of the Amir's territory; but, though nobody had cared to admit the fact, it had undertaken more than it could perform. Like the Russians, we could not cross those 500 miles of mountains. The military authorities had therefore drawn up a scheme based on two main points:

1. A line through Kandahar, Ghazni, Kabul, should be regarded as the "strategic frontier," which must be held by the British Army at all costs.
2. The defence of Afghanistan between that line and the Russian frontier should be left to the Amir's troops.

Kabul is roughly 150 miles from Peshawur and Kandahar is about the same distance from Quetta. Railways had already been pushed some distance forward, and surveys had been made and materials collected for their extension. We could reach the strategic frontier and maintain ourselves there before a Russian army could get anywhere near the same line. But, as in the case of Bloemfontein and Pretoria, the occupation of two cities does not imply control over the whole country. Everything would depend upon the attitude of the Amir and the frontier tribes. This introduced a factor on which no reliance could be placed. As long as the Amir was friendly it was to our interests that he should be strong; we could supply him with munitions and he had sufficient fighting men to put up a formidable resistance against the Russians. Unfortunately there always remained a possibility, almost a probability, that the friendly Amir would be assassinated, and that his successor would turn the rifles we had given him against ourselves. In this case it was to our interest that he should be very weak. Everything therefore depended upon the human factor.

The authors of the scheme were not blind to the facts. The only bright spot was that the Russian advance must be slow and we could not fail to have warning of it. When the time for action arrived we must take stock of Afghan politics and shape

THE NORTH-WEST FRONTIER 165

our policy to fit them; and for some years this had been the attitude of the Government and the military authorities. It must be kept in mind that opinions were very evenly divided. Some people suggested that we ought to abandon our obligations to the Amir and confine ourselves to the defence of our own frontier; others wanted to keep on terms with the Amir without committing ourselves to an advance; others again believed in a strong "forward policy."

Needless to say, Kitchener hated to leave so big a question in a state of suspense. His practical mind wanted a definite policy on which to base definite plans. But before proposing any scheme of his own he was wise enough to study the local situation. Only two months after his arrival he began a tour of the Frontier, and before the first year of his appointment had passed he had personally inspected every station along the whole length of 500 miles between Quetta and Chitral. This of course entailed a tremendous amount of travelling, mostly on horseback, sometimes on foot. Days were spent in consultation with the Political Officers, and in studying the history of our association with Afghanistan. But even after collecting and digesting all the vast mass of detail connected with the question and after holding the office of Commander-in-Chief for six years he had not got much further than his predecessors.

This does not imply that he failed where he ought to have succeeded, but it points to the fact that he was sometimes inclined to criticize the state of affairs in which he found India before he had taken into consideration the difficulties with which his predecessors had been faced.

After eighteen months' study he drew up a paper on the subject, of which the main point was that we should come to a definite understanding with Afghanistan. The Amir Habibullah had only been a short time on the throne, and therefore it was natural that we should raise the question of joint action with him. If he intended to show himself as a loyal ally he would allow British officers to reconnoitre his country and prepare schemes for its defence; if he refused to come to any agreement it would be better to stop the supply of munitions and repudiate all responsibility for the defence of Afghan territory. The Home Government agreed to send a special mission to Kabul for the purpose of sounding Habibullah. His Majesty was intensely jealous of his independence and could not forget that a British Army had occupied his capital some twenty-five years ago. The mere suggestion that officers should be sent into his country inflamed his distrust. So the results of the mission were vague and unsatisfactory; it was resolved to continue the former agreement by which we were responsible for the defence of Afghanistan, but the Home Government refused to demand the concessions from the Amir on which Kitchener laid stress.

In order to finish this rough story of the Afghan problem it is necessary to look forward to the year 1907, when the Amir paid a visit to India. By that time Kitchener seems to have resigned himself to the impossibility of laying down any cut-and-dried policy which could be sealed by formal treaty. He saw that the key of the whole problem lay in the hands of Habibullah himself and therefore it was of the utmost importance to study the character of the man and cultivate mutual confidence. Kitchener's knowledge of Orientals was a real asset in ensuring the success of the visit —there can be no doubt that the impression left on the Amir's mind went far towards the solution of the problem.

Sir H. McMahon was appointed to take charge of the Royal Guest. Habibullah, who had never seen a railway before, showed symptoms of suspicion when he was invited to enter the carriage at the frontier station of Jamrud; it required all the diplomacy of McMahon to prevent him turning back and abandoning the visit. But as soon as he overcame his first reluctance the novel experience filled him with delight.

The Viceroy, Lord Minto, and the Commander-in-Chief met their guest at Agra, where a Durbar was held at which he was to be invested with the Grand Cross of the Star of India.

It was explained to His Majesty that, as soon as he was invested, he should take a seat on a dais one step below the Viceroy, and that the other recipients of honours would take seats below him. This he absolutely refused to do, saying he was a King and would sit below no one. He argued that if King Edward himself had been present his place would have been alongside him, and that he was certainly not going to sit below his representative. As the Amir was obdurate on this point a difficult problem had to be solved, and this was done by arranging that directly he had received his honour he should go straight away.

A big parade of troops revealed to him the power of the British Raj to an extent which he had believed to be impossible; it is said that he was very angry with his followers who had told him that our army was insignificant in comparison with his own. He even threatened to send some of his Sirdars back to Kabul for summary punishment.

The Amir went on to Calcutta and severely tried the energies of his hosts by his ceaseless thirst for amusement and novelty. He rose at dawn and refused to go to bed till some hours after midnight. A great feature of the season was the "Minto Fête," promoted by Lady Minto on behalf of a charity; the stalls of fancy articles and jewellery were a tremendous attraction to the wealthy monarch, who had never seen any shops except in the bazaar at Kabul. He bought everything and only complained that the prices were too low. On one occasion when visiting Lady Minto's own stall he declined to purchase, saying that the prices asked were beneath his royal dignity; returning next evening he found the jewellery priced in thousands of rupees and proceeded to purchase largely. On another occasion, seeing that Lady G——'s doll stall was but poorly patronized, he gave that lady an agreeable surprise, by purchasing, at one vast sum, the whole contents of the stall, by no means a small one, and by making his dignified Sirdars carry off the dolls in baskets to distribute among all the children they could find at the Fête.

After postponing his departure several times Habibullah at last left Calcutta. Before going to the station he insisted on dining at the house of the Commander-in-Chief and appeared to be enjoying himself so well that his host began to fear another postponement. At 10 p. m. a guard of honour was in attendance at the station, and a crowd of high officials had assembled, but when McMahon hinted that a special train was waiting, Habibullah declared that nothing would induce him to go. A message was sent to dismiss the guard and release all those who were in attendance. At midnight Kitchener took his guest by the hand and walked him out to the motor.

The friendship he felt towards Kitchener seems to have been genuine and was maintained by the interchange of letters and gifts. As Sir George Arthur points out, it was "not without its effect on history." Throughout the Great War Habibullah remained loyal to England, and refused to listen to the tempting of German agents; at a time when our garrisons in India were reduced to the lowest possible strength it was of enormous importance that Afghanistan did not seize the opportunity to increase our troubles.

Habibullah was assassinated soon after the Armistice, and the problem of the North-West Frontier had to be examined afresh.

The problem of the Frontier tribes was even more complicated by the human factor. They occupied the strip of mountains which lies between the frontiers of India and Afghanistan—a No-Man's Land of brave and war-like people. Their total strength had been estimated at 300,000 fighting men, with about 90,000 breech-loading rifles. Had they been capable of anything like combined action they would certainly have been a formidable danger, close to our frontier, and within striking distance of towns like Quetta and Peshawur. Fortunately there was no fear of any combination on their part, for the various tribes are not only independent of each other but also at constant enmity with each other; in the Pushtu language the word "dushman" means either "enemy" or "cousin"—because it is inconceivable that a cousin could be anything but an enemy. Each valley is ruled by the Malik, or head landlord, except during outbursts of religious fervour, when the preaching of some Mullah excites their fanaticism and they turn to follow him.

As an example of their mentality a good story is told of the Tirah Maidan, a valley fifty miles south-west of Peshawur. The tribe had no religion of any kind till a certain holy man arrived and converted them by his eloquence to the religion of Mohammed. He taught that a true believer has three duties in this world: to slay an infidel, to build a rest-house for travellers, and to make a pilgrimage to a shrine. Killing an infidel presented little difficulty; in fact most of the tribesmen had already passed this test. No road ran through the valley and therefore a very small hut would provide ample shelter for all the travellers that were likely to appear. But a pilgrimage at first seemed impossible. Being at enmity with all their neighbours they could not cross their boundary except for the purpose of raids; no shrine lay within hundreds of miles. At last after much heart-searching one bright convert hit upon the solution—he killed the preacher and built a shrine over his remains right in the centre of the valley. The deceased by his own account had been exceptionally holy, and therefore little doubt could exist that a visit to his tomb would confer a blessing on the pilgrim. Since that time the happy dwellers in Tirah Maidan have been very proud of their piety.

The policy of the Indian Government towards these unruly neighbours had been chiefly made up of negatives. We did not want to take possession of their country—which would be a difficult and expensive business. We did not want them to fall under the dominion of the Amir, as that would add too much to his fighting strength. Nor did we want them to acquire a high standard of civilization—once they gave up quarrelling among themselves they might learn the value of combination and become a serious menace to us. In 1907 Sir William Lockhart had established a Frontier Militia, to hold the advance posts; it was recruited from the more trustworthy tribes and was controlled by our Political Officers. Besides providing a valuable police force this Militia became an indirect means of bribing the tribes into good behaviour. The pay was fairly good, and, by Kitchener's advice, a pension could be earned; the tribesman did his service and went back to his home knowing that if his friends gave trouble the whole tribe would be put on the black list, and the pension would be forfeited for ever. Therefore his advice would generally be that instead of raiding places under British protection it would be preferable to raid somewhere else.

Curzon took an important step in creating the North-West Frontier Province, consisting of that part of the Punjab which lies beyond the Indus. The idea was that the orthodox forms of government by which the other districts of India were ruled could not be applied to the Frontier. Political Officers were given extended powers to take immediate action, as if the province were under martial law; the Chief Agent, whose position resembled that of a Lieutenant-Governor, was always an officer who had learned by long experience the ways of the tribes.

Kitchener was desperately anxious to formulate a policy which would give lasting results, and spent much time on the subject, but, as in the case of Afghanistan, he was finally forced to admit the impossibility of applying a general rule. When he left India the system was much the same as when he arrived; Political Officers were dealing out bribes to one tribe and threats to another; sometimes punitive expeditions overran a valley and then came away; sometimes a small post was pushed forward to guard an important line of advance. It was all very unsatisfactory in the eyes of those who wanted to reduce government to an academic science; things happened up in those mountains which could not be published in the London Press. But there were great men among the Political Officers. Kitchener recognized their greatness and left them alone. When he was leaving India a writer in the *Pioneer* said "His reforms were wise, but perhaps his greatest wisdom was shown in what he left undone."

But though he could not formulate a definite and consistent policy he added very much to a state of readiness for war; his schemes may be roughly recapitulated as follows:

1. The organization of nine Divisions as self-contained and permanent units tended to avoid anything like the "tangled mess" which had done so much harm in South Africa.

2. The distribution of the Divisions in two lines leading towards Peshawur and Quetta provided for a quick employment on the strategic frontier.

3. The reconstitution of the Indian Army added to its fighting value.

4. Through personal friendship with the Amir the question of Afghanistan was settled as well as could be, and for as long as Habibullah was on the throne.

CHAPTER XIV

THE QUARREL WITH CURZON

THE GOVERNMENT OF INDIA is in the hands of a Council of which the Viceroy is President, and there are Members to represent Finance and other Departments. When Kitchener went to India, the Military Member was in some respects like the Secretary of State for War; that is to say he kept a watchful eye on expenditure, gave his opinion on broad lines of policy, and issued orders to the Army Headquarters in the name of the Viceroy. Though the Commander-in-Chief had a seat on the Council he was not expected to attend the meetings except when matters concerning the Army came up for discussion. The Military Member was always in attendance on the Viceroy to keep him informed and to act as adviser.

But in addition to these advisory duties the Military Member had executive control over the non-combatant services—Supply, Transport, Ordinance, and Remounts. No doubt the original intention of this system had been to lighten the work of the Commander-in-Chief and to enable him to devote his whole time to training of the fighting troops. In fact the Military Member was a glorified Quartermaster General. Having command of these services it was necessary that he should be a regular officer, and consequently the appointment had always been held by a Major-General of the Indian Army. The situation therefore arose that a Major-General was issuing orders in the name of the Viceroy to the Commander-in-Chief, who was his senior in rank. This would have been in accordance with the custom of the Service if he had been merely a staff officer; it is recognized that members of the staff convey orders to officers senior to themselves. But all information and reports from Army Headquarters came to the Viceroy through the channel of the Military Department. The Member could criticize and comment on them; the Viceroy, being a civilian, would naturally rely on his technical knowledge; and so the orders which were issued in the Viceroy's name might really be said to emanate not from him but from the Military Member.

For many years complaints had been made that the existence of the Military Member led to duplication of correspondence and to delay. There was no doubt that jealousy existed between the staff of Army Headquarters and the Department. Sometimes a sharp division of opinion had arisen, but as a rule the Commander-in-Chief and the Military Member had been in agreement on broad questions, and no actual enmity had arisen till the time of Power Palmer. Then the friction became very acute. Perhaps the trouble began through Curzon's honest desire for reform. Everybody agreed that reform was needed. But before deciding on any point the Viceroy must examine every detail for himself, and this made him inquisitive to an extent which sometimes savoured of suspicion and distrust. He took the Military Department under his wing, encouraged its criticisms, and expressed delight when any mistake was brought to his notice. Instead of confining himself to questions of broad policy the Military Member began to investigate matters of discipline and training which had hitherto been regarded as outside his province; in fact he assumed authority equal, if not superior, to that of the Commander-in-Chief. This was the system which became known as the Dual Control.

To Kitchener's mind dual control was an abomination. He did not deny that supreme authority rests with the Civil Government, which decides on the strength of the forces, financial questions, and broad lines of policy. But the Commander-in-Chief is held responsible for the Army, in peace and war, and therefore he should have full power over purely military subjects, and should be the sole adviser of the

Viceroy. The intervention of the Military Department led to duplication of all correspondence, to argument, to delay. Furthermore it was derogatory to the dignity of the Commander-in-Chief that his letters should be submitted to the scrutiny and criticism of a junior officer and his staff. In his opinion the only satisfactory solution was to make a clean sweep of the Military Department.

Curzon's reply to this argument was that there was no dual control, because the Viceroy is sole head of the Army and the ultimate responsibility lies with him. Before deciding on a big question he must see both sides of it and not merely the personal views of one man. He has the right to consult anybody he likes, and he requires an adviser who will be in constant attendance. Secondly, if the Military Member ceased to exist and the Commander-in-Chief became sole adviser, one of two unsatisfactory situations would result—the Commander-in-Chief would either have to give up other duties in order to remain at the side of the Viceroy, or he would continue his other duties and leave the Viceroy in a state of ignorance. No man, however capable of work, can be in two places at one time; the Viceroy might require his attendance while important manœuvres were being held, or even when a frontier expedition was going on. Kitchener himself had desired to introduce a system which would require no alteration on the outbreak of war; it was absurd to suppose that a Commander-in-Chief could give proper attention to a campaign and at the same time keep the Viceroy posted with information and advice.

On this point Curzon was supported by several officers of experience. When Lord Roberts held the command he had complained that the machinery was cumbersome and in need of reform; all the same he pronounced in favour of retaining a Military Member of Council. Still more significant is the opinion of Smith-Dorrien; his book shows that he was a fervent admirer of Kitchener and a strong opponent of the Military Member. Indeed his conflicts with the latter had become so bitter that he insisted on resigning his ap-

THE QUARREL WITH CURZON

pointment as Adjutant-General, and only consented to defer his resignation at the personal request of Kitchener himself. He cannot therefore be accused of any undue tenderness towards the Military Department. But he considered that its abolition would throw too much work on the Commander-in-Chief, who was already overburdened. The trouble lay not so much in the machinery but in the personalities of the Viceroy and Military Member, both of whom interfered much more than was necessary or desirable.

On the second point, control of supply and transport, all military officers agreed. In time of war the Commander-in-Chief must take command of the services in the field; therefore he should organize and train them in time of peace; the Quartermaster-General should be an officer of his own staff, under the orders of nobody but himself. The disadvantages of dual control had been exemplified in the Tirah Expedition of 1897–8. The transport, which consisted of pack animals, broke down. The soldiers complained that the animals were of inferior quality, the saddlery rotten, the native drivers useless: the Military Department retorted that the transport, as supplied, had been of good quality, but was broken down by ill-usage on the part of the soldiers: the animals were overloaded, the marches were too arduous, proper opportunities were not given for watering. There may have been some truth on both sides, but it was impossible to allot the responsibility. Improvement could only be effected by giving the Commander-in-Chief an opportunity to satisfy himself in peace-time that the transport was ready for war. The responsibility would then be on his shoulders.

Even before he left England to take up his appointment, Kitchener had been warned by the Adjutant-General that the Military Department was obstructive, but his first meetings with Curzon were very cordial; many reforms were discussed and on most of them agreement was easy. Three months later he drew up a paper showing that the Military Department gave rise to much unnecessary correspondence and pointing out the danger of dual control. Curzon admitted that there was too much writing, but suggested that the matter should be deferred till Kitchener had more experience in office, and this seemed so reasonable that no objection could be raised. A few months' experience confirmed the first impression. Though his proposals had been accepted, sometimes with eagerness, the tone of the correspondence implied that no reform could pass until it had received a blessing from the Military Department. There was in fact a tone of patronage, which Kitchener probably found insupportable.

In the summer of 1903 a dispute arose over a very trivial matter. Kitchener had drafted an Army Order and in the usual way sent it to the Department to be printed and issued. The Military Member thought the wording was ambiguous, and made a small amendment without further reference to Headquarters. Kitchener regarded this action as unwarrantable interference, and threatened to resign unless the Viceroy called the Military Member to order. Lord Ronaldshay implies that the threat of resignation was rather childish, but I think Kitchener had deliberately chosen a matter of no intrinsic importance in order to get a definite ruling on the bigger point—whether the Military Member had power to override the Commander-in-Chief. He got his own way and his threat of resignation was withdrawn. But the big point remained unsettled, and it seems to have taken hold of his mind till it amounted to an obsession.

Curzon's term of office was due to expire at the end of 1904. Perhaps Kitchener allowed the question of dual control to rest in hopes that the next Viceroy would share his own views, and it could then be settled without violence. But Curzon was given an extension of two years, and in April 1904 he went home on leave, partly on account of ill-health and partly to discuss certain measures with the Cabinet. On June 15 he attended a meeting of the Imperial Defence Committee, and there found a paper written by Kitchener which took him completely by surprise. It contained the views of the Commander-in-Chief on the defence of India,

THE QUARREL WITH CURZON

which of course it was his duty to submit; Curzon's surprise was due to the fact that in pointing out various abuses Kitchener declared that each and all of them arose from the curse of dual control, and drew the deduction that the Military Department must be abolished. Lord Ronaldshay says that this paper "apprised Lord Curzon of the fact that Lord Kitchener intended to take advantage of his absence from India to bring to a head the difference between himself and the Viceroy on the question of military administration."[1]

In order to understand Kitchener's action let us take an imaginary case. The Commander-in-Chief discovers by experiment that all the guns in India are liable to burst when firing a new pattern of shell. This would constitute a terrible danger in the event of a big war. It would be his duty to call attention to the defect, and to repeat his warning if immediate attention is not paid to it. It would be criminal to drop the subject. Now let us put the actual case. By virtue of his office, as well as by reputation, Kitchener was the supreme expert on military subjects. He believed that in the system of dual control he had discovered a source of real danger; therefore it would be criminal on his part to drop the subject. We may think the danger was non-existent or exaggerated—as Ronaldshay and Curzon thought—but we must allow that it was not only his right but his duty to press his own opinion. By offering to resign he had already given the Viceroy fair warning that he meant business. Curzon could not pretend that he had not been given time to consider the subject.

It cannot be supposed that there was any idea of scoring a point behind Curzon's back. Kitchener had sufficient experience of procedure to know that a decision could not be made until after the Viceroy had been given full opportunity to discuss it. He had been asked for his opinion; he could not hold it back. It would have been sheer dishonesty to conceal anything which he believed to be a danger. As a matter of fact he had given Curzon an opportunity to score

[1] Ronaldshay, II, p. 350.

a point behind his back—which Curzon did not fail to take advantage of. He declared that Kitchener's paper did not deal with interior defence, but with the Constitution of the Government of India, and that therefore it ought not even to be discussed. The Prime Minister accepted this view, the paper was withdrawn and once more the question of dual control was shelved.

From this moment the issue seems to have been shifted from the realms of policy into the arena of personal combat. Curzon was furious that Kitchener had attempted to go behind his back, and was determined to prevent any discussion. Kitchener was furious that the strongly-worded paper of a Commander-in-Chief had been withdrawn without discussion, probably to find a resting-place in the proverbial pigeon-hole. There was only one course left; after waiting two months he again tendered his resignation.

The Cabinet could no longer refuse to consider the subject, and if the Ministers had faced their responsibilities the subsequent trouble might have been avoided. The final decision would in any case have to be made by them. Kitchener's arguments were already in their hands; Curzon was on the spot as advocate for the other side; Lord Roberts could be called in to give his experience of the Military Department and suggest a solution. In fact, all the material evidence was at hand on which their decision would be finally based. But the Prime Minister decided to refer the whole question to the Viceroy's Council. Perhaps this course was taken at the suggestion of Curzon; perhaps Ministers hoped that a little delay would give the opponents time to recover their tempers; perhaps it was merely an evasion of an unpleasant responsibility. But there could be little doubt that the resignation of Kitchener would cause a sensation which would not redound to the credit of the Government. The promise was therefore given that his complaints would be considered, and Kitchener withdrew his resignation.

Curzon returned to India at the end of December, but three months went by before the big question came up for decision in Council. These months had been spent by both sides in preparing themselves for battle. Kitchener had drawn up a long minute in which all his arguments were arrayed; he took care to add that his criticism was directed against a system and not against any individual.

The Military Member, Sir Edmund Elles, had also prepared a minute in defence of his own Department. He too disclaimed any personal feeling, but rather spoilt this by saying that the trouble arose, not from the system, but from the way in which it was carried out. He took his stand on the argument that by law every act done by the Military Member is an act of the Governor-General in Council. In taking up this line of defence he was really supporting Kitchener's own argument that the army was under dual control.

These two minutes had been circulated in the usual way to all Members before the meeting, and Curzon had added a long minute of his own. With real eloquence it held up Kitchener as a recognized master of the science of military government as well as of the art of war; during his two years of office he had carried out many valuable reforms, and on every occasion and in every way he had been supported by the Viceroy and Council. But now Kitchener was proposing "to subvert the Military Authority of the Government of India as a whole, and to substitute for it a military autocracy in the person of the C.-in-C." . . . "with great reluctance but without hesitation I am compelled to advise against the acceptance of the C.-in-C.'s proposal."

Everybody expected that Kitchener would make a speech on the subject which he had so much to heart. But to the general surprise "he sat brooding and silent except for a brief statement which he read from paper, regretting that he was in a minority of one and declaring that he was unwilling to discuss the matter further." [1]

He had put into his minute every argument that he could bring to bear; there was nothing to add, nothing to retract.

[1] Ronaldshay, II, p. 377.

The fact that he read out his final words from a paper proves that he knew the majority would be against him, and therefore he considered that further argument was useless. He had made up his mind that if the Home Government supported Curzon he would resign and wash his hands of a responsibility which he considered unfair. Perhaps, too, he was a little afraid of being drawn into a discussion; Curzon's quickness and skill in debate were well known, and in cross-examination he might extract some admission which could be turned to his own advantage. He may also have wished to show that he would not consent to be brow-beaten or heckled before a crowd of civilians who, in his opinion, had no right to decide on a military subject.

In one way his silence may have been wise, but it did not tend to improve the personal aspect of the dispute. Curzon and the civilian members refused to accept the view that the subject was a military one; on the contrary, to their minds it was purely a constitutional question which they had every right to discuss and decide. It is true they had seen Kitchener's arguments in print, but he had not replied to their arguments. By reading his statement from a paper he showed that he knew the verdict would go against him, and thus implied that members had pre-judged the case. No doubt this was true, and nothing he could have said would have altered their vote, but they would have preferred to feel that they were impartial and open to argument. His refusal to discuss the question further implied contempt for the arguments of the other side and some contempt for the Council.

It was a pity that he appeared to take defeat with bad grace. He might have acknowledged the tributes paid to his energy and wisdom, he might have repeated that he did not contest the supreme authority of the Civil Power. Silence left the members under the impression either that he could not answer, or—what was worse—that he would not.

In accordance with Kitchener's prediction the voting was unanimous against him. In due course a dispatch was sent

THE QUARREL WITH CURZON

to Downing Street recording the opinion of the Governor-General in Council.

The final decision now lay with the Cabinet, and unfortunately it took the form of a compromise which Brodrick hoped would satisfy both the gladiators. But it was so vaguely expressed that even Ministers who had assisted in drawing it up failed to grasp its meaning. The Military Department was to be shorn of its powers to criticize the Commander-in-Chief or to give advice, but a Member of Council would be retained, to be known henceforth as the Military Supply Member, in charge of non-combatant services. This sounds clear if unsatisfactory. But an attempt was made at home to show that the Government of India had really been supported; Lord Lansdowne said in the House of Lords:

"We found ourselves in the position of having to decide between the demand of Lord Kitchener that the office of Military Member should be absolutely put an end to, and the view of the Government of India that it should be preserved and that he should remain very much in the position which he had always occupied; and we decided against Lord Kitchener."

But if this was the intention of the Cabinet it was certainly not conveyed to India. Curzon wrote: "The decision about the Kitchener case came the other day. I am under no illusion as to the result. He has practically triumphed although a disembowelled Military Member has been left to prevent me from resigning. I am quite ready to do this."

In fact Kitchener had only got half what he demanded. Supply and transport were still outside his command, and therefore the dual control had not been finally abolished; the vagueness of Brodrick left much room for further dispute. But Curzon's unconcealed annoyance was in itself enough to count as a victory for his opponent. Kitchener remained content without demanding the blood of the new Military Supply Member; that Department dragged out a precarious existence for a few years and was then demolished by the next Secretary of State. Its death was not lamented by anybody.

The next step was to organize the new system, but before that could be done there were several attempts to clear up the situation. Kitchener gave assent to some modifications which seemed to run contrary to his previous demands, and in one note he even admitted that the Supply Member might be available for consultation. Several telegrams were exchanged with Brodrick in a game of cross-purposes and nobody knew what anybody else wanted. One definite piece of news arrived on July 16—that the Secretary of State was about to nominate an officer for the new post of Supply Member. Curzon immediately wired to ask for the appointment of his own choice, Sir E. Barrow. When this request was refused he asked to be allowed to resign. The Cabinet acted with a promptness which showed that the request was not unexpected; they accepted the resignation, and four days later announced that Lord Minto would be the next Viceroy. Curzon left for England in November, rejoicing loudly that he had dared to do right.

Ronaldshay, though ready to give full consideration to Kitchener's arguments, remains unconvinced by them. He points out that the maladministration of the Mesopotamia Campaign in 1915–16 was due to the fact that the Commander-in-Chief, Sir Beauchamp Duff, was unable to combine the duties of advising the Viceroy and superintending the equipment of the Indian forces. Duff himself acknowledged in his evidence before the Commission of Inquiry that while in times of peace one man could discharge the dual function it was more than he could manage in time of war.

The abolition of the Military Department was a question of administration which could be openly debated in Council or elsewhere. On such questions there is always room for divergence of opinion and the strongest arguments may be used without any suggestion of personal feeling. But in this case the dispute was by no means confined to the Council Room, nor was it conducted without personal feeling.

At the outset Kitchener had been welcomed by the Viceroy with enthusiasm, and his first visit to Viceregal Lodge was a complete success. Lady Curzon became an intimate friend; she gave him four beautiful salt-cellars for the set of gold plate which he was collecting, and assisted with the decoration of his houses. Curzon was delighted by his reforming energy. Everything appeared to be *au couleur de roses*. But Curzon could not long be delighted by an energy which was not directed by his own will, and the first impression soon gave way to anxiety. He wrote that Kitchener "is just like a caged lion, stalking to and fro and dashing its bruised and lacerated head against the bars." Again—"He stands aloof and alone, a molten mass of devouring energy and burning ambition, without anybody to control or guide it in the right direction." [1]

The first rift with the Military Member took place over the wording of an Army Order, and though the matter was of no importance it served to publish the fact that Army Headquarters had prepared an attack on the Department which the Viceroy had taken under his wing. India bubbled with excitement over the prospect of a royal row between two combatants, both of whom were known to be capable of hard fighting. The partisans of each side put no restraint on their feelings, and gave rise to much scandal. It was said that members of Kitchener's staff cut members of Curzon's staff in public.

The growing estrangement between the Viceroy and the Commander-in-Chief was increased by an unfortunate incident, which took place during a ball at Viceregal Lodge. In accordance with custom there were two supper-rooms, the smaller of which was reserved for the Viceroy's own

[1] Ronaldshay, II, p. 353.

circle, Members of Council, and distinguished visitors. They were sitting down to table when Lady Curzon noticed that Kitchener was not in the room and no place had been kept for him; this, no doubt, was owing to the negligence of one of the staff. She was horrified to think that such a mistake could have happened and rushed out herself to find Kitchener and put things right. But when she reached the main entrance the wheels of a carriage were heard driving away. In Simla the roads are so narrow that only the Viceroy and Commander-in-Chief are allowed to use carriages—other people drive in rickshaws. Lady Curzon was therefore at once aware that Kitchener had gone off without taking leave of his host and hostess. A lady who was present told me that she had noticed Kitchener, standing by himself, stiff and silent, near the door of the ballroom; suddenly he turned on his heel and strode quickly down the long corridor which leads to the main entrance. Within a few minutes everybody was telling everybody else what had taken place.

Kitchener's best friends were aghast at his precipitate behaviour on this occasion. Hitherto it had been supposed that he knew nothing about the childish personalities in which junior staff officers had been indulging. One moment's reflection would have shown him the interpretation which must be put on his conduct. He would also have seen that an incident of this kind would be widely discussed in every club and drawing-room. Nobody who knew Lady Curzon could for a moment suppose her capable of intentional rudeness. If he had remained for a few moments longer her apologies would certainly have satisfied him on this score. But his abrupt departure implied that in his opinion the slight had been intentional, and constituted a public accusation against his host of grave discourtesy.

Towards the end of the dispute no pretence was made to maintain even the coldest relations between "Snowdon" and the Viceregal Lodge. Correspondence was strictly official. Unavoidable meetings were held in the presence of the full Council or on the parade ground.

THE QUARREL WITH CURZON

Curzon's attitude is not altogether surprising. He regarded his own position, representative of the King, as sacred—in which of course he was quite right. But he was also in the habit of regarding his own opinion as sacred—which was the origin of other quarrels than that with Lord Kitchener. But Kitchener's attitude is much more difficult to understand. It was not the first time he had come into collision with highly placed officials—we have seen what happened at Paardeberg, and the disagreement with Milner and Brodrick over the peace terms in South Africa. He had written strongly-worded Minutes, and on no less than three occasions he had threatened resignation because his advice seemed likely to be rejected. Nevertheless he remained on the best of terms with his official opponents. The quarrel with Curzon was the first time that any personal feeling came into a dispute. The only possible explanations seem to be that his convictions, like those of Curzon, were so strong that they ran away with him, or that the clash was one, not of wills, but of two opposing, yet equally masterful, temperaments.

CHAPTER XV

ROUTINE

THE NEW Viceroy, Lord Minto, arrived in November 1905. He was in every way a contrast to Curzon. He had no preconceived ideas about India or about reform; he could meet army officers on the field of sport, and he was content to leave army problems to the Commander-in-Chief. Consequently there were no more serious disagreements over matters of policy, and the only obstacles to Kitchener's reforms arose from the financial side. It was the Home Government, rather than the council of India, which now stood in the way. The Liberals, who obtained a big majority at the General Election of December 1905, were pledged to retrenchment, and to economy in the fighting forces. The war between Russia and Japan had depleted the resources of the Tsar. It could not be supposed that he would be ready, at least for many years, to undertake another campaign on a big scale. The new Secretary for India, Mr. Morley, laid much stress on this fact, and the Liberal Cabinet believed the situation in Europe to be so calm that an opportunity was open for the reduction of the military budget.

Whatever misgivings Kitchener may have felt, he accepted the Cabinet's ruling, and therefore some parts of his redistribution scheme were held up. Funds which had been earmarked for the re-armament of the artillery and for the construction of new barracks were withdrawn. But like Morley he was ever an enthusiast for economy, and this made a bond of sympathy between the two men, whose views were very divergent in other respects. On one point, however, Kitchener was adamant. He drew a firm line between economy and meanness. He would assent to the reduction of forces justified by the Government's view of our future relations with Russia; but once the strength of the forces had been fixed there must be no reduction of efficiency. While he was a careful guardian of the public purse he did not forget the purses of those under his command. So long as the British Army depends on voluntary recruiting it will be necessary to hold out inducements which will attract a good stamp of officers and men; this can only be done by giving a fair rate of pay.

Twenty years previously the cost of living in India had been low. Officers could live on their pay and get their sport cheap. To those who had no private income the Indian Army held out many attractions. But now it had few or no advantages over service elsewhere. While the cost of living had gone up, the purchasing power of the rupee had fallen. Officers were not prepared to face exile from home unless there were compensations which would make it worth their while. In 1905 a conference of Lieutenant-Generals proposed an increase of pay for junior ranks and suggested that the time had come for a revision of the rates of pay of the whole army. It was three years before the Government assented to the main improvements, but in the meantime Kitchener devised several minor schemes to lighten the burden. The cost of uniform was reduced by abolishing some expensive items of full dress; a grant was given towards the purchase of chargers; travelling allowances were fixed at a rate which would not leave officers out of pocket.

A long list could be drawn up of the various schemes by which Kitchener sought to promote the health and welfare of his troops, and they owed much to his personal energy on their behalf. Fortunately Lord Minto backed up his Commander-in-Chief and reforms went through quickly. But though great credit is due to Kitchener for this valuable work it must not be supposed that he was the only General in the British Army who devoted attention to such matters. Throughout the Service reform was going ahead with rapid strides. The standard of training and efficiency rose by many degrees after the Boer War; regimental institutes, soldiers' clubs, facilities for education and sport, were multiplied; the Temperance Association and other movements for improvement of health and morals were generally encouraged. Kitchener's reforms stood out in a high light because they followed on a period of murky stagnation. He deserves credit, not so much for originality or imagination in devising reforms, as for strength of will in carrying them through.

In the field of practical training he did not see further into the future than other Generals. The troops from India were no better prepared for the new conditions of warfare than those from Aldershot and Salisbury Plain. War is not an exact science like astronomy or mathematics; improvements in firearms and other modern inventions will always produce novel conditions on the field of battle which even the most brilliant student of war cannot foresee, and which cannot be tested in peacetime. It is therefore a recognized principle that hard-and-fast formations and manœuvres cannot be devised to meet all situations. Nevertheless much can be done by way of training in peacetime, if it is carried out under conditions as similar as possible to those that are expected to obtain on active service.

To stimulate interest in training, a competition was instituted known as the "Kitchener Test." Marks were to be given for marching, manœuvre, shooting, and all other branches of training. Every General had to assemble a board, with himself as President, to carry out the examination, and decide which was the best British and the best Indian battalion in his Division. Then each Command carried out tests between the best battalions of each Division. This reduced the competition to four British and four Indian battalions for the final round. These were judged by a special Board from Headquarters. Cups presented by the Commander-in-Chief were awarded to the best British and the best Indian battalion in the Army.

The competition raised the standard of training but it aroused a good deal of jealousy and was by no means popular. Though Kitchener was satisfied that his object had been achieved it was dropped after the first year and nobody regretted its disappearance.

During his six years in India Kitchener claimed that he had travelled 65,000 miles on tours, and this is held to be a proof that his other work did not interfere with the paramount duty of inspection. It is certainly a proof of untiring energy. Except when an accident laid him up for six weeks he spent most of the winter months on tour.

The accident happened after he had been in India just a year. He had taken a house, "Wildflower Hall," at Mashobra, a few miles outside of Simla, and occasionally spent some days there when he wished to work without interruption. The road to Simla runs through a narrow and dark tunnel. Passing through this tunnel Kitchener's horse took fright and bolted, jamming his foot against one of the timber props; the leg was fractured above the ankle. Though he recovered sufficiently to resume work he never regained completely the power of getting about on foot for which he had previously been famous.

In spite of the time he spent in travelling, many officers doubted whether he learnt a great deal about the personal factor which means so much in the British Army, and few of them could flatter themselves that they learnt anything about their Commander-in-Chief. He gave little warning of his visit, arrived by train and expected no ceremonial reception, went back to his train the same evening. It was rather like the visitation of an accountant who comes to audit ledgers. Assets and liabilities were checked by standard measurements; the balance was struck with absolute fairness; there was no petty nagging or bad temper. But on the other hand there was little praise or sympathy. He was too economical of his time. Considering the amount of work he had to get through, this is not surprising; but it left the impression that he reduced everything to the common denomination of technical efficiency and had no interest out of school. The Captain of a regimental eleven was left foaming in mutinous rage: "If the Chief knows nothing about sport why the devil can't he leave it alone? He talked about cricket as if it were a patent medicine to be taken twice weekly for the good of our bodies and souls."

Lord Minto said: "His shy reserved manner may have been somewhat against him . . . he is a curious personality, not attractive in manner, but has a kind heart buried away somewhere, and his inner tastes are much more artistic than military."[1] This is a curious statement regarding a man whose devotion to duty and love of work had raised him to the highest rank in the army. But quite possibly it is true in the sense that Kitchener felt more at ease when he could get away from responsibility and let himself go in an atmosphere of art. Though he never shirked responsibility he felt the burden of it. His letters to the Secretary of State express anxiety about our readiness for war, greater anxiety than could be attributed to his preoccupation with the question of local defence. He placed much faith in the loyalty of native troops, although a few isolated cases of sedition had come to light. There must therefore have been some bigger danger in his mind, and he found it harder to bear because it was impossible to share his suspicions with anybody. However grave the situation, a man in high office may not make any public statement which conflicts with the policy of Government; he must confine himself to confidential warnings. But the great danger which was to arise ten years later lay outside the province of Indian affairs. The whole attitude of Liberal Ministers showed that warnings about a European War would be met with incredulity. Their projected economies depended on the belief that the peace of Europe was secure. Some Ministers held the doctrine that it was dangerous to encourage military enthusiasm even in the Army. It may have been in consequence of this attitude of mind in the Government he was serving that Kitchener never uttered any definite warning of the danger ahead. We cannot say, therefore, how far he foresaw the war with Germany; I

[1] Lord Minto to Lord Morley. Quoted by Arthur, II, p. 189.

have not been able to trace any statement on the subject except in vague terms. But the readiness with which he faced the problems which the Great War created is some evidence that he had given thought to matters which lay far outside the North-West Frontier and the possibilities of unrest in India.

Whatever burden of unuttered anxiety may have lain upon his mind, he was able to find relief and enjoyment in artistic pursuits. Simla offered a wide scope for his tastes. The official residence of the Commander-in-Chief, "Snowdon," required alterations and additions. The planning of a new ball-room demanded technical knowledge of architecture as well as taste for decoration. The garden, though not extensive, was beautifully situated on the slope of a pine-clad hill; its improvement under Kitchener's care exceeded all expectations. He took a childish delight in exhibiting his treasures and hearing them praised. In discussing matters of this kind he stood on the same plane as other people; he was no longer a commanding officer or a schoolmaster, and his stiffness was replaced by an unexpected ease of manner.

His taste for rare china amounted to a passion and gave rise to a good deal of amusement. It has been said that every human being, no matter how scrupulous, has a streak of unconscious dishonesty with regard to some particular thing. Kitchener was surely as honest a man as ever lived; but where a piece of china was concerned, he had the "collector's conscience." Legend says that dealers closed their shops when they heard that he was coming their way. By the time he reached India the collection was a very good one; later on, when he visited Pekin, he added some pieces from the Imperial Treasury.

His hospitality was always lavish. At the Durbars his guests were entertained in tents of Oriental luxury; in Calcutta his dinners were famous. Except at Simla he was under the necessity of maintaining the position and dignity of a Commander-in-Chief. But at "Snowdon" and "Wildflower

Hall" he seemed to be on a holiday, and people who met him there saw a side of him which would have surprised the rest of the world. Smith-Dorrien says:

"Lord Kitchener was always in splendid form, so cheery and happy and such a pleasant chief to serve, I enjoyed it very much. He was most interesting and instructive and much less secretive than I had imagined. He discussed every sort of question with me and told me his views, always searching and far-reaching. He had a fascinating habit when considering a question, of speaking his thoughts, arguing with himself all the pros and cons, then summing-up and coming to a decision."

This view was shared by others who came in touch with him at Simla. Undoubtedly this was the true nature of the man. It was a thousand pities that he was constitutionally incapable of showing the best side of himself on other occasions. "The shy and reserved manner" mentioned by Lord Minto was a bar to popularity and was sometimes mistaken for rudeness. He was too shy to distribute those small courtesies which mean so much to the recipients. The custom was for the Commander-in-Chief to make inspection tours in his own special train, which was put in charge of an English official of the railway. Lord Roberts and Power Palmer never failed to speak a few words or send some message of thanks to those who made arrangements for their comfort. But Kitchener was sadly remiss over such trifles. One youth (who afterwards rose to high position in Calcutta) was overcome with excitement when he was appointed to take charge of the train for part of a tour. He had a reverence for Kitchener's name which amounted to hero-worship, and the smallest attention from the great man would have made him a slave for life. But his existence was entirely ignored. The only message he received was through a native clerk, and it concerned the hour of starting. Hero-worship gave place to feelings of a very different kind. It was a trifle—and yet the outside public builds up its opinions on the accumulation of such trifles. Simla had its glimpses of a man "in splendid form, so cheery and happy"; elsewhere people saw only a grim task-master "shy and reserved."

At the same time it must not be supposed that the Army, officers and men, failed to see that he was a good friend to them. In a hundred ways he watched over their welfare and they knew it. They also knew that he was a good soldier; his judgment was quick and unerring; there was the reserve of force that inspires confidence. When the news was flashed abroad in August 1914 that Kitchener had taken the helm every man who had ever served under him gave heart-felt thanks.

He was given an extension of two years in the Command, and consequently did not leave India till September 1909. Then the Far East called him and he set out on a world tour.

From 1909 to 1914 is a big jump. But since I am not trying to compile a full record of Kitchener's life—that has already been well and truly done by his biographer—I propose to pass rapidly over these five years. A brief visit to China and Japan, three months in Australia and New Zealand, then a tour through America, brought him to England shortly before the death of King Edward VII. There had been a suggestion that he should go back to India as Viceroy, but the Liberal Cabinet could hardly be expected to make a strong-minded soldier the representative of its pacific policy. So there was time for another tour—Constantinople, Cairo, Khartoum, and East Africa—which filled in the months of the following winter. On returning to London, where for the second time he commanded a big parade—at the Coronation of King George V, he was informed that he was to succeed Sir Eldon Gorst as Consul-General in Egypt.

He seemed to be an ideal man for the post. He knew the country which had been for many years his home; tours of service elsewhere had widened his views and given him fresh ideas of government and administration; he had the welfare of the people at heart. Certainly his measures were far-seeing and wide, his hand was strong. It was still noticeable, however, that he could not delegate details of any kind to his subordinates. Nobody knew the inner working of his mind; he was absorbed in schemes which emanated from his own brain, but showed little enthusiasm for the schemes of other people.

One anecdote may be related. The Law College of Cairo was under an English barrister, Mr. (after Sir Maurice) Amos. A proposal was mooted to establish a higher degree, Doctor of Law, which was very popular with the local advocates. After the scheme had been carefully drawn up, Amos took it to the Consul-General for approval. The great man shook his head: "One of these days we shall have to hang some of your friends, and it would be a pity to hang Doctors." Amos returned to the College and gave a diplomatic version of the reply.

In July 1914 Kitchener was in England for the usual summer leave. There is no need to recall the events of that month. But it is strange that the Cabinet did not call in Kitchener earlier to their consultations. He was actually on his way back to Egypt on August 3 when a telegram reached him at Dover with an order for his return to London. England was at war before he came on the stage to take the leading part.

PART IV
THE WAR OFFICE

CHAPTER XVI

SECRETARY OF STATE

NAPOLEON said: "In war men are nothing, it is the man who is everything." This was one of the exaggerations in which he delighted, to emphasize the importance of genius; his own genius, as compared with mere numbers. But the underlying principle, that one man must direct and control, is confirmed by history. Napoleon's great victories at Austerlitz and Jena were won when he was an absolute despot; when he had power to employ the whole resources of France according to his will; when the nation gave him its undivided support, and there was no Parliament to question him and delay action. Alexander of Macedon and Frederick II of Prussia, the other two "Greats" of military history, were likewise heads of their States as well as leaders of their armies. When authority is in any way divided the results are not so good. Allied Councils, however firm and loyal the alliance, cannot arrive at those quick and clear-cut decisions which are so necessary in times of crisis. The seven great Coalitions against Napoleon were chiefly remarkable for mistimed co-operation and wasted effort. The Dutch States-Generals were the curse of Marlborough's campaigns. Wellington has left on record his opinion of the Juntas of Spain. The Aulic Councils are a byword for incapacity. To go still further down the scale of democratic organization for war, we have the flagrant example of the Russian Army in 1917, deciding to govern itself by elected representatives. It shot all the officers who knew anything about their work, made a shameful peace and then disbanded itself; only those men remained in the ranks who had a conscientious objection to earning an honest living.

The British system aimed at something rather indefinite

between despotic slave-driving and democratic anarchy. Up to the end of last century the Staff College held up as a model the Prussian organization of 1866 and 1870. The Imperial Chancellor, Bismarck, was head of the Executive Government: he confined himself very strictly to providing money and issuing orders for the opening of hostilities. Moltke, Chief of the General Staff, dealt with discipline and training, strategy and tactics. Roon, Minister of War, provided equipment, munitions and supplies of all kinds in accordance with the demands of Moltke. The division of labour worked with perfect smoothness and was a big factor in the success of the Prussians.

To illustrate how completely Bismarck refrained from interference a story may be quoted which he himself used to tell about the battle of Königgrätz. The King of Prussia and his staff were looking on at the heavy fighting, and praying for the arrival of the Crown Prince, whose army had not yet come in sight. Moltke, silent as ever, stood slightly in front of the group. Bismarck, realizing that the fate of Prussia hung in the balance, was desperately anxious. He wanted to ask the Commander what hopes there were of success, but was afraid to interfere or show lack of confidence. After a time the anxiety became unbearable; he lit a cigar and passed his case to Moltke saying, "There are two cigars there, one good and one bad—take the good one, I have plenty more on my saddle." With deliberation Moltke selected the good one, and the Chancellor was happy; he knew that a General who could pause at a critical moment to select the better of two cigars must be satisfied about the progress of the battle. Unfortunately few Prime Ministers have such powers of restraint.

The policy of non-interference is perfect in theory. In practice it holds good just so long as the Commander in the field can report success. Throughout 1866 and 1870 Moltke went from one success to another and consequently there was never any attempt to interfere with his plans or even to make suggestions. In 1914 another Moltke, great-nephew of the first, was Chief of the German staff. His plans worked with remarkable success up till September 5; then the battle of the Marne upset them, and he was ordered to hand over his duties to Falkenhayn.

By contrast the British system of command was a haphazard affair. Historians are fond of reminding us that our Constitution has never been defined by Statute, but has been built up by degrees on a basis of precedent and tradition. However admirable the result may have been for the purposes of administration in peace, it did not provide a precedent for a nation in arms. The Committee of Imperial Defence had "made a study" of the question of government in time of war. But it remained a study. No steps had been taken to establish a Supreme Council which could co-ordinate the policy and resources of the State with the demands of strategy. A Cabinet of twenty-three Ministers held collective responsibility for all executive action, and very naturally each of the twenty-three required to be convinced before he would give his assent to measures on which the fate of the country depended. Apart from this executive weakness, the members of the Cabinet in 1914 were not a warlike team. Most of them had hoped that England would not be dragged into a world conflict. Even after the violation of the famous Scrap of Paper half of them wanted to maintain neutrality. Of those who afterwards claimed that they had foreseen the War few were ready to side with the French except on the condition of limited liability.

The Secretary of State for War was not a soldier, and was not expected to have any expert knowledge of the functions of his department. He was a politician. Tradition chiefly required of him that he should control the finance of the army and act as a counter-weight against the ambitions of hot-headed soldiers, though it would be unfair to everlook the constructive services of such a Secretary of State as Haldane. Still, the fact cannot be denied that, compared with the German model, our organization for war was extremely defective. It was not seriously strengthened when in 1904 the office of Commander-in-Chief (then held by Lord Roberts) was abolished and the Army Council took over the administration of the land forces. The Secretary of State for War was First Member, but his colleagues shared the responsibility for all executive action.

It was a remarkable piece of good fortune that the office of the Secretary of State for War was vacant when hostilities began. In the spring of 1914 the Irish question had raised a possibility of civil war. The famous "Curragh Incident" made a flutter in the War Office and brought about the resignation of several high officials, including the then Secretary of State, Colonel Seeley. The Prime Minister, Mr. Asquith, took nominal charge, but in August it was obvious that he would be absorbed in the work of the Cabinet and must hand over the War Office to another Minister. Everything pointed to Kitchener as the man for the job. By good chance he was on the spot; he had had experience of administration; he was known to be careful of expenditure; he was an organizer of genius. Beyond and above all such qualifications he had an almost legendary reputation and prestige. *The Times* of August 3 spoke for the whole country in suggesting that he should be made Minister of War.

It must remain a matter of conjecture how far the call for recruits would have been answered had it come from anybody but Kitchener. Up to the very eve of the war, the country had seemed to be heading for infinitely more terrible calamity. The passions excited by the Government's resolve to coerce Ulster into accepting Home Rule had run higher than any tide of feeling since the Civil War. Such passions do not subside easily, leaving no trace behind them. How could a nation so divided against itself put its whole destiny in the hands of the leaders of either of the two political parties? The Government and the Opposition might agree to bury the hatchet in the face of a common danger. But the Government remained the Government; and neither the Opposition Leaders nor the rank and file behind them could be expected to forget their distrust in the men whom they had been so bitterly denouncing. The appointment of Kitchener made things easy for everybody. He had no political past; his achievements could not be claimed by either party as a triumph of their own principles. The Conservatives trusted him entirely and willingly. The Liberals, if somewhat aghast at the extent of his proposals, were ready to allow him full responsibility. His rule was, therefore, at first supreme in the Cabinet and the War Office, in the Press and the nation at large. At the same time his opinion carried more weight with our Allies than that of any other statesman.

He entered on his duties on August 6, and Sir George Arthur tells a story of his first appearance at the War Office. A specimen of his signature was required; pen and paper were put in front of him, but the pen refused to work. With a gesture of impatience the new Secretary of State flung it from him—"What a War Office! Not a scrap of Army and not a pen that will write!" [1]

The words were lightly spoken, but they may be taken as a serious indication of his frame of mind. With the foresight of an experienced and thoughtful soldier he expected the war to be long and bloody; with the mind of a practical organizer he could not understand how British statesmen could have allowed the army to have remained so absolutely inadequate, while the possibility existed that the nation might be involved in a European war. All the campaigns of modern times pointed to the value of "previous preparation"—a pleonastic term, but one well understood in military circles. Our unreadiness is now admitted by everybody. Kitchener perceived it at the time, when statesmen of both parties were still prepared to limit our participation to the dispatch of Six Regular Divisions. Consequently he regarded these short-sighted statesmen and their War Office with contempt, of which those who had to work with him and under him were soon aware.

This attitude was perhaps natural, but nevertheless it was unjust. No doubt more might have been done, but any

[1] Arthur, III, p. 7.

Government which sought to make preparations on a scale suitable for European warfare would soon have ceased to be a Government. Conservatives as well as Liberals were quite well aware of this, and neither party had dared to bring forward a practical scheme for a big increase in the army. What blame there is attaches to the nation as a whole, not to individuals. Blame has been laid on the C.I.G.S. for not asserting his position as Military Adviser of the Government and calling for an army which could hold the balance in a European War. If we had been able to put a million men into the field (so the argument runs) Germany would never have dared to provoke us, and there would have been no war. This may be true. But if the C.I.G.S. had gone to any Cabinet asking for a million men he would certainly not have got them, and would most probably have lost his appointment. Men cannot be blamed for not deliberately committing suicide.

But Kitchener could not see this. The state of things was wrong, and therefore the Government and the War Office were wrong and there could be nothing good in them. Yet, though he never seemed to be aware of it, a great deal of good work had been done for which the War Office deserves much credit—work which compared quite favourably with his own reforms in India. The good points were the organization of a British Expeditionary Force of one cavalry and six infantry Divisions, the organization of the Administrative Services, and the arrangements for mobilization. So far as these were concerned Kitchener had nothing to do and nothing to alter. The bad points were that no adequate scheme had been drawn up for the expansion of the forces or for an increased supply of munitions. In these two respects Kitchener had to do everything and start from the very beginning. The good points deserve a little more detailed consideration.

Let us take first the administrative Services, dealing with movements, supplies, clothing, transport and billeting of the troops. The work was done so smoothly and so completely

SECRETARY OF STATE

that few people ever realized what it meant. But we have only to compare it with the wretched administration of the campaign in Mesopotamia, which at first was not under the War Office, to see that any mistake or negligence in the Q.M.G.'s Department would have caused a serious breakdown. The credit must be given to Sir William Robertson and Sir John Cowans. Robertson's appointment as Q.M.G. of the B.E.F. was a stroke of genius. He knew that the condition and morale of an army depend very much on the health and comfort of the troops, and he was absolutely determined that as far as his department was concerned nothing should be left undone which could promote health and comfort. Though never careless he was perfectly fearless about expenditure, and saw that money well spent would be repaid a thousandfold. He knew what the army needed and Cowans supplied the needs. Cowans had been Q.M.G. at the War Office long enough to understand the working of a big Department but not long enough to be tied down to the limitations of peace expenditure. And, fortunately, nobody outside the Department knew anything about it. No one could offer criticism or advice; the intelligent politician who knew all about strategy had no idea what a soldier's ration consisted of or where plum and apple jam came from. Robertson and Cowans were left alone—which was just what they wanted. Their system was perfect from the first, and continued with practically no alteration to the end of the war.

Two other men were responsible for the movement of the six Divisions to France. These were Colonel Wilson and Mr. Winston Churchill.

Henry Wilson was one of the outstanding personalities in the war. After holding various appointments, including the command of the Staff College at Camberley, he was made Director of Military Operations at the War Office in 1911. His diary has been widely read, with amusement and indignation, admiration and contempt. Sir Andrew Macphail has exposed without mercy the weak side of his extraordinary character, his ambition, conceit, disloyalty to senior officers and colleagues, and has proved the allegations out of Wilson's own mouth. But with all his faults Henry Wilson was a great man. If we owe to Kitchener the army which afterwards came into being, we owe to Wilson the army which existed in August 1914.

He was desperately in earnest. His belief in the coming war was a passionate conviction which nothing could shake. Statesmen wondered uneasily what the future might hold in store. Journalists like Maxse and Repington were outspoken in their warnings. But for Wilson there was no "possible, probable, shadow of doubt." The future, as he saw it, was a matter of fact. Germany was going to war with France and we were going to fight side by side with the French. Starting from this fact it only remained to make our assistance as powerful and ready as the Government would allow. To this one object he devoted tireless energy, fearless and sometimes insubordinate expostulation. He was well fitted for the task he set himself.

Those who have heard Wilson lecture never forgot his words. He caught the attention of his hearers with a few cheap jokes about red tape; then held it by taking them into his confidence and letting them think that they had found out for themselves the points which he was there to make. He would begin in this way. "In case you should run away with any false ideas from what I say it will be as well to explain that I am a lunatic. I have just been told I am a lunatic by several people in Whitehall. That is a street of offices where all the wise men in England sit at desks and write papers to each other. Of course they don't read each other's papers; they are carefully docketed by a large staff of clerks and then go into pigeon-holes and stay there. I belong to the Office which deals with soldiers. Perhaps you didn't know that we have any soldiers—but we have. You can see two of them in Whitehall any day. On big occasions you may see a couple of thousand on the Horse Guards Parade. At Aldershot we have as many as 20,000 all at once

—mostly nice little boys about 17 years old. And behind this we have Territorials, no less than fourteen Divisions of them; they have few men, fewer officers and no horses—but still there are fourteen Divisions. . . . Last month I paid a visit to Berlin; it was a waste of time because when I came back I found that Whitehall knows all about Berlin. The Germans are a peaceful and hard-working nation, full of culture and human kindness. They have an army which consists of about a million of soldiers in the ranks and about four million trained men in civil employment, mostly waiters in Piccadilly. The object of the German army is to maintain the peace of Europe and every year they maintain peace a little more by adding to their Army. We maintain peace by cutting our Army down—and our way is better because it is cheaper." Wilson will go on for twenty minutes describing the German forces in a conversational tone. "I came back through Paris. There are some Frenchmen who are nearly as mad as I am. They think the German Army is meant for fighting. They are preparing their Army for war and they want us to help them." Another twenty minutes on the French preparation. "But all that is lunacy. The wisest author in England has written a book to prove that War is an illusion, the great illusion. The wise men in Whitehall and the Germans are all determined to have peace, so it is useless for lunatics to argue." But Wilson never stopped arguing.

In spite of his persistence Wilson did not convince everybody, even in his own profession. At the Staff College, where the possibility of war was a constant topic of debate, opinions were evenly divided. I was there, on Robertson's staff, during 1911 and 1912, and I recall our discussions with amusement. Wilson, on his own account, had spent his time at manœuvres, in garrison towns, or in military offices where he met Prussian swashbucklers or French "lunatics." He had little knowledge of international commerce and finance, on which were based the arguments of peace. I remember someone quoting the words of a City merchant: "I know nothing about the German nation, but I know one German who does not want war. My firm has just paid him £60,000 for goods supplied, and next year we shall probably pay twice that sum. Though perhaps he hates England he is not such a fool as to quarrel with his best customer. The War Party may override the students of 'Kultur' but the financiers of Germany have the real power." Many officers, including myself, were inclined to think that the Germans would not throw away the substance for a shadow. The result was that when the war came Wilson's "stock went up." He had been right and we had been wrong. Dozens of officers remembered his prophecies, and those who had disagreed with him were now all the more impressed with his wisdom. It is not too much to say that he carried more weight in the B.E.F. than any other officer. Wilson made the most of his reputation.

Even before 1914 his persistence had effected much. He failed to get an increase in the regular forces but he made the six Divisions ready for war. The mobilization arrangements were far more complete than those which Kitchener had drawn up for his nine Divisions in India. With the help of Directors of the big railway companies schedules were made out for the movements to ports of embarkation. Here the First Lord of the Admiralty, Mr. Winston Churchill, took charge, and the fact that the B.E.F. was never delayed for lack of transport must be regarded as a triumph of the organization for which he was responsible.

Wilson had also been the British representative in the famous "Conversations" with the French staff. Officially our Government had refused to bind us to anything definite, and there were anxious moments in Paris and at the French Embassy in London. But for years Wilson had been talking as if no doubt could exist. "Listen, *mon cher*, three hundred years ago, there was a patriot called Guy Fawkes who meant to blow up Parliament; he bungled it, but next time we shall manage things better. When War comes there will be a big explosion in England and all our peace-loving politicians will hasten to throw off sheep's clothing and become war dogs.

Here are our six Divisions—*je vous en fais cadeau*. Now get on with your job on your side of the Channel and see that the trains are ready to take them to the Front." His convictions were infectious—little wonder that the French loved "ce cher Henri."

Is it surprising that he was proud of his work? Surely we can forgive him for gloating over the compliments that were afterwards showered upon him and that were recorded in his Diary. But though he had certainly seen that England would fight, he unfortunately saw no further. His ideas on the duration of the war and of the possibilities of expanding our forces were just as wrong as his ideas for mobilization had been right.

The work had been well done as far as it went, and as far as the War Office was concerned, but Kitchener either did not appreciate this or at all events he would not acknowledge it. "What a War Office!" It may have been that his mind was too full of bigger things—it may have been that he was constitutionally unable to express satisfaction. But his contemptuous attitude put the senior officers in the position of mere clerks who must henceforward take orders and hold their tongues.

This was especially regrettable in the case of the General Staff. Napoleon said: "It is only by a close study of all the details that a General can make those plans which alone lead to success." This is a maxim even more applicable at the present day than in Napoleon's time because preparations are on a much larger scale. The details which demand study include calculations about the enemy's strength; the number of troops which will be required; shipping and other transport; equipment, supplies, and munitions; geographical details about harbours and landing places, railways and roads. Information on all these points is collected in the office of the C.I.G.S., who is therefore the only authority who can, in Napoleon's words, "make those plans which alone lead to success." When the plan, based on these details, is complete, a *précis* can be made for the information of the Cabinet. It is their duty to decide whether the expedition shall be undertaken or not—in other words whether the game is worth the candle.

By effacing the C.I.G.S. Kitchener allowed this process to be reversed. Decisions were made before the necessary details had been studied, and the C.I.G.S. was then left to make such arrangements as he could. Troops, ships and munitions were diverted in various ways which led to much confusion and accomplished no useful purpose.

I do not intend to imply that the C.I.G.S. is the only person who has any right to propose a plan or to have an opinion on military subjects. Ministers, who are responsible for policy, must retain the right to ask questions and make suggestions. For instance, the Foreign Office might very well suggest that an expedition to the Balkans would encourage our Allies and disconcert our enemies. But any decision should be deferred until the General Staff has given an opinion, based on the facts, regarding the feasibility of the proposal.

Nobody knew better than Kitchener the value of good information. It had been the groundwork of his success in Egypt; lack of it had produced the tangled mess in South Africa. And nobody knew better the vast amount of detail required for the organization of a military expedition. As Secretary of State it was his business to keep the balance between the political experts who decided policy, and the military experts who worked out details. By disregarding the General Staff he allowed a system to grow up in which political considerations and the opinion of amateur strategists outweighed technical knowledge.

The excuse has been put forward that all the higher ranks of the Staff had crossed the Channel with the B.E.F. It was generally believed that the war would be short and sharp, and that the decisive battle would be fought in France at an early date. Apart, therefore, from the natural ambition of every officer to be present at the decisive moment, the Commander-in-Chief would naturally want all the best men with him. Moreover the C.I.G.S., Sir C. Douglas, was in bad health and died a few weeks after the outbreak of war. Kitchener installed in his place Sir J. Wolfe-Murray, who had been serving in South Africa and was out of touch with the machinery of the office. In fact the General Staff had shrunk to such very attenuated dimensions, both in numbers and capacity, that there was good excuse for the new Minister of War to ignore it.

This excuse, however, only covers the first stage of the war. Though the office might be considered empty for the moment there was no reason why it should remain in that condition. If Kitchener had recognized the all importance of the General Staff he ought to have seen to it in practice. He had unlimited power, and in other directions he allowed nothing to stand in the way of organization for a long war. It would have been unfair to the Commander-in-Chief to deprive him during the first critical weeks of Haig, Smith-Dorrien, Murray, Robertson. But there were others whose capabilities Kitchener knew from personal acquaintance: Ian Hamilton, Rawlinson, Maxwell, Birdwood. It is true that these officers were employed elsewhere. But why did they continue to be so employed? The answer seems to be that Kitchener regarded the various appointments they held as more important than appointments to the General Staff. Ian Hamilton commanded the Home Forces, and afterwards went to Gallipoli. Maxwell remained in Egypt. Rawlinson and Birdwood commanded Corps. Kitchener took the whole burden of the War Office on his own shoulders; he did not fill up the General Staff because he did not feel the want of it till a year later.

CHAPTER XVII

EXPANSION

IF KITCHENER had little to do with the move of the British Expeditionary Force there remained for him other and greater work, with which his name will be for ever associated—the expansion of the Army.

Even those prophets who foresaw the war could not claim that they had any idea of the part England would play in it. We had a Navy which would maintain command of the seas—the first essential. We had six Divisions. Haldane had reorganized the Territorials for the purpose of Home Defence, thus releasing the British Expeditionary Force for service abroad. This was the limit of our horizon. The war would be over before any other forces could be collected or trained. The extension of railways in Europe would bring the opposing armies face to face in a few weeks and the first battle would be decisive. If not—well, a peace of some kind must be patched up or all Europe would be bankrupt. Soldiers said so, Henry Wilson said so, financiers said so.

In these circumstances it was unnecessary to think of anything beyond the regular army. Far from encouraging our Auxiliary Forces the War Office had regarded them with politely concealed contempt. Military authors, Wolseley and Henderson, had held up the American Civil War as an example of the folly of those who send undisciplined soldiers into battle. The Prussians gave their recruits two years of very severe training. The French had raised their term of compulsory service to three years. Our Territorials were a good lot of fellows; some of them could hit the bull's-eye at Bisley; they knew the mechanism of their rifles and had a smattering of drill. But a fortnight in camp will not turn civilians into soldiers. It takes time to ingrain

EXPANSION

discipline, and without discipline an army is a mob. It would be massacre to send these gallant fellows against Continental soldiers. Or so the professional experts believed.

Two people thought otherwise. One was a Frenchman, General Foch. In 1909 he was discussing with Wilson plans for co-operation, and a question came up about the strength of the British Expeditionary Force. Foch then spoke the words which have been so often quoted: "It matters little what you send; we ask for only one corporal and four men; but they must arrive at the very beginning. You will give them to me, I promise to do my best to get them killed; from that moment I shall be happy for I know that after that the whole of England will come as one man." [1]

The other prophet was Kitchener, and the salvation of England and her Allies lay in the fact that his prestige was high enough to enable him to carry through his plans in spite of sceptical opposition. This fact is now so well recognized that there is no need to lay further stress upon it.

His big idea was to raise our forces up to seventy Divisions. This would mean about 1,200,000 troops in the fighting line, with reserves ready to replace casualties and sick. Such an army would require a huge number of men on the lines of communication; staff for railways, transport, and hospitals; a score of minor departments, such as the Post Office, which in a small force are insignificant, but for seventy Divisions must employ thousands. For the maintenance of such an army abroad there must be an equivalent increase in the arsenals, workshops and equipment stores at home. Roughly speaking, everything must be multiplied by at least ten—it afterwards turned out that guns, ammunition, and shipping had to be multiplied by a much higher figure. Looking back we congratulate ourselves on a magnificent national effort. But in August 1914 Kitchener was the only Englishman who could look forward to it.

The conception of this tremendous idea proves Lord Kitchener's powers of foresight and imagination. But it re-

[1] Huguet, p. 38.

mains a matter of dispute whether in realizing it he made the most of the existing machinery. Lord Haldane argued that the expansion should have been carried out by means of the existing Territorial organizations. As this was his own pet scheme he was naturally biassed in its favour and resented the fact that Kitchener practically ignored it. But other competent critics agree with him that the machinery of the Territorial Associations might have been well employed. Every County had its Association, composed of prominent men, leading citizens, landowners, employers of labour, familiar with the local conditions, the buildings, rifle-ranges, parade grounds and manœuvre fields in the vicinity. The framework of the Division was in existence, with guns, rifles, and wagons. The ranks would have been filled on the first day that recruiting was opened and the Division could have marched off into camp, or into barracks vacated by the Regulars, to complete their training. With such a good start it would have been ready to move to France within three months; some battalions were ready even sooner. And before it left the country the Association would have formed a second Division to take its place, good enough to act at once in the scheme of Home Defence and to go abroad in due course. In this manner an even flow would have been maintained at least for the first year, a flow which would only have been limited by the difficulty of providing arms and equipment.

There would have been other advantages besides the immediate collection and training of recruits. The Association could have taken off the hands of the War Office an immense amount of clerical work. A record must be kept of every man's service; the date of his enlistment, his next-of-kin, family allowances, admission to hospital, and other details. This work was done by Kitchener's organization, and on the whole it was well done—but only by heavy labour much of which might have been saved by a better and less centralized system. Each Association had its own paid secretary, its office, and a staff of clerks—by no means sufficient to deal with the increase but experienced enough to act as instructors to additional clerks who could easily have been collected.

Other arguments, of no little weight, have also been adduced. Inadequate as the training and equipment of the Territorials had been, they contained the most warlike material in the country. Many of the officers, and N.C.O.'s, had put in a great deal of their spare time in learning all that they could about the art of war, in preparation for this very emergency. In most of the Territorial regiments a very high degree of *esprit de corps* existed—the most valuable of all essentials to a fighting force. It was galling in the extreme to these enthusiasts, who had prepared for war while the rest of the nation amused itself, to find themselves put into the second place, their units starved of equipment, their regular staffs too often taken away and replaced by retired "duds," and the whole Territorial organization regarded with something like contempt by the mushroom New Army.

The County Associations were not abolished. They continued their work and, during the first year, dealt with 460,000 recruits. But "Kitchener's Army" was in a sense a rival and a favoured institution. It deprived the Associations of much of their influence. Leading men thought that they could do more for the country, and perhaps incidentally more for their own credit, by leaving the old organization to take up work with the new. The result was scattered effort instead of systematic combination.

Two arguments have been brought forward on the other side. First, the Territorials were enlisted for Home Defence and could not be sent abroad without their own consent. This argument is very weak. The Territorials never hung back; forty-seven battalions left England before the end of 1914; Kitchener had only to say the word and every man would have gone. Secondly, many of the men held important posts in civil life and required time in order to provide substitutes before they left the country; it is therefore claimed by the protagonists of the "new armies" that it was better to make the first call on recruits who could more easily be spared. This is true—but surely the Associations could have a few simple regulations to overcome the objection.

It cannot be said that Kitchener was ignorant of the arguments on both sides. As he had never held a command of any kind which brought him into touch with the Auxiliary Forces, it is curious that he did not consult those Generals who were serving at home at the time. Some of them offered advice, and it may be taken for granted that his colleagues in the Cabinet pointed out the value of an organization which was already in working order. But for some reason Kitchener decided to build his "new armies" from the very foundation. His reasons are matter for speculation. Partly, no doubt, they lay in his own character. Working on the gigantic scale he had set himself, with his own unique vision of what he wanted and was determined to get, and with the strange incapacity he always showed for sharing his plans with others, he no doubt felt instinctively that the organization must be wholly his own. Perhaps, too, he had a sense of what might be called the "publicity value" of the New Armies. A man might resist the appeal to identify himself in time of war with an organization which he had refused to join in time of peace, and had thought of (however unjustly) as a form of "playing at soldiers." But he would find it much harder to resist the appeal to join an organization created specially for him, on the grandest model, by the most famous soldier of the day. If Kitchener perceived this, he was no mean psychologist.

Several critics have suggested that as Kitchener foresaw a prolonged war which would demand all the resources of the nation he ought to have insisted on universal service at once. Looking back with the knowledge of after events we may think that much trouble would have been avoided if we had accepted from the first the principle that every man in time of war owes service in some form or other to his country. The burden would have been more fairly distributed. As it was, those who volunteered so readily in 1914 deserved more and got less reward than those who stayed at home. By the time compulsory service became necessary the wages in various industries had risen to high rates. The temptation was great, especially for those who had families dependent on them, to make money instead of shouldering a rifle.

But in trying to fathom Kitchener's reasons we must shut out of mind all that took place later and get back to the situation as he saw it and as others saw it in August 1914. He wanted men, and no doubt he considered the possibilities of universal service. He may have foreseen what would happen, but he knew that other people could not yet see with his eyes. The Liberal Cabinet had not even been unanimous in deciding to embark on the war. Lord Morley and John Burns resigned; others gave only a half-hearted assent. Many were disturbed even by the first call for volunteers. A proposal to enroll the manhood of the nation would have met with serious antagonism both in the Cabinet and in the country. The most patriotic business men would have been staggered, if they had been told that all their employees were liable to be taken at a moment's notice. Patriotism is deeply rooted but it is a plant whose growth cannot be forced.

We may believe that Kitchener saw that the main thing was to keep the nation together and to avoid giving a handle to those who were secretly against him. The first battles would excite in the heart of the people a fierce desire for victory—and after that the talkers might say what they liked. Whether this was in his mind or not it was certainly the way in which things went. The first volunteers enlisted from sheer love of the glorious adventure—they were the flower of the country's youth. The employer allowed a percentage of his men to go; instead of grumbling about compulsion, he felt a glow of virtue over doing his bit. The rich merchant, whose chauffeur had enlisted, sweated virtue as he walked to office. Everybody felt the uplift which comes from voluntary service. Those who could not or would not do anything had the grace to keep quiet. As the first stories of Mons and Ypres came through, the response became still more general. Kitchener got more men in the first three months than he could equip and arm, house or train. And there was no opposition.

The second phase came later. As the long struggle took on a grimmer and deadlier character, the first and almost joyous enthusiasm was replaced by a stern determination to see the ordeal through. It was that change of spirit which made the introduction of compulsory service possible in a country devoted to the tradition of individual freedom. Even so, the final acceptance of conscription waited on the proof of military necessity, and was opposed by men whose opinion would have carried much greater weight in the early days of the war.

In spite of the fact that Kitchener had been little in England during the previous forty years he seems to have known a good deal about the temper of the country.

So good a judge of the situation as the Foreign Secretary, Sir Edward Grey, was of the same opinion. "Conscription" he says "in the early days of the war was impossible; public opinion was not ready for it; it would have been resisted. Voluntary enlistment gave the country a good start in good-will and enthusiasm; conscription would have given a bad start." [1]

The full details of the expansion of the Army can be found in the War Office publication, *Statistics of the Military Effort of the British Empire during the Great War*. A few figures are sufficient to indicate the work which Kitchener took on his shoulders. Before he arrived at the War Office the House of Commons on August 5 authorized an increase of 500,000 in the Regular Forces; Reserves were

---

[1] *Twenty-five Years*, by Lord Grey of Fallodon, II, p. 70.

EXPANSION

called out and the Territorials were embodied. The Secretary for War had thus a free hand to begin collecting recruits. On August 7 posters were issued all over the country calling for 100,000 men to form the First New Army of six Divisions. Fortunately there were in England over 500 officers on leave from India. Kitchener detained these to act as instructors.

Recruits poured in, and the first 100,000 were enrolled in a few days. The half-million had been completed by September, a million by February 1915, a million and a half by September 1915. The Dominions came forward with offers, and the War Office accepted, as a first instalment, 20,000 from Canada, 20,000 from Australia, 8,000 from New Zealand.

Two complete Divisions (Lahore and Meerut) were ordered home from India and began to embark on August 24. Garrisons from Malta and elsewhere were collected to form extra Divisions of the Regular Army, the 7th, 8th, and later 27th, 28th, and 29th.

CHAPTER XVIII

THE OPENING MOVES

TRADITION and common sense put a strict limit on the duties of the Secretary of State—as soon as an army takes the field the strategy and tactics must be left in the hands of the Commander-in-Chief. Though the British Government had firmly refused to make any definite engagement with the French, our General Staff had been allowed to discuss with the Grand Quartier Général the means of British co-operation. It was clearly understood that our Expeditionary Force would be best employed on the left of the French line, and the transhipment had been worked out accordingly. Once the forces were assembled in France the Commander-in-Chief would take command. Further interference from the War Office would be regarded as irregular.

All this had been settled before Kitchener became Secretary of State. He changed nothing, and everything points to the fact that he intended to leave the strategy and tactics to the Commander-in-Chief without even disturbing him by suggestions. But on September 1 he found himself forced to intervene. The reasons for his action on that date can only be understood when the course of events, as seen by him at the time, has been taken into consideration.

The German plans were simple, and apart from questions of international honour, exceedingly sound. They were based not so much on theory as on concrete facts.

They calculated that Russia, big, unwieldy, badly-organized, would not be able to bring any real weight into the field for six or eight weeks. During that time a strong offensive might crush France entirely; once that was done the combined forces of Germany and Austria could turn

THE OPENING MOVES 219

at their leisure to deal with Russia; after that they would dictate their own terms to the whole of Europe. Everything therefore depended on a quick and decisive movement into France.

The next question was to decide the line of their advance. The frontier between France and Germany, from Longwy to Belfort, is about 150 miles in length. On the French side there lay fortified zones, including Verdun, Toul, Epinal, Belfort—of modern type, heavily armed. Behind these a row of second-class fortresses—La Fère, Reims, Langres, Besançon. These two lines formed serious obstacles and commanded all the railways.

Further north there is a bit of frontier, 60 miles long, from Longwy to Givet facing the Ardennes. Here the roads and railways are few and the wooded ground is unsuitable for manœuvres of large masses.

Still further north, from Givet to the coast at Dunkirk, is a stretch of rather more than 100 miles. It contains no natural obstacles. There are a few forts round places like Maubeuge and Lille, but only of old-fashioned type. Plenty of roads and railways exist; in addition, the most direct line from Berlin to Paris runs through Cologne, Liège, Namur, and so into France at the point on the frontier nearest to Paris. Moreover, a movement through Belgium would outflank the northern end of the line of big fortresses.

There were two objections to this move. First, Germany herself had signed a Treaty guaranteeing the integrity and neutrality of Belgium; but, as all the world knows, that Treaty became a scrap of paper in German eyes. Second, a wanton violation of Belgium soil might arouse the Belgians to defend it, and might even awaken the British. The Belgians, however, would hardly dare to provoke the wrath of a powerful neighbour whose troops could be poured into their country before any succour could be expected from outside. The British had nothing to gain by interfering and were quite unprepared for Continental warfare. We had certainly a navy, but the German Army was as safe

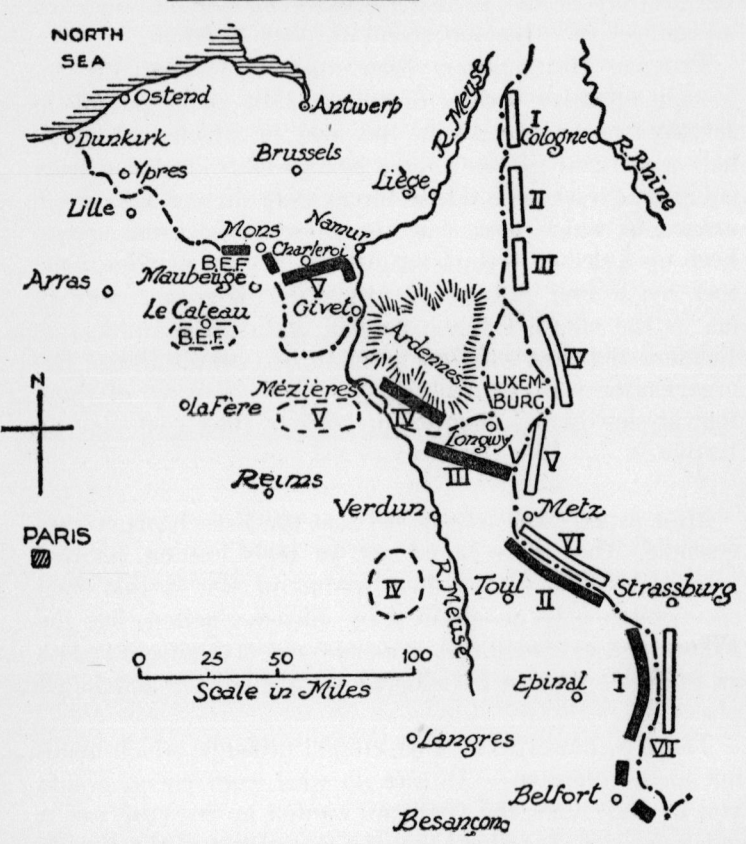

THE OPENING MOVES

from our Dreadnoughts as an elephant is from a whale. Our land forces consisted of only six Divisions, and the rest of the nation was, according to Prussian standards, untrained and unmilitary. Therefore, even if the very pacific Liberal Government decided to support the French, the hostility of the British forces would not outweigh the advantages of a big movement through Belgium.

Prussian Headquarters drew up plans accordingly for a main offensive in this direction. They could put about seventy-two Divisions into the field of which more than half were "active," the others being well-trained and fully equipped "reserve."[1] These forces were divided into seven armies, of which three came into line at the south end to keep up a demonstration against the French frontier. Further north four armies, of forty-four Divisions, were to act as the offensive mass, moving at first westwards into Belgium and then wheeling southwards towards Paris. The organization was perfect, and the mighty impetus of those four armies carried them within sight of their goal—but no further.

Most experts are now agreed that the French plans were unsound. They were based not on facts but on "eternal principles." One of the first maxims of war is that final success can only be attained by offensive action, but the French had extended this principle and crystallized it into an inflexible law, to be adhered to at all times and in all places.

There is, however, another eternal principle which ought not to be forgotten—"Do not do what your enemy wants you to do." What the Germans wanted in this case was a quick decision. It follows that the first object of the French should have been to delay the decision, for at least a couple

[1] The Prussian unit was the Army Corps, but the Corps in the opposing armies varied in strength; for purposes of comparison it is convenient to talk of Divisions. In the German and British armies a Division numbered about 18,000 of all ranks. The French Division was weaker.

of months, during which their initial unreadiness could have been repaired and steps arranged for a counter-stroke on a grand scale. They knew that the Germans would have superiority of numbers at first, but every day would shift the balance in favour of the Allies. The Russians, if undisturbed and unhurried, could produce a force in two or three months which would demand serious attention. British forces were hastening towards France from India and the Colonies.

There was ample strength for the erection of a barrier to stem the German rush—not in the form of a single rigid line, but as a deep and elastic system of defence, outposts well forward to prevent surprise and hold up reconnoitring patrols; a first-line strong enough to repel feints and demonstrations; a main line based on natural obstacles and strengthened with field works; heavy artillery in masked positions; reserve lines in rear. They could put into the field about sixty-two Divisions, divided into five Armies. The eastern front, strong in the fortified zones from Belfort to Verdun, could easily be held by the I and II Armies; the III could be extended along the Meuse up to Namur; this would leave two complete armies for action further north or wherever the German main attack developed. They might be in time to join hands with the Belgians and save Brussels; failing this they could hold on to the line Namur, Maubeuge, Lille, Dunkirk, and stop the invasion of France. It must be remembered that the Germans were staking everything on a quick decision—they could not afford to mount an attack with all the elaborate detail which experience afterwards suggested; they would have poured out their ammunition and advanced in mass across the open. Their casualties would have been colossal and a check at the outset would have been very damaging to their prestige.

The advantages of such a scheme for delaying action are easily seen by the light of the knowledge and experience we now possess. It is easy to be wise after the event; but it is a fact that there were just a few military experts who had thought of it even before the War.[1]

An entirely different view, however, was held by the French Operations Section. This was the 3ᵉ Bureau, which had been called the *"nouvelle École"* or more irreverently *"les jeunes Turcs."* As a matter of fact they were far from being a new school; on the contrary they were slaves of the Napoleonic doctrine a hundred years old. When Napoleon was struggling in 1814 to save Paris against heavy odds he never thought of a defensive battle. Swinging his little army to and fro between the Prussians and Austrians who were converging on him he hit a flank or threatened a rear, and trusted to the maxim that surprise is the deadliest weapon in the hands of a commander. His lightning strokes aroused the enthusiasm of military critics and were hailed as the ideal form of warfare. This idealism fitted in with the temperament of the French nation and with the well-known *élan* of the French soldier. Though there was none of the over-weening optimism that flooded Paris on the eve of war in 1870 everybody looked to Joffre for a strong and successful offensive.

The French training had been based on the same principle with the object of fostering "the true offensive spirit." The idea was that when bullets are flying about the instinct of self-preservation will drive men to seek cover; but if once the soldier thinks that he is not expected to attack he will dig himself in as deep as he can, and that will be the end of all manœuvre. Training should therefore be directed to overcoming this instinct and maintaining the principle of movement. The *"nouvelle École"* laid it down that even with inferior numbers attack is always the best means of defence; surprise and manœuvre can win any battle. A suggestion for defensive action was held to be a sign of weakness, of a lack of self-confidence. Entrenchments were regarded with suspicion as tending to cramp liberty of movement. Serious preparations for a steady retreat would have been branded as

[1] See Lanrezac, Chap. I.

sheer cowardice. As a result of such teaching the French had never thought out or practised anything like delaying tactics.

That this obsession is by no means exaggerated can be proved from the writings and sayings of French military authorities. The words of Foch have often been quoted—"My right is broken, my left is broken, my front is broken. Situation excellent. I attack." In 1903 he had published *Les Principes de la Guerre,* which is a continuous reiteration of the same doctrine. He preached it when he was head of the French Staff College; he put it into practice in the war. The glamour of it is dazzling, but the cost was terrific.

The British teaching, though not quite so dogmatic, followed the same lines. In studying the brilliant offensives of Napoleon and Moltke we had lost sight of our own history. Wellington, when the odds were against him, thought it no shame to retire into the lines of Torres Vedras; with cold-blooded patience he could await the moment when the chances would be in his favour—rightly has he been called the Iron Duke. In the Waterloo campaign he fell back and stood on the defensive till his allies could co-operate in a counter-stroke.

In addition to these lessons from history we had actual experience of the advantages of the defence under modern conditions with quick-firing rifles and guns. In 1899 a British Army attacked at Colenso and was defeated with heavy loss; attacks were made at Modder River, Magersfontein and Paardeberg; in each case troops in the open suffered terribly while the enemy sitting still under cover lost very little from gun-fire and practically nothing from rifle-fire. With such experience to guide us we had less excuse than the French for persisting in the doctrine of eternal attack. Sir John French acknowledges our ignorance:

"It is easy to be wise after the event; but I cannot help wondering why none of us realized what the modern rifle, the machine-gun, the aeroplane and wireless telegraphy will bring about. It seems so simple when judged by actual results. The modern rifle and machine-gun add tenfold to the relative power of the defence as against the attack . . . I feel sure in my own mind that had we realized the true effect of modern appliances of war in August 1914 there would have been no retreat from Mons."

The theory of *"attaque, attaque"* had become so fixed in the minds of the French that they scarcely seem to have taken into account the possible action of the Germans. The Napoleonic doctrine was: "seize the initiative and instead of allowing the enemy to develop his own plans force him to conform to yours." So the French were formed up for the purpose of invading Germany; even the V Army was no further north than Mézières when the attack on Liège was reported.

As Wellington said, the art of war consists in knowing what the fellow on the other side of the hill is doing. Napoleon in his early days possessed this gift to a very high degree and made the most of it in Italy and Austria. Later on he seems to have lost it; in 1812 he persisted in believing that the Russians would do what he wanted them to do, and at Waterloo he persisted in the same blind obstinacy with fatal results.

As soon as the first German troops crossed the Belgian frontier there was a clear inference to be drawn from that simple fact, though little was yet known about their strength. By that time it was certain that the invasion of Belgium would bring England into the war; it should have been obvious that the Germans expected the invasion to give them some result big enough to compensate for the hostility of England. Such a result could not be obtained by sending a weak force to make a demonstration. And from this it follows that the German strength must be sufficient to brush aside the Belgians and penetrate into France. In fact this move, if not their main effort, must at least be a formidable thrust.

It seems incredible that the Grand Quartier Général could miss so obvious a deduction, and yet as late as August 14

Joffre said "Nous avons le sentiment que les allemands n'ont rien de prêt par là." [1] These words can only mean that he was so absorbed in his own plans that no heed was paid to the other side of the hill. The only other solution would be that German agents had succeeded in duping the Intelligence Bureau. But of this there is not a shred of evidence.

The truth must have come as an appalling revelation. The Germans had no less than forty-four Divisions in Belgium, of which twenty-six were on the north bank of the Meuse. By August 16 something of the truth was known, and the V Army (Lanrezac) had orders to march towards Mons and Namur. But the plan for a general offensive was not changed; on the 20th the I and II Armies advanced between Metz and Strassburg while the III and IV plunged into the wooded ravines of the Ardennes. These moves played into the hands of the Germans whose front line fell back a few miles. But even had they been driven back fifty miles it would not have hurt them; indeed, the more deeply the French were committed to an advance in the east the more certain would be the success of the German thrust in the north.

Then came the great revelation of the effect of modern fire. Headlong assaults on well-posted troops broke down everywhere and entailed hideous slaughter. By August 22 the French line was back at its starting-point. The casualties prove that the men had fought with real heroism. It was not to be expected that the Grand Quartier Général would accept the blame; so it fell on those who had failed to carry out the orders—that is to say on the unhappy commanders of Armies and Corps who were between the fire of the enemy in front and the reproaches of their own authorities in rear.

Even then the strategical error might have been repaired if there had been any knowledge of the principles of delaying action. Rearguards could have held positions which would force the enemy to deploy and waste time while the main bodies got some rest and prepared for further defence. Instead of this the only idea of the French was to turn on their

[1] Lanrezac, p. 77.

THE OPENING MOVES

pursuers with repeated attacks, thus tiring out their men, incurring heavy losses, and effecting nothing. Such was the situation at the end of August. Theories based on false estimates of the German strength and false calculations of the effect of fire had broken down; the senior officers were grappling with a situation for which they were untrained and unprepared; the troops, worn out with marching, fighting, and counter-marching, were retreating as well as they could.

We must look straight at this black situation, because it is only after seeing the depths that we can measure the full height of the magnificent recovery which followed—a recovery that in completeness and dramatic suddenness has no equal in the history of war. But before turning to the bright side of the picture we must see what was happening to our own "contemptible little Army."

On August 12 an important meeting had been held in the room of the Secretary of State at the War Office. It marks the first divergence of opinion between Kitchener and the General Staff. During the "conversations" between the French and British staffs all arrangements had been made for the British Expeditionary Force to concentrate near Maubeuge in accordance with the plans of Joffre. Kitchener thought this was too far advanced. Though he had not given study to the detailed reports and appreciations regarding the German plans he felt instinctively that the enemy would develop his main attack through Belgium and north of the Meuse. In this case the left of the allied line would have to retire, and in his opinion a retrograde movement at the outset would have a depressing effect on the morale of our troops. He proposed that the concentration should be round Amiens, some fifty miles further back.

But, as we have seen, the French plans were cut and dried. They were determined to take the initiative and make a general advance, and this could only be successful if every available man was thrown into the attack. The British Expeditionary Force had been allotted a position on the left of their line; a very natural and proper decision, as they would have the ports of Calais and Boulogne behind them. No anxiety was felt lest the position at Maubeuge should be in any danger. The officers present at the meeting, especially Sir John French and Henry Wilson, were ready to give assurances that the French scheme had been worked out on good information; it would have a very bad effect on our Allies if they thought the British were hanging back or if we tried to upset the arrangements on which they were depending. Though Kitchener remained unconvinced, the last argument certainly carried weight and he yielded to those who had given more detailed study to the plans. The British Expeditionary Force after crossing the Channel went by train to an area round Le Cateau, from which place it was intended to march forward as soon as possible.

Sir John French and his staff arrived in Paris on August 15 and he was received with the graceful courtesy for which the French are famous. On the following day he motored to the Grand Quartier Général and for the first time met General Joffre.

THE BRITISH EXPEDITIONARY FORCE

Commander-in-Chief: Field-Marshal Sir J. French.
Chief of Staff: General Sir A. Murray.
Sub-Chief of Staff: Colonel H. Wilson.
Adjutant-General: General Sir C. N. Macready.
Quartermaster General: General Sir W. Robertson.
Cavalry Division: General Allenby.

> I Corps. General Sir D. Haig.
>   1st Division. General Lomax.
>   2nd Division. General Monro.
>
> II Corps. General Sir H. Smith-Dorrien.
>   3rd Division. General H. Hamilton.
>   5th Division. General Sir C. Fergusson.

THE OPENING MOVES 229

> 19th Infantry Brigade. Brig.-General Drummond.
> > 4th Division. General Snow. (Arrived August 25.)
> > 6th Division. General Keir. (Arrived in September.)
>
> The 4th and 6th Divisions formed the III Corps under General Pulteney.

"There was a complete absence of fuss and a calm deliberate confidence was manifest everywhere. I had a long conversation with the Commander-in-Chief . . . he certainly never gave me to suppose that any idea of 'retirement' was in his mind . . . his main intention was always to attack."

With this impression Sir John went on to his own Headquarters, where the troops were assembling round Le Cateau. By the 22nd he had moved up to Mons. It was understood that the centre of the French V Army lay at Charleroi and the intention was to advance in a northeasterly direction. But during the day news came in that Lanrezac had fallen back with some loss, thus leaving the British right flank exposed. Very wisely Sir John refused to commit himself to further movement till the situation developed; he agreed to stand fast for twenty-four hours. This brought about the battle of Mons.

On Sunday morning, August 23, the German I Army (Von Kluck) came up against the British line. No serious preparation had been made for defensive action, as Sir John still had hopes of making a forward move. But in spite of the overpowering strength of the German guns the British infantry had a good fight—in fact, when we had time to think about it afterwards, Mons turned out to have been a very good fight indeed. Certainly there had been a lot of shells flying about, but they did wonderfully little harm against even rough cover. And as for the targets presented to the infantry—the worst shot in the regiment, who had never hit a bull's eye in his life, had killed a thousand Huns—more or less. After a year

THE RETREAT FROM MONS

THE OPENING MOVES

at Ypres men looked back to Mons as a picnic where there was no sitting about in ditches and where we had something to shoot at. As Sir John said, there need have been no retreat if we had fully realized the effect of fire.

But though the Germans in the immediate front of the British had received a nasty shock they were pressing round both flanks unopposed. On our right the V Army had fallen back, on our left there were only some scattered French Territorials. It was obvious that the British Expeditionary Force must retire or else it would be surrounded. And so the great Retreat began, along the dusty roads which ran like white ribbons ever southwards towards Paris.

By the evening of the 25th a line had been reached stretching east and west through Le Cateau. Sir John had hopes that a stand might be made here, but during the day reports showed that the Germans were still pressing round our west flank; orders were therefore issued for the retirement to be continued on the 26th. But General Headquarters was back at St. Quentin, twenty miles away, and Sir John had no idea of the scene of confusion which was being played out in the darkness. The II Corps had been directed to extend westwards from the little town of Le Cateau. Some brigades reached their ground by 6 P.M. and got a few hours' rest; others were not so fortunate. The 4th Division (Snow) had arrived at Le Cateau by train on the 25th, and was pushed forward to Solesmes (6 miles to the north) to assist Allenby's Cavalry and the rear-guards of the II Corps. A bottle-neck of roads in that village got hopelessly blocked by the wagons of refugees getting mixed up with the military transport, and a serious rear-guard action was fought until dark. Then the rear-guard and the 4th Division tried to find their way back across country to the places allotted to them at Le Cateau. It would be impossible to say at what hour the various units reached their ground. Some never reached it at all, and throughout the night scattered parties were trickling in. The 4th Division was certainly not in place before dawn next morning.

Smith-Dorrien was on the spot. Like the Commander-in-Chief he was anxious to resume the march next day and about 10 P.M. orders were sent out accordingly. But at 11 P.M. Allenby came to Corps Headquarters to report that German cavalry was within a couple of miles of our line and unless we could march before daylight the enemy would be upon us. Hamilton, commanding the 3rd Division, was consulted, and his opinion was that as many of his units were only now coming in it would be impossible to start before 9 A.M. This left Smith-Dorrien with no option, for it was useless to think of starting another march before the first one was completed. Not from choice, but from dire necessity, he issued the order to stand fast.

At 3:30 A.M. a message was sent to General Headquarters at St. Quentin, informing Sir John of this decision. The reply, timed 5 A.M., was as follows:

"If you can hold your ground the situation appears likely to improve. 4th Division must co-operate. French troops are taking offensive on right of I Corps. Although you are given a free hand as to method this telegram is not intended to convey the impression that I am not anxious for you to carry out the retirement, and you must make every endeavour to do so." [1]

Unfortunately this message was not nearly precise enough. It evidently did not convey what was in the mind of the Commander-in-Chief, for he afterwards wrote:

"In more than one of the accounts of the Retreat from Mons it is alleged that some tacit consent at least was given at General Headquarters at St. Quentin to the decision arrived at by the Commander of the II Corps. I owe it to the able and devoted officers of my Staff to say that there is not a semblance of truth in this statement."

But Smith-Dorrien derived from the message the comforting assurance that General Headquarters knew his intention

[1] O.H., 1914, p. 136.

and gave him a free hand to use his own judgment. It was one of those cases which are common enough in war—the man who cannot see the actual situation must either put complete trust in the man on the spot or else he must take all responsibility on his own shoulders and issue definite orders. A message which can be mis-read is worse than none.

Le Cateau was a repetition of Mons. With the help of civilian labour some very civilian trenches had been scratched in the ground; otherwise there had been no time to prepare the position. But the troops were well posted and frontal attacks of the enemy's infantry were held off without difficulty. Both flanks, however, were in the air, and as soon as the traffic left the roads clear Smith-Dorrien issued orders for the retreat. The Germans had suffered too heavily to follow up or interfere with the march.

The casualties at Le Cateau amounted to 8,482 and were chiefly borne by the 4th Division (3,158), 5th Division (2,631), 3rd Division (1,796), and the 19th Brigade (477). Forty-two guns were abandoned because their teams had been killed.[1]

At this stage of the war such losses seemed to Sir John excessive and unnecessary. In a telegram to the War Office he used the expression "I do not think that you understand the shattered condition of the II Corps." These words show that he took a very gloomy view. The next three weeks, however, proved that the II Corps was far from being shattered. Without a rest it went on for over two hundred miles and fought in two of the big battles of the world's history. Maybe it was not pretty to look at. Officers found it hard to keep the footsore men from straggling; they wanted to stop at every cottage to ask for *low* (useful French word, meaning water), some had dropped their equipment in desperate anxiety not to be left behind. It is the pet privilege of an old

---

[1] O.H., 1914, p. 224. In "1914," page 78, Sir John says: "The actual result was a total loss of at least 14,000 officers and men, about 80 guns, numbers of machine guns." He does not quote his authority for these numbers.

soldier to grumble—Napoleon loved his Grognards of the Old Guard—and the boys who had fought at Mons and Le Cateau already considered themselves old soldiers. They had plenty to grumble about; they cursed the Huns, and the heat, and their boots, and the company cook. But in spite of their physical distress the spirit within kept them going. These footsore grumblers were in fact intensely proud of themselves. They had stood up to a hail of shells that no British Army had ever seen the like of; they had only gone back when they got the order to go; and they knew they had taken very heavy toll of the enemy. They were proud of themselves and proud of their regiments. There was none of the feeling that someone had blundered. The Huns had got round our flanks, and that was all about it.

Losses can be reckoned up in definite figures, but it is hard to put any definite value on morale. The question how far gains balanced losses must therefore remain unanswered. Historians may take what opinion they choose. The remnants of the old II Corps look back to Le Cateau with greater satisfaction than to any other day in the war.

But if the troops were well pleased with themselves the Staff was not so happy; it was realized that matters were not developing "according to plan." The situation led to a distressing incident of a personal nature. On the principle that "all is well which ends well," and out of respect for the memory of Lord French, the trouble might have been passed over in silence or with the restraint shown in the Official Account.[1] But unfortunately Lord French himself reopened it in his book by his severe criticisms of Smith-Dorrien, whom he deprived of his command, and by his adverse reflections on Kitchener. This gives the right of reply to those who, like myself, look on these two officers as the saviours of the situation.

Three times during the next few days Joffre visited General Headquarters and had interviews with the Commander-in-Chief. The first visit was on August 26, while the battle of

[1] O.H., 1914, p. 244.

Le Cateau was in progress. He had begun to collect a new VI Army under Maunoury, to prolong the left of the line, and his plans were still for an immediate offensive. Lanrezac, who was present, says that Sir John was "manifestement de mauvaise humeur, et cela s'explique." [1] As far as the British Commander could see, when Joffre issued an order for one thing the French did something else. Later in the day news came in from Le Cateau and put any idea of an offensive out of the question, at least for some time. The Retreat went on without further fighting except for insignificant rearguard actions.

By August 30 the relative positions of the British Expeditionary Force and V Army were reversed. On August 23 Lanrezac had been a full day's march in rear. The British went back without a stop for five days and on the 28th the line was fairly straight. They continued their retreat on the following days. But on the 29th the V Army turned round to attack. With true French heroism the weary soldiers flung themselves on the head of the German vanguard and drove them back a few miles. This action, known as the battle of Guise, was in accordance with the French idea—"battre en retraite." But as Lanrezac had only four Divisions against seven of the enemy he was soon forced to resume the retreat. He was thus two days' march behind the British, and a gap had been left in the Allied line between the French V and VI armies. This gap became the cause of trouble.

On the 29th Joffre again visited General Headquarters, then at Compiègne. He had information that the Germans had detached a "considerable force" to face the Russians, and he was anxious to take advantage of this by attacking at the earliest possible moment. Sir John could not promise to assist for some days. "I assured the French Commander-in-Chief that no serious gap should be made in his line by any premature or hasty retirement, but I imperatively demanded the necessary time to refit and obtain reinforcements."

It was another instance of the old trouble which arises

[1] Lanrezac, p. 210.

LEFT OF THE ALLIED LINE
NIGHTS OF AUG: 23RD & 29TH

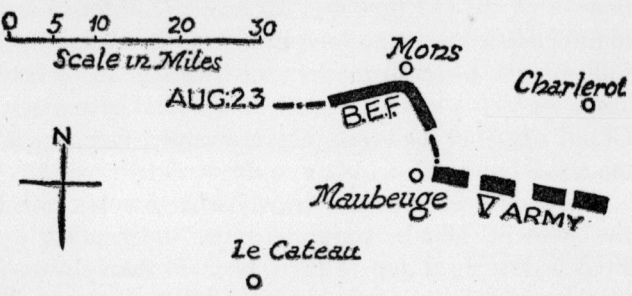
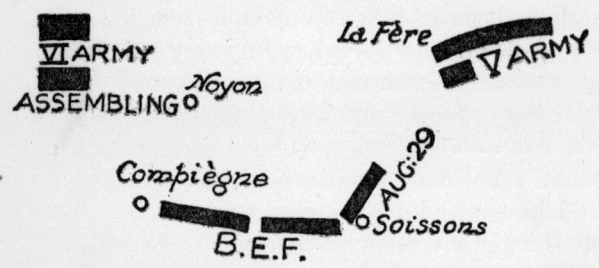

from divided command and divided responsibility. "One bad commander is better than two good ones"—so says the adage, not without a germ of truth. Sir John had a responsibility to his own Government and nation. His instructions clearly laid down that while he was to support and co-operate with the French Army his command was an independent one. The responsibility lay heavily upon him at this moment. He believed that the II Corps was shattered; Joffre was calling on him for offensive action; the French troops were continually falling back; he could not get away from the too well founded suspicion that a serious miscalculation had been made at the Grand Quartier Général. Little wonder that he was "de mauvaise humeur."

His book does not state clearly what was his intention at the moment. Did he mean to retire independently of the French, leaving a gap in their line? Probably not—but he was determined to retain his own liberty of action, because he had found that the plans of the Grand Quartier Général were very indefinite and its orders were never carried out. Probably he meant to retire steadily and see how the situation developed before taking any drastic action. Certainly he was determined not to be rushed into any action by Joffre until he saw what the V Army was going to do. But whatever his intention may have been he failed to make it clear in his conversations, letters, and telegrams. A careful study of these shows that he had no right to complain if they conveyed the impression that he meant to retire and leave a dangerous gap.

On August 30 he wrote to Kitchener: "I have been pressed very hard to remain, even in my shattered condition, in the fighting line; but I have absolutely refused to do so. . . ." This was written after the interview with Joffre on the 29th. "Absolutely refused" sounds like plain speaking. Joffre took it to mean that a gap would be left. So definite was this impression that he took the very strong step of appealing to the French President, M. Poincaré, who passed on the appeal to the British Ambassador, Sir F. Bertie. The Ambassador sent a message to General Headquarters. No record has come to light of its actual wording, but there can be little doubt that he appealed urgently to the British Commander-in-Chief to conform to the wishes of Joffre. Nor has any record been kept of Sir John's reply—he says curtly, "I refused." Further messages were flashed over the wire to Whitehall. They brought Kitchener in haste to Paris.

CHAPTER XIX

THE PARIS INTERVIEW

It is not too much to say that the interview on September 1 between Lord Kitchener and Sir John French was the most critical hour both in the history of the Entente, and in Lord Kitchener's own career.

After bidding good-bye to the General Headquarters staff on its departure for France the Secretary of State could only await news. Not that his days were spent in idleness—far from it. Every morning he was at his desk by 9 A. M. There reports were put before him. From time to time he had to grant interviews—which he did with obvious impatience. From time to time he had to cross over to the torture-room in Downing Street where precious hours were wasted in listening or pretending to listen to his civilian colleagues of the Cabinet. He never left office before 8 P. M. and messengers pursued him throughout the night. On the map on his wall little flags showed the distribution of the forces.

During the first two days reports from General Headquarters were cheerful and reassuring. On August 17 Sir John wrote: "I am much impressed by all I have seen of the French General Staff. . . ." The whole letter was cheerful in tone. Another letter of August 22 said: "The strength of the German movement in Belgium is about six and a half Corps." As the V Army had five and a half Corps and the British Expeditionary Force had two Corps, the Allied total came to seven and a half Corps, giving them at least equal strength. On receipt of this, Kitchener was much relieved—he did not know till later that the Germans had twelve Corps (twenty-six Divisions) north of the Meuse.

Then come notes of doubt which deserve careful consideration:

Sir John French to Lord Kitchener, August 30.

". . . I cannot say that I am now happy in the outlook as to the further progress of the campaign in France . . . my confidence in the ability of the leaders of the French Army to carry this campaign to a successful conclusion is fast waning, and this is my real reason for the decision I have taken to move the British Forces so far back . . . I feel most strongly the absolute necessity for retaining in my hand complete independence of action and power to retire on my base when circumstances render it necessary. I have been pressed very hard to remain, even in my shattered condition, in the fighting line; but I have absolutely refused to do so, and I hope you will approve of the course I have taken. Not only is it in accord with the spirit and letter of your instructions but it is dictated by common sense . . ."

A telegram dated August 31 was even more disquieting:

"I have let Joffre know plainly that in the present condition of my troops I shall be absolutely unable to remain in the front line as he has now begun his retirement. I have now decided to begin my retirement to-morrow in the morning, behind the Seine, in a south-westerly direction, west of Paris."

The natural impression which these messages and other information conveyed was that:

(1) Joffre had pressed Sir John to remain in the fighting line and Sir John had refused.

(2) The British Commander-in-Chief certainly intended to move south-west of Paris, which would leave a gap in the Allied line.

(3) He further had in mind a possible retreat to his base—which had been transferred to St. Nazaire, at the mouth of the Loire, 240 miles from Paris.

(4) The French Government had made an appeal which Sir John had also refused.

The seriousness of the situation so created was not hid-

THE PARIS INTERVIEW

den from Kitchener, and on August 31 he sent the following telegram to Sir John:

"I am surprised at your decision to retire behind the Seine. . . . What will be the effect of this course upon your relations with the French Army and on the general military situation? Will your retirement be a gap in the French line or cause them discouragement of which the Germans might take advantage? . . ."

This telegram shows that the Secretary of State, far removed from the hustle of the retreat and undisturbed by the thousand questions which were being pressed on the Commander-in-Chief, was able to take a wider and clearer view of the effect of a British withdrawal.

He saw first of all the effect on the French nation. A movement of five khaki-clad Divisions could not be hidden from the eyes of the populace; all the world would ring with the story how the British marched away, leaving open the road to Paris. And if Paris fell would the Entente bear the strain?

Hardly less serious would be the effect on the French Army. Military co-operation between the French and the British would be rendered excessively difficult. Furthermore, British withdrawal might have unexpected consequences on the French Command. Joffre's plans for a big offensive all along the line had broken down—Kitchener did not yet know how badly they had broken down, but he knew enough to see that the French Government had taken alarm. Joffre's position as Commander-in-Chief probably hung in the balance. If Paris fell somebody would have to be the scapegoat. But if the French could point to the defection of the British as the cause of failure it would at least save their national pride to some extent. Joffre could prove that he had pressed Sir John to remain in line; the French President and the British Ambassador could add their evidence. We know now that the Germans were not aiming at Paris during the following days—they were aiming at the left flank of the

French line, that is to say of the V Army. But Kitchener had every reason to suppose that they were aiming at Paris.

Finally, there was the effect on the Germans. They would soon know that the British had not only been "shattered" but by leaving the field had actually acknowledged the blow as a "knockout." Berlin would not fail to make the most of such news. Even if they could not take full advantage of the situation to defeat the French Army the Germans would have at least the enormous moral advantage of having defeated the contemptible British.

Even now such an idea strikes us with horror; it is no wonder that it drove every other consideration out of Kitchener's head. It would be better that every man of those five Divisions should die fighting. Immediately after sending off his telegram Kitchener consulted his colleagues and then telegraphed again:

"Your telegram 162 submitted to the Cabinet. The Government are exceedingly anxious lest your force, at this stage of the campaign in particular, should, owing to your proposed retirement so far from the line, not be able to co-operate closely with our Allies and render them continual support. They expect that you will as far as possible conform to the plans of General Joffre for the conduct of the campaign. They are waiting for the answer which you will no doubt send to my telegram of this morning and have all possible confidence in your troops and yourself."

The reply to this was received at midnight. It was a long message chiefly repeating former statements about the shattered condition of the II Corps and the necessity for refitting. But though the British Commander-in-Chief could not undertake any offensive action it contained the extraordinary suggestion that "an effective offensive movement now appears to be open to the French." There was no assurance that the Commander-in-Chief would conform to the plans of Joffre. "I think you had better trust me to watch the situation and act according to circumstances."

THE PARIS INTERVIEW

Kitchener was not prepared to give Sir John a free hand until a more definite assurance had been received. If he did not intend to desert the French, well and good—five minutes' conversation would clear up the mistake and no harm could come of it. On the other hand if the telegram of August 31 was a literal and accurate expression of his intention, if the British Commander was persisting in a movement west of Paris, then the authority of the Secretary of State as representing the British Government must be enforced to prevent disaster. A telegram was dispatched to arrange a meeting at the British Embassy at Paris. A destroyer was in waiting to convey Kitchener across the Channel, and the momentous interview took place at 7 P. M. on September 1. Besides the British Ambassador there were present M. Viviani (the Prime Minister) and M. Millerand (Minister of War). The British Commander-in-Chief was accompanied by his Chief-of-Staff, Murray, and the French Liaison Officer, Huguet.

Kitchener left no record of what actually took place. Various accounts have been given. Colonel Repington claimed to have heard the "true version," though he does not relate it. But Sir John goes into the matter at length. His book shows that even after he had full time for reflection the appalling significance of his own words about a retirement never came home to him. His mind seems to have been pre-occupied. To use a well-worn expression he could not see the wood for the trees. There were a good many trees to distract his attention. The heavy casualties caused him real distress; everybody who served under him knows how deeply he felt for the suffering of his men. Then the French plans had all gone wrong. He had been left in the air at Mons and Le Cateau, orders and counter-orders aroused his suspicion that Grand Quarter Général had lost grasp of the situation; he did not give Joffre and the French Army credit for the power of recovery which came to light during the next few days. He was wrong. But if we look back over the events of August his mistake seems very natural; not one single calculation had turned out correct, not a single order had been carried through with success. Joffre's appeal to him to attack was manifestly unreasonable. The appeal to the French President added fuel to his "mauvaise humeur" and Kitchener's visit sent him into a rage. He makes no concealment of the fact that he regarded the intervention of the Secretary of State as a personal affront.

"I deeply resented being called away from my Headquarters at so critical a time. Two important actions were fought by considerable detachments of the Army under my command during this day, over which there was no one to exercise any co-ordinating control. Either might have brought on a general engagement."

These words are sufficient to show his frame of mind. The two "important actions" were small rear-guard encounters—sharp little fights which lasted for less than an hour. The Official History, which does not err on the side of brevity, devotes only three pages to them. But to the harassed commander they loomed so large as to shut out questions of infinitely greater importance.

When he entered the Embassy at Paris the first thing that struck him was that the Secretary of State wore the uniform of a Field-Marshal. Next Kitchener "announced his intention of taking the field and inspecting the troops." Why this should have appeared so distasteful is not explained; two months later Lord Roberts in the uniform of a Field-Marshal visited the British Expeditionary Force and was welcomed. Kitchener probably wished to give the French Ministers the impression that he had come on a friendly visit to congratulate the British Expeditionary Force on its gallant fighting; when he saw it would give annoyance to Sir John he was quite willing to abandon his proposed visit to the troops. But Sir John was by no means pacified.

"In the conversation which followed between us all Lord Kitchener appeared to take grave exception to certain views

THE PARIS INTERVIEW

which I expressed as to the expediency of leaving the direction of the operations in the field in the hands of the military chiefs in command in the field. He abruptly closed the discussion and requested me to accompany him for a private interview in another room. When we were alone he commenced by entering a strong objection to the tone I assumed."

For the first time Kitchener seems to have recognized that personalities could not be avoided, but as he left no record of the private conversation we must turn again to Sir John's account.

"Upon this I told him all that was in my mind. I said that the command of the British Force in France had been entrusted to me by His Majesty's Government; that I alone was responsible to them for whatever happened, and that on the French soil my authority as regards the British Army must be supreme until I was legally superseded by the same authority which put that responsibility upon me. I further remarked that Lord Kitchener's presence in France in the character of a soldier could have no other effect than to weaken and prejudice my position in the eyes of the French and my own countrymen alike. I reminded him of our service in the field together some thirteen years before, and told him that I valued highly his advice and assistance, which I would gladly accept as such, but that I would not tolerate any interference with my executive command and authority so long as His Majesty's Government chose to retain me in my present position."

This was strong stuff—but entirely outside the matter Kitchener had come over to discuss, which was whether the Commander-in-Chief did or did not intend to withdraw from the fighting-line. Was the subject ever mentioned? If Sir John's account is to be credited, not a word was said about it. He concludes by saying: "I think he began to realize my difficulty and we finally came to an amicable understanding." It is obvious, however, that the great question must have been put and that the answer must have been satisfactory. The proof lies in Sir John's subsequent action. All idea of quitting the line was certainly dropped from this date. Instead of moving west of Paris, as had been his intention when he sent off his telegram of August 31, he moved well to the east of it. Further, we can be sure that Kitchener would not have come to an "amicable understanding" until he had received complete assurance on this point. It was for the sake of this assurance that he had come to Paris. Immediately after the interview he dispatched the following telegram to the Government in London:

"French's troops are now engaged in the fighting line, where he will remain conforming to the movements of the French Army, though at the same time acting with caution to avoid being in any way unsupported on his flanks."

He sent a copy of this telegram to Sir John and added: "Please consider it as an instruction."

Sir John himself was satisfied that he had got out of the interview all he wanted.

"It is very difficult for any but soldiers to understand the real bearing and significance of this Paris incident. If the confidence of the troops in their commander is shaken in the least degree or if his influence, power, and authority are prejudiced by any display of mistrust in his ability to conduct operations, however slight the indications of such distrust may be, the effect reacts instantly throughout the whole army. This is more than ever true with troops who, at the moment in question, were being subjected to great and severe demands upon their courage, endurance, and, above all, faith in their leader. Then again there was the effect which might have been produced on the French Ministers and Generals who were present and witnessed Lord Kitchener's apparent assertion of his right to exercise the powers and authority of a Commander-in-Chief in the field. Fortunately the incident terminated in a manner which led to no regrettable publicity. Kitchener realized his mistake and left Paris that night."

Sir John was disturbed at "the effect which might have been produced on the French" by Kitchener's assertion of authority, but he never thought about the effect which might have been produced on them by his own refusal to comply with the wishes of Joffre and with the imperative message of the French President. Yet though he does not seem to have been aware of it the interview had a decisive effect on his own conduct. There were no more refusals, and the British Army was present at the battle of the Marne instead of being somewhere south-west of Paris on the road to its base.

CHAPTER XX

THE MARNE

GENERAL JOFFRE puzzled those who had dealings with him, and remains a puzzle to those who have written about him. A big, burly, white-haired man, to all appearance of simple manners and fixed ideas, full of confidence in himself and his army, a despot, jealous of his own authority. But the outstanding trait was *mutisme*. Dictionaries say this means "silence" or "reserve," but neither of these words gives the full sense. Joffre never argued or explained. He would allow others to talk, he would listen much as a learned professor might listen to the prattle of a child—sometimes without troubling to follow the meaning of what was said. But his words conveyed *mutisme* even more than his silence. French officers have a thousand stories to tell of "Papa Joffre." One will serve as a sample of the rest.

Once upon a time a Colonel Carence came to Grand Quartier Général. He was an expert and enthusiast about heavy artillery, and wanted to argue for an increase in that branch of the Service. He was admitted to the presence. "Je t'écoute, Carence, parle." For half an hour the enthusiast poured out a stream of eloquence on the value of heavy guns. Then he paused for Joffre to take up the argument. The great man, who had not yet uttered a word, gave him a friendly tap on the shoulder. "Ce sacré Carence, il a toujours beaucoup aimé l'artillerie; c'est bien ca"—and the expert found himself dismissed.[1]

Over trivial matters Joffre was given to bursts of irritation. An officer late for dinner would be greeted with a frown

[1] From the book of M. Pierrefeu, a well-known journalist, who was taken on the staff to edit the News Bulletins. This duty brought him into daily touch with Joffre, Pétain, and others. He has given a lively and outspoken account of his impressions of Grand Quartier Général.

of offended dignity. The staff, who were devoted to him, busied themselves, often without success, in nursing the humours of their Chief. Yet in the hour of crisis this irritable veteran remained supremely calm—not with the forced calm which masks agitation, but with the true serenity which comes from unshaken confidence.

The victory of the Marne will always be associated with his name. Some French authors have given a big share of the credit to Galliéni, Foch, and Maunoury; it has also been hinted that the manœuvre was hatched in the brains of the staff. However that may be, it remains true that the real honour for such a battle is due not so much to the brain which conceives the plans, nor yet to the men who carry it out, as to the Chief who shoulders the responsibility.

Think of the courage of the man. He issued an order for the IV and V Armies and the British to retreat right down to the Seine. We must look at the map and remember the history of the French nation before we can grasp the full meaning of such an order. It admitted the failure of all the roseate illusions with which the campaign had been opened—the failure of the dashing attack which was to fling back the enemy from the frontier. But there was much more in it than that. Though the order was secret, streams of refugees told a story which could neither be concealed nor misread. A nation—and of all nations in the world the French—must look on while invaders swept down through the country, down into the very heart of it, right down to the gates of Paris. The Tsar Alexander I could order a retreat and abandon Moscow to Napoleon—but his people were mere ignorant serfs. In Paris every man and woman is a politician, and a very free-thinking politician. Three times in history the dynasty of the Buonapartes had crumbled when the Capital was threatened by invaders. Could a Republican General allow the Germans to come so near without fighting at least one pitched battle?

Perhaps it was the lightning quickness of the whole thing

that saved the situation. The masses had scarcely time to realize that a storm was brewing before it veered round, without bursting on them, and left the sky clear. But the confidence and *mutisme* of Joffre were real assets. People who wished to appear wise shook their heads mysteriously and whispered to each other that Joffre "avait une idée." Of course there was excitement, but it was repressed into a sort of cold stupor; the Government packed up for a move to Bordeaux and Paris sat down to await a siege.

It was true that Joffre "avait une idée." But a siege of Paris was no part of it, though at first appearances seemed to point that way. The one bright spot was in the east where the fortified zones from Verdun to Belfort enabled the I, II and III Armies to block the German advance; they could even afford troops to help further west. Half a dozen Divisions were sent round by train to join the VI Army north of Paris. Whatever the theories of the Operation Section may have been, they were adepts at practical organization. The movement of those Divisions, during the hustle of the retreat, was a masterpiece. General Galliéni, Governor of Paris, brought out four Divisions from the garrison of the city. With the addition of odd units Maunoury's Army was brought up to the formidable strength of 150,000 men. It was gradually collected on the northern outskirts of Paris, while the Germans were being drawn into the net spread for them.

Paris and Verdun were now to be the *points d'appui*. Between them the Allied line, the IV and V Armies and the British, had orders to sag down southward, down to the Seine if necessary. Then Maunoury was to lead off with a blow from the west while the whole line turned about and attacked. This was the great manœuvre of the Marne.

By September 4 everything was ready and Joffre issued his orders.

The Marne is held to be one of the decisive battles in the history of the world. It warded off the threat to Paris:

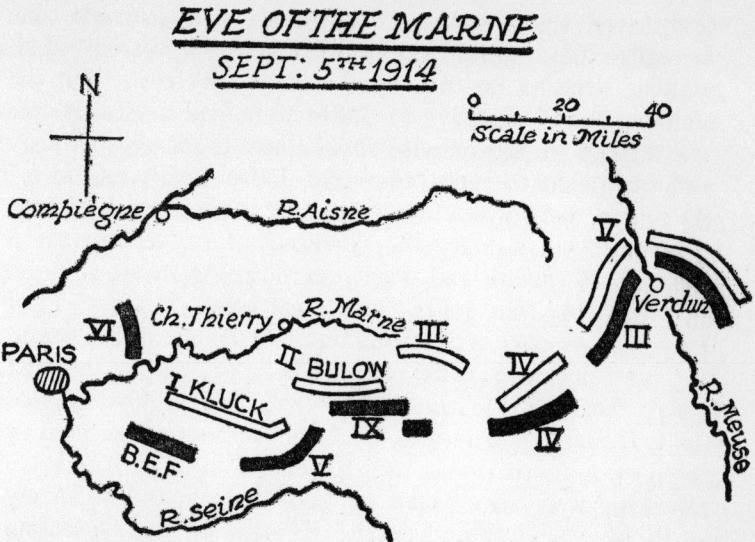

it thwarted the enveloping movement which would have rolled up the French line: it upset the great scheme of the Prussians and deprived them to a large extent of the advantages they hoped to reap from well-matured organization. Though the defeat of the enemy was far from complete, the moral ascendancy of the Allies was established. It was now the turn of the Germans to abandon illusions and conform to the enemy's plans. The battle was continuous from the 5th to the 9th of September on a front of 120 miles.

The decisive factor which forced the enemy to retreat in haste was the little army of five Divisions which wedged itself into the long German line. Yet, curiously enough, the severe fighting did not fall on the British and they cannot claim the lion's share of the glory. To understand how this could come about we must turn to the map.

About August 30 Von Kluck gave up the idea of going round the west of Paris and turned south-east, trying to force his I Army behind the left of the French, to cut them off from Paris and drive them into the jaws of the other

German forces in the east. While the French VI Army was being collected north of Paris Von Kluck was allowed to advance and every day his prospects of success seemed brighter. By September 5 he was well south of the Marne (see sketch) leaving only one Corps on the north bank.

On September 4 Joffre had decided to stop the retreat and launch his counter-stroke—the reason being that the VI Army was now reported to be ready. It was indeed something of a motley crowd—Regulars, Territorials, garrison troops, Marines, a Moroccan brigade, and the remnants of Sordet's Cavalry Corps; but they called themselves "the Army of Paris" and they meant to fight. No matter that they had few guns and no transport, no matter that they had been flung together under an improvised staff. For four days without a pause they were at close grips with the enemy and earned immortal fame. A complete success would have brought Maunoury right behind the German I Army, but Von Kluck hastened to parry the blow. He turned about and then using his west flank as a hinge swung round to face the VI Army. Thus a gap was left between Von Kluck and Von Bulow's II Army, held only by cavalry. This was the gap into which the British penetrated.

At 3 A. M. on September 5 Sir John received the instructions from the Grand Quartier Général. His troops were at that moment marching southwards in accordance with the previous order. By 9 A. M. they came to a halt, rested a few hours, and then turned about and began to retrace their steps. During the 6th, 7th, and 8th they pushed back the German rearguards. On the 9th they crossed the Marne, between La-Ferté and Château-Thierry. The III Corps on the left had a stiff fight before they reached the north bank, but the Cavalry and the I and II Corps found themselves, much to their surprise, marching unopposed over perfectly good bridges—then up a wooded slope and on for two or three miles. They were well in between the German I and II Armies.

Meanwhile the French were doing great work. Maunoury

had stood up gallantly to Von Kluck; the V Army, now under Franchet d'Esperey, had found its way into the gap at Château-Thierry. Foch with a newly formed IX Army was attacking further east. And the Germans had to fall back on the whole line; not till they reached the Aisne, 25 miles to the north, could they pull themselves together for a stand.

Though the battle did not fulfill all Joffre's hopes it was a glorious victory for the French arms. The extent of the German demoralization may be inferred from the fact that they lost 38,000 prisoners and 160 guns. Moltke had calculated that the decisive moment would be "between the 36th and 40th days." September 9 was the 38th day of the war. It was certainly decisive—especially for Moltke himself. He was removed and replaced by Falkenhayn.

Although the brunt of the fighting fell on the French, but for the wedge of the British Expeditionary Force in the German line the enemy might well have made a stand along the river. If Kitchener had not insisted that the British should co-operate with their Allies the battle of the Marne could hardly have been won. As he sat in his room at the War Office, he may well have congratulated himself on the result of his interview in Paris with Sir John French.

Kitchener had little to do with the operations of the next month. The Germans retreated to the Aisne. The Allies exaggerated their success and believed that continuous pressure would force the invaders out of France. But, as Sir John says, it was in the fighting on that river that the eyes of all of us began to be opened. Frontal attacks were held up everywhere. Joffre determined to turn the western flank of the German line. New armies were formed, stretching northwards from Soissons, first as far as Amiens, then successively to Arras, Béthune, and finally to the coast. The British Expeditionary Force was pulled out of position on the Aisne to take its place in the line north of Béthune; later on it spread up to Ypres.

But the eyes of the Germans had also been opened to

the futility of frontal attacks. While Joffre was trying to turn their flank they were trying to turn his. The result was that the new French Armies, instead of getting round the flank, found themselves face to face with new German Armies. Both sides fought themselves to a standstill. Then they sat down where they were to dig the first of the line of trenches which afterwards became opposing barriers, withstanding all assault for over three years.

The British Expeditionary Force had its full share of the fighting in the terrible first Battle of Ypres, which lasted continuously from October 15 to November 21. During the first ten days the Allies were hoping to break the German line. Sir John says: "I did not expect I should have to fight a great defensive battle." Orders were issued for the advance to Menin, 12 miles east of Ypres; also for an advance "via Thourout, with the object of capturing Bruges." Neither of these movements got further than a couple of miles—and it gradually became evident that the enemy had brought up strong reinforcements.

From October 27 to November 1 the Germans made their big attacks and were repulsed with heavy losses though the thin British line was more than once pierced. Further attacks were made almost daily up to November 21, when the enemy's force was spent. Both armies then sat down to spend the winter in icy mud.

CHAPTER XXI

THE RIFT WITH G.H.Q.

In December the barometer of our hopes, which had been rising and falling in the most spectacular fashion for four months, settled down to dismal wintry weather. This was the beginning of the stalemate on the Western Front.

Both the British and the French Headquarters clung to the belief that the enemy's line could be broken; and this belief governed their policy throughout 1915. Kitchener was not so impatient. He had never expected to conquer the Germans while they still had superiority in men and munitions. Even the first of his New Armies would not be ready to go abroad before May. In the meantime he did not want to squander the little nucleus of trained men whom he was retaining as instructors for his recruits. This brought about a difference of opinion which Sir John French does not conceal. On December 20 he crossed the Channel for an interview with the Secretary of State. In his book he gives an account of this meeting.

"Lord Kitchener met me there [at Folkestone] with his motor and we drove together to Walmer Castle where Mr. Asquith was then staying. I had not seen Kitchener since our memorable meeting at Paris in September, but he met me in the most friendly manner, and said many kind things about our work in France . . . we discussed the situation fully . . . the question of munitions and the fear of invasion formed the basis of our long conversation at Walmer . . . with deep sorrow I recall the fact that this was the last of all the many days of happy personal intercourse which I spent with my old South African chief. As a soldier and a commander in the field I had always loved and venerated him; in his capacity as a politician and Minister

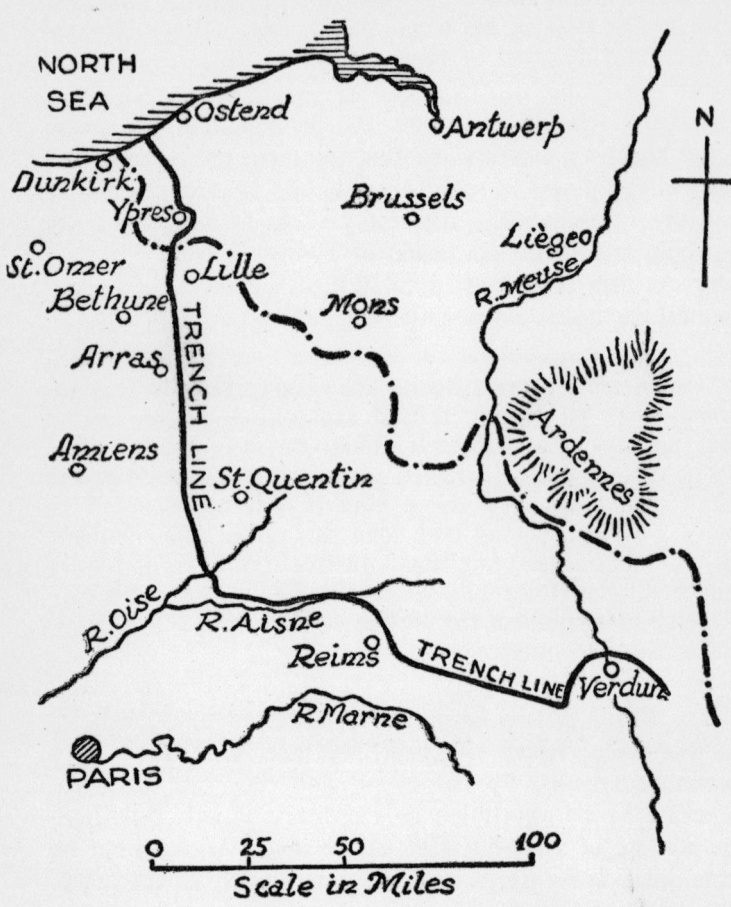

THE RIFT WITH G.H.Q.

my sentiments and feelings towards him were never the same.

"I am willing to admit that our differences—which were great and far-reaching—may have been to some extent my own fault; but be that as it may, our subsequent relations, down to the time of his tragic death, were always clouded by a certain mistrust of each other."

Mistrust—the word is not too strong—had its origin in the honest convictions of the two men, convictions diametrically opposed to each other. It had begun even earlier than the Paris incident, and the process of its growth can be easily traced in the pages of Henry Wilson.

Sir A. Macphail hints that Wilson's diary was a confidential document not intended for publication.

"The book is a cruel book. The cruelty lies not in publishing what Sir Henry Wilson says about others, but in what he says about himself. What he says about others will be disbelieved or believed according to the taste of the reader: what he says about himself will be accepted as true. . . . If an enemy had done this publication it might fairly be alleged that any man's furtive scribbling, if wholly published, would do him discredit. But it must be rare for a friend to publish the writings of a friend and thereby exhibit him as a public spectacle."[1]

Very likely Wilson would have hesitated to publish it; the prophecies which he cheerfully uttered in 1914 were invariably falsified by the event, and they are distinctly damaging to his reputation as a military expert. But there was nothing of a confidential nature in the book; what he wrote down in its pages he was saying openly in the office, in the mess, to the staff, to French officers and to anyone he met on the roadside. He was always ready to talk, in fact he rarely stopped talking, and of course everybody was ready to listen. While others of the staff were wrapped

[1] Macphail, p. 9.

in official mystery, "Henri" was always willing to answer questions and disburse news; he was cheery and amusing; he knew many officers by sight, hailed them by nicknames, and always seemed glad to see them. The result was that his news and opinions passed from mouth to mouth and the whole of the British Expeditionary Force knew what he was saying. The diary, even in its most indiscreet pages, was no revelation to anybody who served in France in those days.

The first difference of opinion with Kitchener took place as early as August 7. Wilson, as Director of Military Operations at the War Office, had wired to France on August 5 asking that an officer of the French Staff might be sent over to discuss plans. General Huguet arrived early on the 7th and Wilson writes:

Friday, August 7. "Long talk with Huguet,[1] who then returned by special train and boat to France to see Joffre and to return here on Wed. morning. Lord K. sent for me 1.45 p.m. and was angry because I had let Huguet go, and angrier still because I had told Huguet everything about our starting on Sunday. I answered back, as I have no intention of being bullied by him, especially when he talks such nonsense as he did today."

This gives us a clear idea of the situation between the two men. Wilson, as D.M.O., was making arrangements for the movement of troops; he wished to be assured by Huguet that everything was ready on the French side of the Channel —landing-places, rest camps, railways; it was absolutely necessary that the French should know when our troops would begin to arrive in order that their preparations might be completed. He regarded any interference by the Secretary of State as unnecessary and harmful. Kitchener, on the other hand, was not disposed to abrogate his authority or to allow

---

[1] Huguet had been Military Attaché at the French Embassy in London for several years. He became Liaison Officer at General Headquarters. He was well known and very popular with the British Army.

THE RIFT WITH G.H.Q.

Wilson to issue important orders which had not been approved by himself or the Cabinet. Just as the Paris interview left its aftermath in Sir John French's attitude towards Lord Kitchener, so did this incident affect Wilson's relations with his chief. He became definitely hostile, and everybody, except perhaps Kitchener himself, was soon aware of the fact.

The retreat from Mons was of course a bitter disappointment to the optimist, but after the Marne his hopes grew stronger than ever and he had no hesitation in proclaiming and recording them. When the Allied armies had just arrived on the Aisne he visited the Grand Quartier Général and writes:

September 13. "Berthelot [Joffre's Chief-of-Staff] asked me when I thought we should cross into Germany, and I replied that unless we made some serious blunder we ought to be at Elsenborn in four weeks. He thought three weeks."

September 15. "If we drive in the force in front of us we won't have any more trouble till we get to the Meuse."

Every available man must be sent out from England at once and rushed into the line to keep up the pressure. Nothing else mattered. This was the object which Wilson kept before him and to which he applied all his arguments, sarcasm, and powers of intrigue. In front of junior officers he poured ridicule on Kitchener's scheme and denounced the cowardice, weakness, and ignorance, of everybody who did not agree with himself.

"Kitchener's shadow armies, for shadow campaigns, at unknown and distant dates, prevent a lot of good officers, N.C.O.'s and men from coming out. It is a scandalous thing. Under no circumstances can these mobs now being raised, without officers and N.C.O.'s, without guns, rifles, or uniforms, without rifle-ranges or training grounds, without supply or transport services, without morale or tradition, knowledge or experience, under no circumstances could these mobs take the field for two years. Then what is the use of them? What we want and what we must have is for our little force out here to be kept at full strength with the very best of everything. Nothing else is any good."

A few days later he wrote:

"His [Kitchener's] ridiculous and preposterous army of 25 Corps is the laughing stock of every soldier in Europe. It took the Germans forty years of incessant work to make an army of 25 Corps with the aid of conscription; it will take us to all eternity to do the same by voluntary effort."

Wilson was wrong in saying that every soldier in Europe was laughing at Kitchener's effort. No doubt there were very few who could foresee what that tremendous effort would amount to, or realize the possibilities of those amazing new armies. Few could look forward to the crisis of 1918 when the old regiments had practically ceased to exist and Kitchener's recruits finished the war. But there were many officers who had realized that the regular forces would not suffice, that new units must be raised, and that we wanted an many as we could get. Far from pouring ridicule on Kitchener's effort, these officers were anxious to do everything in their power to assist it. And even those who had not much faith were still sufficiently loyal to refrain from discrediting the policy which had been adopted. Wilson had no faith and no hesitation in saying so.

He propounded his views to everybody he met. On September 27 Churchill visited General Headquarters and the diary says: "Saw Winston for five minutes, but he talked such nonsense about the shadow forces that I got to grips at once." Churchill remained unconvinced, and wrote subsequently:

"I could not share the universal optimism of the staff. It was fully believed and loudly declared on every side that, if all the reinforcements in officers were sent to the Army without delay, the war would be finished by Christ-

THE RIFT WITH G.H.Q.

mas. Fierce were the reproaches that the W.O. were withholding vitally needed officers, instructors, and material for the purpose of training vast armies that would never be ready in time. . . . Taking a complete survey I consider that this prudent withholding from the Army in the field, in face of every appeal and demand, the key men who alone could make the new armies, was the greatest of the services which Lord Kitchener rendered to the nation at this time, and it was a service which no one of less authority than he could have performed."

Wilson's optimism survived the Aisne. On October 3 he wrote: "I still think that the war will be over in February or March." By October 13 the II and III Corps had been moved to the north and were in the front line from Béthune to Armentières. The diary says: "We must push, push, push as we have nothing in front of us." As a matter of fact more than three German Corps were already there and others were gathering fast. Wilson's ignorance was largely due to the scorn and disbelief with which he received any reports which did not fit in with his own views. He was travelling all over the country and talking as much as ever.

"My dear boy, we *know* the Germans are on the run; the Russians are knocking them, the French are knocking them; of course your men are weary, but not half so weary as Fritz, and you ought to be able to kick a cavalry rearguard out of your way—there is nobody behind it."

If this cheery optimism had been confined to keeping up the spirits of the troops it would have been very excusable. By the end of November Sir John might well have said that the original British Expeditionary Force was shattered. There was not a regiment but had lost more than half its Commissioned and Non-Commissioned officers, and some had lost all. It was a difficult business to keep a regiment going with a completely fresh staff which joined one day and went into the trenches on the next. It must also be remembered that those who had fallen were the comrades with whom we had been living for years, our oldest and nearest friends; in this respect the Regular Forces were harder hit than new units which came together for the first time in 1914. The British Expeditionary Force maintained its splendid morale because the men had become conscious of their own fighting power. But the strain was heavy, the work incessant, and the discomforts of weather and mud depressing. Wilson's unflagging energy and cheeriness were a valuable asset.

But unhappily his energy did not stop with the encouragement of the troops. It was exerted to prevent a defensive spirit. While his optimistic views were shared by General Headquarters no preparations were made to meet the terrific attack which is known as the first battle of Ypres. No position was selected, no entrenchments were dug, no reserve line was chosen, and such a thing as barbed wire had not yet been thought of. Worse still, any officers who suggested defensive measures were regarded with suspicion. We must "push, push, push," and none of the reports received from the front line could alter this policy. I am convinced that the hostility of Sir John French towards Smith-Dorrien, which afterwards culminated in the dismissal of the latter, began at this time because the Commander of the II Corps did not show sufficient eagerness to fling his infantry against the unbroken line of German machine-guns.

But the facts were too strong for even Henry Wilson.

October 19. "Our news tonight is not so good, though there is nothing to be anxious about. But the Germans are crowding up against us, and I am afraid that, from the fact we have not pushed as hard as we ought during the last week we are now going to find the boot on the other leg. We shall know more tomorrow. I still think the campaign will be over in the Spring. Owing to nothing but absolute incompetence and want of regimental officers we have lost the finest opportunity of the war and are now being thrown on the defensive. Maddening and perhaps disastrous."

THE RIFT WITH G.H.Q.

By the light of after events we all know that Wilson and French and General Headquarters were wrong. A few more officers and a few more battalions, even a few more Divisions, would not have broken the German line at that time. Kitchener seems to have known this from the first. It is a matter of conjecture how far he was aware of the feeling at General Headquarters. He had not the faculty of drawing people out, he never encouraged tale-bearers. It is possible that he knew little or nothing of the personal feelings entertained towards himself. Certainly he would have cared little about them, if he had known. But he took deep interest in the facts, and by the middle of December they spoke for themselves. The losses had been terrific. In addition to the original six Divisions the British Expeditionary Force had been reinforced with four Divisions and many battalions of Territorials. General Headquarters still demanded more. What use would be made of them? From Sir John French's letters there was no doubt about the answer to this question. "Attaque, attaque, attaque." Kitchener was prepared to admit the necessity of "keeping up the pressure," especially as the Russians were at this time heavily engaged and looked to us for help. But the spasmodic efforts made in November and December had only encouraged the Germans. What Kitchener wanted to do was to store up troops and munitions for a move on a wide front that would give at least some prospect of success.

There can be little doubt that his faith in Sir John had been seriously shaken. This was not because the British Commander and his little army failed in fighting—Kitchener had never expected a sudden and decisive victory—but because the staff at General Headquarters appeared so hopelessly incapable of judging the situation. The mistakes are down in black and white: "We shall be in Germany in four weeks," "The war will be over by Christmas," "There is nothing in front of us." The comparison of such language with the facts reveals a terrible lack of knowledge. The fog of war makes some mistakes excusable. If Sir John had admitted that his information was defective and unreliable no one would have been surprised. But when the staff repeatedly made confident statements which afterwards turned out to be ridiculously remote from the truth, "mistrust" necessarily resulted. Kitchener would have been neglecting his duty if he did not act on it.

According to Wilson,[1] who got the information through Foch, the idea of relieving the British Commander-in-Chief had been raised while the Battle of Ypres was still in progress. On November 1 there was an important meeting at Dunkirk, at which Poincaré, Joffre, Foch, and Kitchener were present; the Minister of War proposed to send Ian Hamilton to command the British Expeditionary Force but the French were opposed to any change. The joint success at the Marne had brought about happier relations between General Headquarters and Joffre; Foch in particular had established a firm hold on Wilson, and through him on Sir John; a change in the command of the British Army would not have suited the French at all. In face of their objection to his proposal Kitchener could not insist, but he was evidently determined to make a change of some kind at General Headquarters.

Murray was suffering from overwork. All the office correspondence, orders, appreciations, dispatches, fell on his shoulders while the sub-chief of Staff ran about the country in a motor. He was a magnificent worker but he had not the gift of delegating to others anything that passed through his office. On one occasion during the Retreat he broke down, and though he resumed his place the strain was heavy. Sir John wanted to appoint Wilson and, during one of his visits to England, proposed the change; but when he returned to General Headquarters he had to break the news that the suggestion did not meet with favour from high quarters.

Wilson, who had certainly expected the appointment, gives vent to his annoyance with the usual lack of restraint:

[1] Wilson, I, p. 186.

THE RIFT WITH G.H.Q.

December 23. ". . . Sir John said the Government and Kitchener were very hostile to me. That I was the principal cause of all the Ulster trouble and was therefore dangerous. In short, neither Kitchener nor Asquith will have me. . . . I care not a rush for the opinion of either of these men . . . anyhow, the net result is that Murray is more firmly established than ever and Sir John hinted that the less work I did the better. I might go to Russia and see what they were doing there. How funny! I cannot get up any sorrow at not serving him or Asquith or K. as Chief of Staff. He said this Government would soon be out and then it would be all right. So there are politics in our Army."

Disappointment was natural enough. But it is amusing to see Wilson, who was a politician above all things, objecting to the political influence. In this case, however, his suspicions were entirely wrong. However angry Asquith may have been over the Curragh incident, it is monstrous to insinuate that he allowed memories of it to rankle in his mind when the fate of England was in the balance; later on he took Carson, a much more prominent figure in Ulster affairs than Wilson, as a member of the Cabinet. If the War Minister and Sir John had pressed for Wilson he would not, in fact he could not, have stood in the way. Kitchener had never bothered himself about the Curragh incident. Like the Prime Minister he was looking forward, not backward. What they both wanted was a Chief-of-Staff who would loyally support not his own fancies but the policy of the Government. Wilson's opposition was too openly declared for the idea of his appointment to such a position to be entertained.

Murray was replaced in January by Sir William Robertson. Unlike Wilson the new Chief-of-Staff had not committed himself to loud prophecies and assertions. Though convinced of the necessity of keeping up the pressure as far as possible he preferred to study the means at his disposal before deciding on action. He was not one of the "push push" enthusiasts who flung attacks about piecemeal without artillery preparation, without reserves, without any kind of considered plans. Above all he was a man of unwavering loyalty. He expected, though he did not always get, a definite statement of the Cabinet's policy; so far as he got it, he supported it without reserve. If he thought the policy wrong, he was not slow to speak his mind. But he never did so except to his superiors. No junior officer, no French General, ever heard from his lips abuse of those in authority such as Henry Wilson poured out so cheerfully. He held the appointment of Chief-of-Staff till December 1915, when Kitchener called him to the War Office.

Wilson became liaison officer with French Headquarters, and it must be admitted that his work in that capacity was of real value. Relations between ourselves and our gallant Allies had not been improved by the events of 1914. On our side of the Channel we knew little about the French, and perhaps even now we scarcely appreciate what they did in that first year. Our own losses, our own efforts, absorbed all our attention. We were justly proud of what our soldiers had done, of the rush of enthusiastic recruits, of the voluntary workers who offered service in every capacity. Later on in 1917 the British saved France when the French had been bled white. But during that first year the chief share of the fighting fell on the French, and we ought not to forget it. We cannot blame them for being a little sore. They had taken every man for the army and the whole nation was concentrated on the one object of defeating the enemy. They knew little of the great effort preparing across the Channel. But they knew that we had not introduced compulsory service, and they had heard something about "business as usual." They could not see the Grand Fleet, the shoals of scouts that kept ceaseless watch and ward over the North Sea. All they could see was a little army holding 34 miles of the line against the 350 miles held by their own troops.

It was the question of frontage which raised friction between General Headquarters and Grand Quartier Général.

THE RIFT WITH G.H.Q.

The prestige which Joffre had gained by the battle of the Marne, was barely enough to carry him through the next few months when he failed to drive the enemy out of France. There was an intrigue to replace him by Galliéni. Naturally he wanted every man he could find to put into his attacks, and constant appeals were made for the British to take over an extra stretch of line. Sir John, fortified by Robertson, was adamant in refusing to do anything which might endanger any Channel ports; Antwerp had fallen, Ostend had fallen— but at all costs we must hold on to Calais and Boulogne. Joffre was willing to guarantee that French reserves should be forthcoming if the Germans made another heavy attack, but Sir John wanted to have the British line independent of French reserves. The intermixture of armies during the battle of Ypres had led to several complications not only in the front trenches but also in the railways, roads, and billets in rear.

As each successive attack failed Joffre became more and more insistent. It almost appeared that he wanted to be given definite command over the British Army. Wilson was certainly useful in keeping the peace. He could argue or flatter, cajole or chaff, as the circumstances required. He had no scruples about making promises for the future if only the immediate trouble could be tided over. In this respect he was more accommodating than Robertson, who never made a promise until he saw the means of carrying it out. Robertson's deeds were better than his words. Wilson was all words. But even words are useful at times.

CHAPTER XXII

GALLIPOLI

WHILE Joffre and Sir John were planning fresh offensives in France the Cabinet in England had begun to look in other directions. Mr. Winston Churchill, in his book *The World Crisis*, has devoted a chapter to the "Blood Test," proving, with many statistics and great argumentative skill, that offensives were always more costly to the attack than to the defence. His inference is that instead of making frontal attacks on the lines in France, where the Germans were at their strongest, we ought to have sought a flank where the opposition would be weak.

"Although the Central Powers were working on interior lines this advantage does not countervail the superior mobility of sea power . . . Britain could at any time in 1915, for instance, have moved 250,000 men (if available) to suitable points on the shores of the Eastern Mediterranean in a fraction of the time required to send an equal number of Germans and Austrians. . . . Moreover the selection of these points would remain a mystery to the enemy up to the last moment." [1]

The arguments on the other side have been effectively marshalled by Sir William Robertson. They are based on the premise that "when you cut down the trunk of a tree the branches will fall." Lopping off twigs does little harm, and even the fall of big branches is not fatal. This is proved by the fact that the Allies lost several big branches without fatal consequences. The enemy occupied a large slice of France, overran Belgium and Serbia, forced Russia and Rumania to ask for peace, and in fact broke down the

[1] Churchill, 1915, p. 31.

GALLIPOLI

TURKEY

N

To Constantinople
100 miles

ÆGEAN SEA

Gallipoli

Sea of Marmora

Suvla Bay
Anzac Cove
Achi Baba
Cape Helles
Kum Kale

Chanak

DARDANELLES

ASIA MINOR

0 10 20 30
Scale in Miles

← To Mudros
50 miles

Allies everywhere except on the decisive field—and there they were beaten.

It is not for me to enter into the controversy between such champions. But on one point there can be no controversy. The first essential in war is to settle where the main decision is to be sought. The Cabinet never settled that point and "throughout the winter of 1914, so far from being required to submit plans for the next year the General Staff were kept in almost complete ignorance of the various courses under discussion by the Cabinet." [1]

During 1915 no less than 400,000 troops were sent to Gallipoli and our casualties in that expedition came to 120,000. Besides this, there was an enormous expenditure of ammunition and supplies of all kinds, and a large quantity of shipping was continually employed. On the other side of the ledger it is claimed that the Turks had double that number of casualties, and that the Gallipoli adventure prevented any attack by the enemy on Egypt and the Suez Canal. These advantages, however, were not sufficient to outweigh the losses. It was recognized that the campaign had been a dismal and expensive failure, so much so that the Government appointed a commission to investigate it. Statesmen, sailors, soldiers, were examined and cross-examined at length. The report says:

"It is impossible to read all the evidence or to study the voluminous papers which have been submitted to us, without being struck by the atmosphere of vagueness and want of precision which seems to have characterized the proceedings of the War Council." [2]

One Minister, however, had very clear ideas and the courage of his convictions—the First Lord of the Admiralty, Mr. Winston Churchill. He had been much impressed with the improvements which science had made during the last

---

[1] O.H., *Gallipoli*, p. 47.
[2] Report of Dardanelles Commission, p. 21.

few years in artillery. The forts of Namur, which were expected to hold up the Germans for a month, had been demolished in twenty-four hours; the forts outside Antwerp, of the most modern type, had collapsed like cardhouses—he himself had been there and had seen them. Surely the British Navy could do equally well against the Turkish forts in the Dardanelles. Ships, guns, ammunition, were all available—why not use them? He painted the advantages of success in gorgeous colours.

"The striking down of one of the hostile Empires against which we are contending, and the fall to our arms of one of the most famous Capitals in the world, with the results which must flow therefrom, will—conjoined with our other advantages—confer upon us a far-reaching influence among the Allies, and enable us to ensure their indispensable cooperation. Most of all it will render a service to an Ally unparalleled in the history of nations. It will multiply the resources and open the channel for the re-equipment of the Russian Armies. It will dominate the Balkan situation and cover Italy. It will resound through Asia. Here is the prize and the only prize which lies within reach this year. It can certainly be won without unreasonable expense, and within comparatively short time. But we must act now and on a scale which makes speedy success certain."

This was the dazzling opportunity opened to the War Council by the persuasion and brilliant eloquence of one of its members. Ministers were in a frame of mind that inclined them to jump at anything which would offer a means of escape from the stalemate in France. They cannot be blamed. Every consideration—political, economic, humanitarian—underlined the urgency of some speedy and decisive success. The prospect of a "break through" on the Western Front had become ever more remote. They would have been more than human had they been able to smoke their cigars like Bismarck and leave the soldiers alone.

For some time Kitchener had been convinced that the break through was impossible. He wrote to Sir John:

"The feeling here is gaining ground, that, although it is essential to defend the line we hold, troops over and above what is necessary for that service could be better employed elsewhere . . . what are the views of your Staff? . . ."

The Commander-in-Chief sent a long reply to the general effect that as France was the main theatre of war all our resources in men and guns should be turned in that direction; he was opposed to diversions of any kind.

On January 2 the British Ambassador at Petrograd telegraphed that the Russians, being hard pressed by the Turks in the Caucasus, begged for a demonstration against Turkey in some other direction. This gave Mr. Churchill an opening to bring forward his favourite scheme.

"Demonstration" seems to have been the fatal word which lured Kitchener into the first stage of agreement. A "demonstration" would not interfere with the main theatre of war in France and would not commit us to anything. But this was as far as he intended to go. He wrote to Churchill:

"I do not see that we can do anything that will seriously help the Russians in the Caucasus. The Turks have evidently withdrawn most of their troops from Adrianople and are using them to reinforce their forces against Russia, probably sending them across the Black Sea. We have no troops to land anywhere. The only place where a demonstration might have some effect in stopping reinforcements going East would be the Dardanelles. We shall not be ready for anything big for some months."

This was perfectly plain. And this was the first stage of the Gallipoli adventure.

After the demonstration had been promised the First Lord telegraphed to the man on the spot, Admiral Carden, to ask for his views as to the practicability of forcing the Dardanelles by the use of ships alone. On January 13 his reply was produced. It was to the effect that "it was impossible to rush the

Dardanelles, but that, in his opinion, it might be possible to demolish the forts one by one." And on this "Lord Kitchener thought the plan was worth trying. We could leave off the bombardment if it did not prove effective." But he stated that there were not and would not be for some months any troops available for the operations. Lord Fisher, First Sea Lord, said nothing. "Some of those present at the meeting left without having any very clear idea of what had or had not been decided."[1] Mr. Churchill, however, understood that the Admiralty was to prepare plans for a naval bombardment in February.

At this moment the Chancellor of the Exchequer, Mr. Lloyd George, produced a rival scheme which centred round Serbia and later on involved us in the Salonika adventure. Serbia was being threatened by Austria. Greece promised to join the Allies and move to the defence of Serbia on the condition that Allied troops should first be sent to her assistance. The advantages of having Greece on our side were strongly emphasized. The cost would be very small, so small as to be barely noticeable; just one Regular Division, the 29th, and perhaps one Territorial Division. Kitchener agreed that these should be sent. But on February 15 Greece suddenly refused to join the Allies after all. The Serbian adventure was dropped for the time being.

Another step, however, had been taken on the downward path to Gallipoli. Originally the Secretary for War had said that no troops were available; now he had offered the 29th Division. As it could not be used in Serbia why not send it to Gallipoli? Not to take the forts—the Fleet would do that— but to exploit success when they were taken. And by this time the Anzac Corps was assembling in Egypt. Why not send that too? As soon as Constantinople had fallen the troops could come to France.

According to Mr. Churchill, "the genesis of this plan and its elaboration were purely naval and professional." It should, however, be noted that Lord Fisher, though he had not denied

[1] Report of Commission, p. 21.

the possibility of forcing the Dardanelles, was entirely opposed to the plan, and by January 25 had made his position clear on this point. For all practical purposes he was left out of the proceedings and arrangements were made direct with Admiral Carden, who commanded the ships in the Ægean Sea.

February 16 is an important date. Up till then the discussions had been vague and the Commissioners found difficulty in declaring what actual decisions had been taken. But on February 16 it was definitely settled at a meeting of the War Council that:

(1) The 29th. Division should be sent to Mudros to be ready for operations in the Dardanelles.

(2) Preparations should be made for a Force to be sent from Egypt to the same place.

(3) The Admiralty should arrange transport and the various tugs and horse-boats required for the landing.[1]

The naval demonstration had thus grown into a combined naval and military operation. After the War Council had given assent all the details should have been left in the hands of the technical experts. They could have worked out joint plans to secure the two objects which form the essential part of every attack—first that the weight of all available forces should be applied simultaneously, and second, that the enemy should be surprised. Unfortunately no attention was paid to either of these two essential points. The attack was made piecemeal, and the Turks were given full warning. As early as November 3, 1914, British and French ships had bombarded the entry to the Dardanelles, apparently for the purpose of testing the range of the guns in the forts. The effect was that the Turks very naturally took steps to improve their defences in every way; batteries were masked; fresh mines were laid down. It is true that this extraordinary mistake was made before the definite decision taken on February 16. But even after that date the orders for the naval bombardment were allowed to stand, although it was known that the troops would

[1] O.H., *Gallipoli*, p. 68.

not be on the spot for at least a month. It was, as we have seen, on February 16 that the War Council agreed to the dispatch of troops. The naval bombardment began on February 19, without waiting for the troops.

It is evident that Mr. Churchill did not think that the troops were indispensable. And on March 2 he wrote to Kitchener:

"I have now heard from Carden that he considers it will take him fourteen days to enter the Sea of Marmora counting from March 2. I wish to make it clear that the naval operations cannot be delayed for troop movements."

The operation of February 19 was entirely the affair of the Navy and Admiralty. Nevertheless it is not possible to absolve Kitchener from a share of the responsibility for the subsequent disaster. His consent to the use of troops should have been accompanied by an absolute condition that no action should be taken by the Fleet until the troops were on the spot. There was still a possibility of effecting a surprise if plans were carefully made. The Anzac Corps was in Egypt; its embarkation, ostensibly for France, would be a natural proceeding, and need not have pointed to Gallipoli. At the same time the 29th Division could have been embarked in England, ostensibly to relieve the Anzac Corps in Egypt—also a perfectly natural proceeding. Meanwhile the Fleet could have made a demonstration in some other direction. Then, when all was ready, a sudden concentration would have had some chance of catching the Turks unawares.

The second naval bombardment, which began on February 19, was broken off a few days later without effecting anything.

The dispatch of the 29th Division was delayed by disturbing news from other quarters. The Russians were doing badly; Joffre was afraid that if they gave way the Germans would soon be turning their attention to the West. Kitchener still regarded the Gallipoli expedition as a subsidiary one which must not be allowed to jeopardize the situation in France. He therefore decided that the 29th Division could not be sent eastwards until better news had been received. This led to an "acute difference of opinion with Churchill," who although he would not wait for troops was very anxious to have them; he considered that Kitchener had pledged himself and had no right to detain the Division. On March 10, however, the situation was more reassuring, and once more orders were issued for the embarkation. Kitchener was able to inform the War Council that the "forces available against Constantinople" would be approximately 128,700 men. In this number there was included a Russian Army Corps—about which the information was very indefinite. The other troops were the Royal Naval Division, the 29th Division, the Anzac Corps, and one French Division.

Sir Ian Hamilton was appointed to the command and the instructions given to him were dated March 13. They opened with the statement: "The Fleet have undertaken to force the passage of the Dardanelles."

March 13 is another important date. By this time the troops were definitely under orders, the commander was appointed, and the date of the concentration could be worked out exactly. But once more the naval attack was launched, on March 18, without waiting for the land forces.

Just previous to this Carden fell ill and his second-in-command, De Robeck, took charge. The attempts to force a passage was a failure; out of sixteen ships engaged three were sunk and three were crippled. De Robeck reported that several forts had been silenced; the casualties were 100 British, 600 French; the battleships lost were of obsolete type and of no great value. The failure was due to an unknown minefield and some masked batteries.

Mr. Churchill has argued that the operation might have led to complete success had the 29th Division been on the spot. It could have landed under cover of the guns; many of the forts could have been occupied; a firm footing could have been gained at all events on the south end of the Peninsula; observing posts could have been established to direct gunfire on the forts at the Narrows. Perhaps the Turkish defences would have collapsed altogether. All this may well be true. The Commissioners evidently agreed that the 29th Division would have been of inestimable value. Their report says with reference to its detention: "The favourable moment was allowed to lapse." They appear to have considered that this was Lord Kitchener's fault. But Kitchener was not responsible for the action of the naval authorities. Information about the troops had been given to the Admiralty on February 16 and on March 10. On March 2 the First Lord had told the Secretary of State that the naval operations could not be delayed for troop movements. It is not easy to come to any other conclusion than that the indispensability of the land forces was not perceived until after the ships had failed.

The disappointment was heavy, but the First Lord would not give up hope. A few obsolete ships would be a small price to pay for Constantinople. He urged that the attack should be resumed at once, but did not go so far as to issue a definite order. De Robeck, on reviewing the situation, decided that another attempt would only result in further losses without bringing success; and this opinion was backed by Lord Fisher, Admiral Sir H. Jackson, and the Admiralty. The naval attack was therefore abandoned, and De Robeck began to concert plans with Ian Hamilton for landing the troops.

This again marks a very distinct stage in the growth of the expedition. It was now to be a military attack under cover of naval guns. The object was to secure the high ground overlooking the narrows of the Dardanelles; once the heights were in our hands the forts could be silenced, and the Fleet would then make another attempt to get through. The cost, far from being negligible, would be high, and, even more important, it had become an accepted decision that there could be no withdrawal. Failure could not now be thought of. Our prestige in the Near East was at stake; the Russians were clamouring for help; Italy, Bulgaria, Greece, were hovering on the brink of war and their action would be influenced by the event. It was no longer a gamble with a small stake. It was a case of unlimited expenditure to avoid total loss.

As soon as Ian Hamilton arrived he got into touch with the officers who had been studying the local conditions—De Robeck, from the naval point of view; Sir J. Maxwell, who commanded in Egypt, and had all the latest information about the Turks; Birdwood, commanding the Anzacs, who had been consulting the Fleet and examining the ground. None of these officers had any illusions about the difficulties in front of them. Before the naval attempt of March 18 both Maxwell and Birdwood had expressed serious doubts about its chances of success. Hamilton himself inspected the position on the day of the naval attack, and reported in the following terms:

"*March* 19. Yesterday we steamed close along the whole western shore of the Gallipoli Peninsula. There are landing places here and there but except at Cape Helles all are commanded by elaborate networks of trenches. . . . Enemy are entrenched line upon line behind wire entanglements, sometimes fifty yards broad."

The defences were more formidable than anything we had yet encountered in France because the trenches had been carefully sited and ample time had been available to construct them. Very different were the conditions on the Western Front, where digging had to be done under constant fire and the trenches were patched up as opportunity occurred.

But in spite of these obstacles Hamilton was not without hopes.

The dismal story of the successive attacks, only relieved by the heroism of the troops, has been retold many times. I do not propose to recall more than is necessary to explain Lord Kitchener's subsequent action. The first landing took place on April 25. By the magnificent effort of the Fleet's boats 29,000 men were landed on six beaches, from Cape

GALLIPOLI

Helles to a point thirteen miles round the coast which became known as Anzac Cove. After fourteen days' heavy and continuous fighting the advance had been pushed foward in some places about 5,000 yards. But the dominating height, Achi Baba, was not reached, and the hopes that the position could be rushed were now extinguished.

Kitchener then asked Hamilton what reinforcements he would require in order to break down the Turkish resistance. The reply, dated May 17, asked for two Corps, considerable drafts for the units already there, and a large amount of ammunition. This marked another stage in the growth of the expedition. Reinforcements on such a scale would mean that the Gallipoli campaign, far from being a side-show, must be regarded as a major operation. The diversion of so many troops would make a very appreciable difference to our strength in France, and consequently to the plans of Joffre and Sir John French, who wanted to know what they could rely upon in the way of new Divisions.

No immediate decision was made because at the end of May the Liberal Cabinet gave place to a coalition, and the new Ministers were busy settling into their places. Mr. Churchill handed over the Admiralty to Lord Balfour, and Mr. Lloyd George became the head of the new Ministry of Munitions. The Dardanelles question remained in abeyance till June 7, when Kitchener brought three alternatives up for discussion.

(1) To withdraw.

"This would put an end to an operation the difficulties of which had been under-estimated . . . but the actual tactical operation of withdrawal would be one of great difficulty and danger, involving certainly much loss of life. . . . More permanent disadvantages would be the abandonment of all hope of further co-operation from the Balkan States, the surrender of Constantinople to Germany . . . and last but not least, a blow to our prestige which would resound throughout every portion of our Empire and create serious difficulties and dangers for us in every Moslem country."

These fears were generally entertained at the time. Lord Kitchener cannot be blamed for sharing them. But it is curious that while his foresight amounted to genius in other matters, such as the duration of the war and the creation of the new armies, in the case of the Dardanelles he was no wiser than others. In the end the withdrawal cost only one life, and no serious dangers arose in Moslem countries.

(2) To seek an immediate decision. This meant giving Hamilton the reinforcements he wanted. Men and ammunition could only be spared at the expense of the Western Front.

(3) To continue to push on and to make such progress as was possible. This involved no immediate blow to our prestige and kept alive hope, a rather forlorn hope, of something happening in the Balkans.

The decision of the Council was to send out three Divisions of the new army. Three Territorial Divisions had previously been dispatched. The total strength of the expedition now came to eleven British and two French Divisions.

Throughout June and July fighting had been practically continuous without result. Proposals had been mooted for a landing on the Asiatic side of the Straits but were eventually dropped. Hamilton decided to use the three new Divisions for a surprise landing in another place, Suvla Bay, four miles north of Anzac Cove. While this was being done a general attack along the whole line was to hold the attention of the Turks.

The landing was effected on August 6. Hamilton claimed that the big operation very nearly succeeded, and would have succeeded if the attack at Suvla Bay had been pressed with more energy. But the Divisions of the new army were tried very high. In France fresh troops were gradually brought into line, generally into a quiet sector, and were given time to settle down and learn to take care of themselves before being thrown into big attacks. This could not be done in Gallipoli; new Divisions were put ashore to face the full blast of fire for the first time in a pitched battle. Thy suffered intensely from thirst and from all the discomforts which can only be overcome by experience. They were tired and bewildered. In spite of some extraordinary gallantry the big battle was another failure. Hamilton reported that the Turks had now 110,000 men opposed to his own 95,000; for another general attack he would need new formations as well as drafts. His total further regiments came to another 95,000 men.

Upon this Kitchener reluctantly came to the conclusion that success was beyond our reach. And this marks yet another stage of the expedition; the only question now remaining was whether to evacuate or to hold on. Hamilton thought evacuation would be disastrous—"It would not be wise to reckon on getting out of Gallipoli with less loss than that of half the total forces as well as guns, which must be used to the last, stores, railway plant and horses."

It was this terrible forecast from the man on the spot which delayed the decision. A loss of life can be faced in a battle where there is a possibility of something to be gained, but to give up all those attractive hopes and at the same time to lose perhaps forty thousand men, required more resolution than the Government could yet muster. The decision was delayed from August to December.

During these months various expedients were proposed. The French Government offered to send four Divisions under General Sarrail to make a landing on the Asiatic side. But Joffre was preparing an offensive and he succeeded in holding up this offer until the result of his offensive should be known. Then the Salonika project came up again and the French decided to withdraw from Gallipoli altogether. Advice was asked from various quarters. General Munro was sent out to relieve Hamilton and report "whether in his opinion, on purely military grounds, it was better to evacuate Gallipoli or to make another attempt to carry it." He arrived in Mudros on October 27 and four days later he sent in his report. The pith of it was contained in two sentences: "It is my opinion that another attempt to carry the Turkish line would not offer any hope of success. . . . On purely military grounds I recommend the evacuation."

In search of comfort the Government turned to Robertson but got little of it. In a very outspoken memorandum dated October 25 he pointed out that the first essential in war is to settle where the main decision is to be sought. This had not yet been done.

"Having settled this, keep it in the first place and subordinate everything else to it. . . . It seems to me that if you lose the war in the west you lose it all the world over . . . I should have thought that the Dardanelles Expedition was no longer serving any useful purpose. Its object was to open up the Bosphorus and Dardanelles, but with both Turkey and Bulgaria against us we can hardly hope to do that . . . Personally I should advise withdrawal, firstly, because if I do not withdraw I shall probably be driven into the sea before I can prevent it, and secondly, I am serving no useful purpose where I am . . . Withdrawal undoubtedly means loss of men and material, though perhaps not so much as is imagined . . ."[1]

The advice of these two experienced Generals was, however, not immediately accepted. Hesitating to confess failure the Government requested Lord Kitchener to go out and study the situation on the spot, in the hope that he might find some alternative to evacuation. But before we come to discuss the problem which confronted him in Gallipoli, it is necessary to turn to other events, in France and elsewhere, which had a bearing upon it. The conclusion forced itself upon him that further sacrifice would be useless. Orders were issued to evacuate the Peninsula. The operation was carried out very successfully on December 20 and January 9.

It may make for clearness to recapitulate the various stages of the Expedition.

(1) A demonstration by ships alone. Object to assist Russia. Carried out on February 19 and March 18.

(2) Addition of an auxiliary force of troops. Object, to occupy Constantinople after the Fleet had forced the Dar-

[1] Robertson, I, p. 134.

danelles. This was detailed and dispatch began on March 10.

(3) A land attack. Object, to capture the high ground above the Narrows and thus enable ships to get through. April 25 and following days.

(4) A further and bigger land attack. Object, to avoid loss of prestige. August 6 and following days.

(5) An occupation of the southern fringe of the Peninsula. Object, to avoid the casualties involved in evacuation and to postpone the confession of failure. August to December.

(6) Evacuation. December 20 and January 9.

Who was responsible for the failure? Mr. Churchill has described the Gallipoli Expedition as a legitimate gamble. Everybody admits that there can be no such thing as certainty in war. Risks must be faced, and therefore every operation is to some extent a gamble. But it is only legitimate when success will pay the cost and when adequate measures have been taken to ensure success. In Gallipoli the first of these conditions was fulfilled—success would have been worth even more than we paid. The second condition was not fulfilled. Mr. Churchill says: "Not to persevere, that was the crime." [1] But surely the crime had been committed earlier. There were indeed two crimes. The first was the fatal miscalculation about the fire of naval guns. This was excusable. Robertson puts his finger on the real and inexcusable crime. "The first essential in war is to settle where the main decision is to be sought . . . having settled this keep it in the first place." This was never done. The Expedition began as a subsidiary operation with a naval bombardment; it grew, by patchwork, into an operation of the first magnitude.

Whatever Lord Kitchener's share in the responsibility may have been, it was not his alone, nor (we may think) primarily his. But since he lost his life before the sittings of the Dardanelles Commission began, we cannot know how he regarded the matter as he had no opportunity to defend himself.

[1] Churchill, 1915, p. 169.

CHAPTER XXIII

SHELLS

THE GRAVEST charge that has been directed against Kitchener, in fact the only one that was published during the war, was that of failure to ensure an adequate supply of munitions in neglect of the warnings and applications which came from General Headquarters.

Sir John French devoted the last chapter of his book to this subject; he was clearly under the impression that the fault was due to the negligence of Kitchener.

"From the beginning of the Aisne up to the close of the battle of Loos, at the end of 1915, the scanty supply of munitions paralysed all our powers of initiative and at critical times menaced our defence with irretrievable disaster . . . I exhausted every effort by urgent official demands in the W.O. and personal appeals to Lord Kitchener and such other Cabinet Ministers as I came into contact with. When these efforts got no response I gave interviews to the Press. . . . During my term of office as C.I.G.S. from March 1912 to April 1914 I had urged the vital necessities upon the Government, but my demands were steadily opposed by the Finance Department and the Treasury."

The Press correspondent to whom Sir John refers was Colonel Repington, who represented *The Times*. In many ways he was a privileged individual. He had been in the Army; after passing through the Staff College he saw service in Egypt and held appointments in the Intelligence Branch of the War Office and as Military Attaché at The Hague. Thus he had not only expert knowledge but an intimate acquaintance with the higher ranks of the Service. Sir J. French, Sir A. Paget,

Sir J. Cowans, and Sir A. Murray were among his friends, and he took care to make the most of their friendship.

His diary, like that of Henry Wilson, is very outspoken, but in the eyes of some people it loses much of it value on account of the many pages which he devotes to the lighter side of London Society. Every day he took lunch with a countess at the Ritz, tea with an actress (Lydia Kyasht or Doris Keane), dinner with a duchess at the Carlton; he describes bridge and tennis parties, theatres, and the charms of his lady friends. All this, however, was part of his job as a journalist. Politics and personal intrigues were big factors in the war and Repington was a keen student of both these subjects. When would Sir John French be recalled, and who would replace him? What had Churchill or Lloyd George said about Gallipoli? When would compulsory service be introduced? These were the topics of conversation at every dinner table. Duchesses and countesses were not seldom able to impart "exclusive information." Such sources of knowledge are not to be despised by an ambitious journalist who has the good fortune to find them at his disposal.

But Repington was something more than a mere gossip monger. He knew his way round the corridors of the War Office and had the entry into other offices in Whitehall. Even people like Kitchener and Robertson, who did not want advertisement for themselves, were ready to make use of the Press to educate the British public. As soon as Kitchener had taken command he set himself to awaken the nation. In an interview he gave Repington an outline of his proposals which duly appeared in *The Times* of August 15. But though the new Minister of War was a member of the Cabinet he had very little knowledge of party politics. He did not know that Liberal editors, with a Liberal Government in power, expected to get "inside information" at least as soon as, if not sooner than, other newspapers—even *The Times*. The gift of exclusive information to *The Times* was therefore a breach of party tradition. Repington of course knew this, but it was no part of his business to enlighten the simple soldier. After the article had appeared the indignant editors complained to the Prime Minister, who explained to his Minister of War the nature of the offence.

Kitchener no doubt realized that advantage had been taken of his innocence. At all events he was careful not to repeat the offence, and he refused to see Repington again. This, however, was another error of ignorance on his part. He failed to realize that finding his door was shut the journalist would have to go elsewhere in search of information and might possibly fall into the company of his enemies. This was what actually happened. Repington went off to Sir John's mess at General Headquarters and made himself useful and agreeable. He was allowed to visit the troops; he picked up the views of the officers, and was shown a good deal of the working of the Staff. He did not accept all the views of General Headquarters, in fact he by no means supported the theories of Wilson and the French, but in respect of the shortage of guns and munitions he became the mouthpiece of the Commander-in-Chief. We need not discount his motives. "I was determined" he says "to expose the truth to the public, no matter at what cost." [1] But it is not very clear what the "cost" could be, unless it was Lord Kitchener's reputation—an asset of some importance to others besides Lord Kitchener.

How was it that Sir John arrived at the conclusion which he has stated so definitely? By the end of 1914 the trenches were practically continuous and fixed. The line had never been chosen with a view to defence, it simply marked the positions in which the foremost troops happened to be when the two sides had fought themselves to a standstill. In many places it could be overlooked or enfiladed from the enemy's side. By the aid of aeroplanes a map was compiled showing in full detail the system of trenches on both sides. This map became the joy of the Staff and the curse of the Regimental Officer. An advance on our line for even fifty yards was hailed as a victory; a loss of fifty yards of untenable mud generally meant that somebody was *dé-gommé*. Any proposal to draw

---

[1] Repington, I, p. 36.

back for fifty yards in order to get on to firmer ground, or to avoid casualties from enfilade fire was a dastardly crime. It is difficult to explain why, after the long retreat of 150 miles, there should have been such desperate anxiety over a few yards of mud. But so it was.

The case of the Ypres Salient is the most outstanding example. When the battle fizzled out on November 21 our front line formed a big salient with its apex at Zonnebeke, 5 miles east of Ypres. Early in the year the British forces had been reorganized into two Armies, commanded by Haig and Smith-Dorrien. The II Army took over the Ypres section. Owing to the many casualties which occurred in the Salient suggestions were made for a withdrawal to a line further back. This would have been easy. Before the move the new position could be dug, sand-bagged and wired in a way that would make it comparatively comfortable. The communications with Ypres would no longer be subject to concentrated fire from three sides. Since the town was already within range of the German artillery it would not have suffered further harm than before.

Sir John French, however, could not see anything except the weakness of surrendering ground. A letter which he wrote some time later is a clear indication of his ideas. He was being pressed, as usual, to take over more line from the French, and was writing to explain that he could not spare troops:

"I understand that it has been suggested that in order to obtain the required troops for the relief of Castelnau's Army we should withdraw from the Ypres Salient. I am very strongly opposed to such a withdrawal . . . it would involve the abandonment of a greater extent of ground than has ever been voluntarily resigned to the enemy. The moral effect on our troops and on the Belgians would be very bad; it would shorten the German lines more than our own. . . ."

This is precisely the sort of opinion that might be expected from anyone who looked at a map but never spent a night in the "Bloody Salient." "It would shorten the German line more than our own." I will not stress the point that the Germans, having plenty of guns, did not keep so many infantry as we did in the trenches. The curse of the Salient was not in the front line, though that was bad enough, but in the approaches to it. From Ypres to Zonnebeke there was no cover of any kind; every night fatigue parties had to carry ammunition, rations, water, sand bags, to the line; for the whole of the way they were under concentrated fire from three sides. Of course the Germans were not under the same disadvantage. "The moral effect on our troops would be very bad." As a regimental officer I can assert emphatically that a straightened line, far from lowering the morale, would have raised it. Our men were ready to face fire when they could get to grips with the enemy. During that nightly trudge to the trenches they saw nothing, and could make no reply. They hated it.

Smith-Dorrien was always ready to listen to any suggestions for saving casualties or lessening the discomforts of his men. He knew what they were suffering and I believe he favoured a withdrawal. But that would have spoilt the map; and the French might have made scornful remarks. So we hung on to the Salient until the German gas attack in April straightened it out for us. On May 2 the Commander-in-Chief wrote:

"It has now become necessary to retire our forward line. This operation is now in progress and the new line will have the effect of retiring the east end of the Salient about 2,500 yards to the west."

The II Army said "Thank God no more Zonnebeke for us." But the map had to be corrected and somebody must suffer for that. Smith-Dorrien was sent home.

It was the determination not to yield a foot of ground that first gave rise to complaints about the shortage of gun ammunition. Our men were sitting in ditches, misnamed trenches, under the fire of artillery which sent over about half-a-dozen rounds to every one of ours. This heavy handicap was the subject of discussion in every billet, and Repington heard about it wherever he went. But he reserved the use of his information until matters came to a head. They were brought to a head by the failure of the offensives undertaken in the early part of 1915.

Joffre was determined to maintain an offensive attitude. As France had already put her full strength under arms, he saw little reason for any delay; like Wilson he had no great faith in the shadow armies. He believed that the German line could be broken— "Les événements ont prouvé que tactiquement on peut rompre le front allemand." Sir John French said, "My views are in complete agreement with those of General Joffre." Though Kitchener was content to wait for results till his new armies could take the field he saw that an attitude of passive defence would re-act badly on the Russian situation, and in view of the opinion of the two Commanders he could not discourage their plans for the Spring of 1915.

The first offensive started on March 9 and is known as the battle of Neuve Chapelle. It was really a small affair large as it seemed at the time. The I Army attacked with the 7th, 8th and Meerut Divisions. The first results were satisfactory; after a bombardment the infantry advanced and took about two miles of line, penetrating to a maximum depth of 1,000 yards. We lost 12,000 men and consoled ourselves by computing the German loss at 15,000 to 16,000. There could be no question about the gallant fighting of the troops, and from that point of view the operation can justly be called the glorious battle of Neuve Chapelle. The final results, however, were not glorious. An excuse had to be found for failure. The excuse found was lack of shells and particularly of high explosive shells. Henceforward it became the excuse for everything.

Undeterred by this setback the Commanders began to lay plans for what Sir John calls the *"big* operation." There were many difficulties to be overcome. Joffre continued to demand, rather imperiously, that the British should take over more of the line. This meant "spreading out thin" and trusting to the

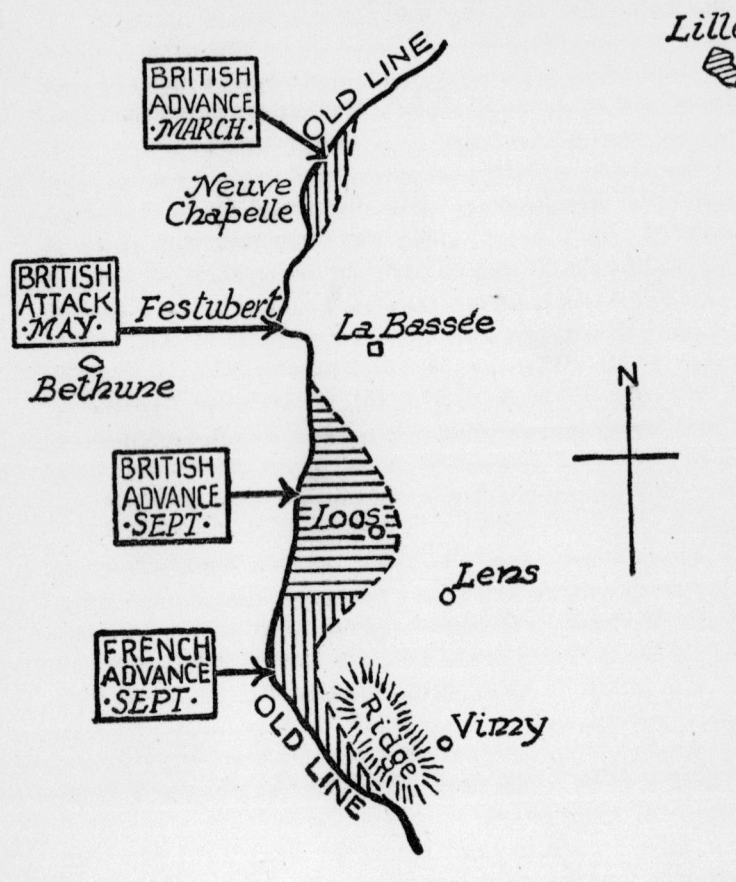

French to bring up reserves if the Germans attacked in strength. Sir John insisted that the British line must be self-supporting, and the reliefs were constantly put off.

Another cause of delay was the gas attack on April 22, which, but for the heroism of the Royal Canadians, might have led to disaster. Several days went by before the line could be arranged. It seems pretty evident that neither of the Commanders was quite as ready as he wished to appear, and each was inclined to make the other responsible for the delay. But finally the arrangements were completed for a combined attack by the I Army, under the immediate command of Haig, and by the French on our right under Foch.

On May 9 was launched the attack known as the Battle of Festubert. It was probably the worst setback we ever had in France. In later offensives we had learnt by bitter experience not to expect too much, but on this occasion we expected or at least hoped for everything. It is necessary to lay stress on this point in view of what happened afterwards. A few quotations will reveal the hopes entertained at General Headquarters.

Wilson's Diary. *April* 10. "This morning Robertson came to my room and we had a long discussion about the coming attacks. We have 10 Divisions and 600 guns, of which a hundred are heavy. Foch has 14 Divisions and 950 guns of which 230 are heavy. I can't help thinking we ought to succeed. . . ." [1]

There is more to the same effect, but not one word about shortage of ammunition.

Sir John French to Lord Kitchener. *May* 2. "I was with Foch some time this morning and am now making all arrangements for the *big* operation . . . the ammunition will be all right." [2]

The troops of the I Army were equally hopeful. I met many of them soon afterwards. All agreed that they had gone over

[1] Wilson, I, p. 222.
[2] Arthur, III, p. 236.

the top in the best of spirits, expecting, after the terrific bombardment, that nothing would be left in the German trenches but corpses.

Foch, having plenty of ammunition, shelled the position for twenty-four hours before launching his infantry attack. Haig had less ammunition and kept it for one heavy burst; he believed that Foch by beginning twenty-four hours earlier would give the enemy time to collect reserves opposite the French attack, and perhaps they would thin out the line opposite Haig. It was calculated that forty minutes shooting at the rate of nearly a thousand rounds a minute would clear the wire and prepare the way for infantry. Our attack would come as more of a surprise than that of the French.

Everything was carried out according to plan, but without any success. Our infantry got into the front trench at several points. Then German guns opened and blew them out again. By the evening the I Army had lost 10,000 men and was badly shaken by the failure. The accumulated store of shells was practically used up; and even the big-scale map could not show the smallest advance anywhere. The French, who had nearly four times as much ammunition to expend, made some progress at very heavy cost. In the hope that the Germans had exhausted most of their ammunition Foch made some further attempts on the following days, but at no time was there any prospect of a break through.

Sir John came back to General Headquarters bitterly disappointed with the result. There he found a telegram from the War Office which served to increase his ill-humour. It ordered him to hold twenty thousand rounds of shells in readiness for dispatch to Gallipoli. The reason for this apparently strange request was that a ship was waiting at Marseilles ready to start for Mudros. Sending the shells from the reserve in France would mean a saving of time; they were replaced immediately from England.[1] In view of what had happened to the French attack it is absurd to suppose that these shells

---

[1] O.H., 1915, p. 331. The 20,000 shells were replaced on May 12 and 13. 2,000 rounds of howitzer shells replaced on May 16.

would have made any difference in the result of the battle. But naturally enough the telegram came as a shock to the Commander-in-Chief. He interpreted it to mean that deliberate measures were being taken to thwart him; and he determined to make his protest to the British nation.

Repington had been present to watch the attack, and the failure gave him the opportunity for which he had been waiting. He sent off a telegram, which appeared on May 14, stating that "the want of an unlimited supply of high-explosive shells was a fatal bar to our success." *The Times* published a leading article which attracted much attention, but did not fix the blame on Kitchener. The *Daily Mail*, however, made a direct attack on the Secretary of State. Though Repington was not directly responsible for this, there can be little doubt that it was inspired by his view, which he was repeating all over London.

In the course of the following week the Cabinet was rearranged on a Coalition basis. How far this change was due to the shortage of shells is a matter of argument; only those in the confidence of Mr. Asquith knew the truth and their accounts do not seem to be always in agreement. The Dardanelles Expedition had given rise to recriminations. Fisher had insisted on resigning his position as First Sea Lord. The question of conscription was becoming urgent. Though Unionists had refrained from any definite action that would embarrass the Government, criticism could not be altogether repressed. Asquith may have felt that it would be better to admit Unionists to a share of the responsibility, and turn the leading critics into colleagues. It is possible the question of shells may have brought the matter to a head. But Sir John French thought that the question of shells was the only effective factor, and declares that it was his action which brought about the fall of the Government.

Colonel Repington claims for himself the credit of arousing the nation to a sense of its danger. "Away the fateful telegram went, containing in one little phrase enough high explosive to blow the strongest Government of modern times into the air."[1] In publication his message had been shorn of some of its details. "I had been furious about the censoring of the telegram, and hastened to London to expose the facts ... I neither minced matters nor concealed my feelings." He saw Lloyd George and several of the Unionist leaders. It was known that he was a friend of Sir John French and that he had come direct from General Headquarters. Everybody was therefore ready to listen to his denunciations. Their substance can be given in his own words: "Kitchener did not comprehend the importance of artillery, took no effective measures to increase our supplies of it, and concealed the truth from his colleagues in the Cabinet."[2]

This imputation of wilful ignorance, carelessness, and deliberate concealment of the truth must be considered in detail.

"Kitchener did not comprehend the importance of artillery."

The importance of artillery was a revelation to everybody. Even the Germans, who had made a careful study of the effect of guns in the Russo-Japanese War, were soon forced to increase their heavy ordnance. Like everybody else, Kitchener had to revise his estimates from time to time. But the original miscalculation was made in the first place by the very people who afterwards brought the charge against him. Sir John French and Henry Wilson had been at the War Office before August 1914. They both claimed to have foreseen the war and to have made preparations for it. But the question of ammunition had certainly been treated very lightly. Sir John claims that he "had urged these vital necessities upon the Government but his demands were steadily opposed by the Finance Department." This was of course the common fate of proposals for military expenditure. It would be interesting to know what his demands had amounted to. He might have asked for 100,000 rounds. These would

[1] Repington, I, p. 37.
[2] Repington, I, p. 34.

certainly have been useful, but they fade into insignificance compared with what Sir John calls "a reasonable demand" for August 1915, which came to over 900,000 rounds *monthly*. When war was declared the Finance Department had no longer any right of veto. If Sir John had then urged the "vital necessity" of an enormous increase in ammunition his opinion would have carried tremendous weight. During the meetings at the War Offices and in Downing Street in August 1914 he could have put forward his demands as Commander-in-Chief. It is true that those meetings were chiefly occupied with the immediate question of mobilization. But a matter of vital necessity could surely have been raised. Munitions were, in fact, not mentioned at them.

Henry Wilson had been Director of Military Operations for four years. His Diary contains about seventy pages devoted to that period. There are countless entries on the subject of preparing the British Expeditionary Force for war; demands for horses, transport, railway time-tables, and so forth. There is one short entry of two lines on the subject of munitions: "Haldane is inclined to fight Johnnie French over a demand for ammunition which we three Directors have put forward. We will knock him." [1] But after that the subject was apparently dropped. Even when war was declared Wilson seems to have had no anxiety on the subject—at all events there is no mention of it during the first six months.

These were the two men on whom had rested responsibility for preparing for the war which they regarded as inevitable. I do not suggest that they can be blamed for their lack of foresight, because the war produced conditions which surprised everybody. But they had no conceivable right to throw stones at Kitchener. If their estimate had been accepted—that six Divisions would be the limit of our contribution and that the war would be over by Christmas—there would have been neither men nor shells at the time when Sir John made his complaint.

[1] Wilson, I, p. 112.

The second charge, again in Repington's words, is that Kitchener "took no effective measures to increase our supplies."

It was the first duty of the Secretary of State to watch the needs of the Army, many of which could only be learnt from actual experience in the field. It was his duty to accept the opinion of the men on the spot. There is no doubt that General Headquarters made urgent appeals for more shells. Did Kitchener take any "effective measures"?

The question is difficult to answer because the answer depends upon the meaning of "effective measures," and on a mass of information of a very intricate and technical kind. Fortunately the Official History has dealt fully with the subject; its figures and facts are based on the secret files in the office of the Master General of Ordnance.[1] They show that while Kitchener was planning to raise the Army to a strength of seventy Divisions he did not forget that an equivalent increase must be made in munitions. France and Germany had calculated for the maintenance of large forces and therefore their factories were numerous and well equipped; skilled labour was plentiful. But in England the delay in production arose from the fact that before guns and shells could be made the plant must be erected for their manufacture.

Without going into details of the growth of the work we can take a short cut by comparing the state of munitions at two dates. In August 1914 there was one Government Ordnance Factory in England, at Woolwich. The estimated production of shells, with the assistance of private firms, amounted to 30,000 rounds a month. By October 1915 orders had been placed in the United Kingdom by the War Office which involved over 2,500 manufacturers; production amounted to 1,200,000 rounds a month.

At this later date the supply was under the control of the Minister of Munitions, Mr. Lloyd George, who took full credit for the result. The British Commander-in-Chief evi-

[1] See O.H., 1914, Introduction, and 1915, Chap. III.

dently thought that no credit was due to anybody else. He wrote:

"The successful solution of the problem came when Lloyd George applied to it that matchless energy which has enabled him to come through the great ordeal as England's most valued leader in her direst hour."

But the truth is that those 1,200,000 shells which were delivered in October had all been ordered before the Ministry of Munitions came into existence. The Official History sums the matter up in these words:

"The foundations of the great organization which, in later years of the War, was to give the Army not only a sufficient but an almost embarrassing supply of munitions may be said to have been well and truly laid." [1]

The third, and not the least serious, charge in Colonel Repington's indictment was that "Kitchener concealed the truth from his colleagues in the Cabinet."

Now it was not the business of civilian members of the Cabinet to study the technical side of munitions, the difference between guns and howitzers, between shrapnel and high explosives. Very probably the Minister of War had said little to his colleagues on these subjects. But they could not plead ignorance of the fact that there was a shortage. Sir John himself had said that he made personal appeals to such Cabinet Ministers as he came into contact with. At Walmer Castle in December 1914 he met Asquith and "the question of munitions and the fear of invasion formed the basis of our long conversation." Other Ministers had the subject brought more immediately to their notice because a Cabinet Committee had been formed in October, including Mr. Lloyd George and Mr. Winston Churchill, to study the resources of the country. They had access to all information, including the secret files which gave par-

[1] O.H., 1915, p. 38.

ticulars of the contracts placed and the estimated production; they knew the deficiencies of plant, furnaces, materials, and labour. If they had remained in ignorance it would have been due to carelessness on their own part. But neither of them has supported Repington's statement or made any suggestion that Kitchener concealed the truth. Mr. Churchill has done full justice to the Secretary of State in this respect.

Repington taking his tale of distress to Lloyd George "was astonished at his ignorance of the facts." There were two facts of which Mr. Lloyd George was no doubt ignorant: first that a bombardment of 40,000 shells made little impression on the German defences; secondly that Kitchener had ordered 20,000 rounds to be dispatched to Gallipoli. One may conjecture that he expressed some surprise on hearing about this, and that Repington jumped to the conclusion that Kitchener had deliberately concealed the truth. Mr. Lloyd George's "ignorance" was one ground for the charge. Another was a public utterance of the Prime Minister. "Mr. Asquith, immediately before, doubtless on the faith of false information supplied to him, had declared at a speech in Newcastle, that we had no lack of shells." [1] It is true that the Prime Minister had used words to that effect, but his information came from no less authority than the British Commander-in-Chief. The newcastle speech was based on the following letter from Kitchener.

"MY DEAR PRIME MINISTER,

I have had a talk with French. He told me I could let you know that with the present supply of ammunition he will have as much as his troops will be able to use in the next forward movement."

Kitchener could scarcely have made a mistake about such an important statement, but if any confirmation is necessary we have only to turn to Sir John's written words

[1] Repington, I, p. 39.

on May 2—"The ammunition will be all right." As in the case of the Paris interview Sir John seems to have forgotten his own words, or at all events he did not realize the impression those words must leave on the minds of other people. Repington, ignorant of what French had said, assumed that Asquith had been primed with false information by Kitchener. But it is impossible not to conclude that though Sir John had been complaining about the shortage of shells he had managed to accumulate what he considered sufficient for the "big operation," and that he believed the attack would succeed.

There are few situations so distressing as that of a Commander who sees a carefully built plan come crashing to the ground. The loss of ten thousand gallant lives, the shock of personal as well as national failure, the revelation of the enemy's unsuspected strength—these were enough to shake the strongest nerves. Sir John was a man of moods. He had been thrown into black gloom by the Retreat and the "shattered II Corps." Indignation had mastered him at the "interference" of Kitchener in Paris. His spirits soared on the promise of the Marne. During the first months of 1915 he fretted at the diversion of troops to Gallipoli and the rejection of some of his own plans. The "big operation" was to put everything right, to confirm his position, to justify his forecasts. The collapse of his hopes made him only too willing to put the blame on another man's shoulders.

It seems that Repington, no doubt unwittingly, was the villain of the piece. He was entirely ignorant of the steps that were being taken to build up the supply of munitions, he knew nothing of the conversations and letters which had passed between Kitchener and French. In fact he knew only what was obvious to everybody on the spot—first that the Germans had more shells than we had, and second that the attack at Festubert had failed. When he found Sir John in a state of distress he was ready with the comforting suggestion that the failure was due to causes beyond the control of General Headquarters. Kitchener had taken no effective measures to increase the supply of ammunition. Sir John then realized that this was the cause of all the trouble and his disappointment gave way to righteous anger. He decided "to take drastic measures to destroy the apathy of a Government which had brought the Empire to the brink of disaster."

Repington's attack, in which he "neither minced matters nor concealed his feelings" missed fire as far as Kitchener was concerned. But for a few days there was a possibility that it might succeed. The Cabinet had to face a strong Press campaign and was apparently willing to throw Kitchener to the wolves if it could save itself. Mr. Churchill says:

"Up to Monday it had been determined that Lord Kitchener should be transferred from the W.O. . . . but on Tuesday it was realized that his hold on the confidence of the nation was still too great for any Government to do without him."

After that his position was stronger than ever. The country knew that he was the man who had created the New Armies without which there could be no hope of victory—and that outstanding fact was sufficient to establish him as the one man who could carry us through. The King conferred on him the highest honour of Knighthood, the Garter, as a token of unwavering trust.

The attack must have aroused in Kitchener astonishment more than any other feeling. He had in his pocket the letter which would have been a full and convincing answer to the charge—"The ammunition will be all right."[1] It would have confounded his critics and annihilated his accusers. But with Kitchener the greater always included the less. The one thing that mattered was the steadfast pursuit of victory. Until that was achieved there was no time for

[1] The letter is in Arthur, III, pp. 235–6. I am not aware that it had previously been published.

recriminations. He did not even remind Sir John of the latter's own words, and contented himself with an order that Repington should not be allowed to visit General Headquarters again.

Though the charges against Kitchener were unfounded it must be admitted that the Press campaign did good in other ways, in rousing labour and the country generally to a fuller sense of the efforts required. The Ministry of Munitions was virtually in existence when the War Office handed over its functions. Its machinery had been constructed; what Mr. Lloyd George brought to it was oil to make the wheels run more smoothly. His subordinates were not afraid of him, as they were of Lord Kitchener. He had the power of infecting them with his own enthusiasm; he appeared to welcome those who had to be granted interviews, he caught at suggestions. When the statistics are examined they show that the increased supply of munitions was the most wonderful of all our efforts in the war. If Kitchener laid the foundations Mr. Lloyd George is not without a substantial share of the credit for the completed building.

CHAPTER XXIV

SALONIKA

The second attempt to find a way round was through Salonika. For three years it dragged out its weary length; all through 1916 while the struggle was going on at Verdun and the Somme; through 1917 while British troops were pouring out blood at Passchendaele in the heroic effort to save the French; through 1918 to the very end. But though it lasted all that time and was mixed up with many other things it can best be understood if we regard it as an interlude.

Salonika was the pet project of M. Briand, and his own words show it in the most attractive form. The following extract is taken from *La Loire Républicaine,* one of Briand's organs, dated August 1919.

"C'est en janvier 1915, exactement le 1er. janvier, que M. Briand, qui était alors garde des sceaux et ministre de la justice dans le cabinet Viviani, a fait au président de la République et aux membres du gouvernement la proposition d'organiser, en collaberation avec les Anglais, une expédition de 300,000 hommes qui, débarquant dans un port de l'Adriatique serait allée joindre les Serbes, dont l'armée venait de remporter sur les Autrichiens une grande victoire, consacrée par la prise de plus de 50,000 prisonniers.

L'idée fut adoptée en principe par les membres du gouvernement, mais MM. Millerand, Ministre de la guerre, et Delcassé, Ministre des affaires étrangères, ont fait des objections et ont demandé que le G.Q.G. fut appelé à donner son avis. Il en fut ainsi décidé.

Quelques jours après, le G.Q.G. addressait au gouvernement un rapport dans lequel il concluait a l'impossibilité absolue de cette expédition.

Plus tard, la Bulgarie ayant attaqué la Serbie et celle-ci

se trouvant en péril, on dut envoyer des troupes à son secours, mais il était trop tard; elles ne purent pas joindre l'armée serbe, qui fut menacée d'une destruction totale. C'est alors que les Anglais voulurent renoncer totalement à toute intervention dans les Balkans et ramener les troupes en France. Beaucoup d'hommes politiques étaient de cet avis, et l'on se rapelle toutes les attaques violentes qui furent dirigées contre M. Briand, alors devenu président du conseil, lorsqu'il persistait à maintenir les troupes françaises envoyées l'a-bas, à en augmenter le nombre et à obtenir des Anglais qu'ils consentissent à suivre cet exemple.

On sait qu'il parvint à triompher des résistances du maréchal Kitchener, et c'est là la veritable origine de la grande expédition de Salonique qui, dès l'année 1916 libéra le canal de Suez des entreprises de la Turquie, barra à l'empereur Guillaume II la route de Constantinople, sauva l'armée serbe de la capitulation et permit de s'emparer de Florina et de Monastir.

Pendant ce temps nos alliés russes, libérés des troupes turques rappelées vers Salonique, s'emparait en Arménie d'Erzeroum et de Trébizonde; les Anglais reprenaient Kout-el-Amara, et prenaient Bagdad; et le roi de Hedjaz, rompant avec les Turcs, se rangeant à nos côtés, s'emparait des Lieux-Saints et de la Mecque, ce qui eut, dans le monde mussulman de nos possessions algérienne, tunisienne et marocaine, une influence considérable.

Une outre conséquence—et non des moindres—de l'expédition fut que la Roumanie déclara la guerre à l'Allemagne."

The above extract is valuable because it shows that the war policy was decided in Paris in much the same way as in London. That is to say, the Minister of Justice proposed the plan, the other Ministers, with two exceptions agreed; *after* that the project was referred to the Military Staff; the Grand Quartier Général reported the "absolute impossibility of this expedition"; but the civilian Ministers became so fascinated with the bait that they continued to nibble at it; finally the expedition was launched.

On our side of the Channel the procedure was very similar. In January 1915 the project was put forward by the Chancellor of the Exchequer, Mr. Lloyd George. He had come to the conclusion, as he afterwards told Robertson, that the soldiers were lacking in imagination, and he evidently intended to supply them with some. He imagined the entire British Expeditionary Force withdrawn from France, "where it was doing no good," and transported bag and baggage to the Balkans. This was at least a thoroughgoing proposition. Apparently he could get his colleagues of the Cabinet no further than imagining what Joffre and the French would say when the proposal to withdraw all British troops from France was put to them. That was enough. The thoroughgoing proposition was dropped, and that was the end of Mr. Lloyd George's first essay in imaginative strategy.

After that the General Staff wrote many papers on the subject of Salonika. It is only necessary to quote two or three of the main arguments to show that our soldiers were in complete agreement with the Grand Quartier Général that the expedition was impossible.

The first obstacle was geography, which nothing could alter. Robertson says:

"A tour made in the Balkans in 1906 had convinced me that of all the countries in Europe none was defensively stronger and therefore none less favourable to offensives than the Balkans." [1]

The only harbour connected with a railway is Salonika. Thence the line runs north to Belgrade, 350 miles. As far as Nish, 220 miles, it is single, badly laid, easily demolished; beyond Nish it is doubled; rolling stock is very limited. Under war conditions the railway would of course be demolished if it was intended to contest an advance. The country is hilly, roads are few and bad. No force of any

[1] Robertson, II, p. 88.

size could be supplied at any distance from the railroad. There was therefore only one possible line of advance and no wide manœuvre could be thought of. Even under the most favourable peace conditions a single Division would take over a month to reach Belgrade.

This consideration led to the second argument, that there could be nothing in the nature of a surprise. The forces must be provided with special equipment and transport for mountain warfare; and ships must be collected. All this would take time, but by good management secrecy might be maintained up to this point, and during the voyage the destination would remain unknown. But once the first troops were ashore there could be no further concealment; and before they could hit the enemy's army or invade his territory two, three or more months must elapse.

The geography and the impossibility of surprise were impassable objections from a military point of view, quite apart from the question of what the enemy might do. This question of course led to many ramifications. If we advanced with a small force the enemy could concentrate a larger force to smash it. If we took a large army the enemy might retire without fighting and force us to prolong our line of communications until eventually the army was brought to a standstill by its own unwieldiness. Here the difference between Salonika and Gallipoli is accentuated. In Gallipoli the Turks could not retire even twenty miles without giving up positions which would open the gate to Constantinople; they must therefore fight and hold at all costs a position close to the shore. The battle could be fought on the very day of landing. But at Salonika there was no vital reason why the enemy should hold any ground south of the Danube; he might even retire further north if the odds were against him. We could force a battle. That means that the initiative was left to the enemy. He could choose his ground; he would have full information of our numbers, and ample time to make and carry out his plans.

Nothing could be more advantageous to him from a military point of view.

There was one more argument of a definite kind. Entrenchments, barbed wire, and modern firearms had proved to be insuperable obstacles in France. We should certainly meet with the same obstacles in the Balkans, or in Austria, or indeed anywhere. Therefore the "way round," far from being any easier, would probably be more difficult, because our army, with guns and munitions, would have to be transported by ship, rail, and march to some indefinite spot about 3,000 miles from England, there to attack the same kind of entrenchments and perhaps the very same troops, as might be found within a hundred miles of our own coast. The disadvantage of those 3,000 miles is obvious. Reinforcements could not be rushed out to meet a sudden emergency, forces in Serbia could not be brought back to meet an emergency in France.

Though the first proposal was dropped it continued to reappear in minor shapes. The first of these was inspired by diplomacy. Greece was wobbling. King Constantine's position was an uneasy one. Whether he really wished to join Germany is doubtful; he may have only wanted to be left in peace. But German diplomatists were not without strong arguments. Though the mailed fist was some distance away, Turkey and Bulgaria were uncomfortably near. There were three courses open to Constantine, and each course had its peculiar danger. If he joined Germany he would be safe from Turkish and Bulgarian menaces, but exposed to the British Navy. If he threw in his lot with the Allies—which was the policy urged by the Prime Minister, Venezuelos, and his supporters—he would have to reckon with Turkey and Bulgaria. If he remained neutral, he would have to face the probability—as events proved, the certainty—of Civil War.

On January 20 an important telegram was received in London from Athens. Greece would join the Allies provided that she was given direct military assistance and was assured of Bulgarian neutrality. The advantages of having Greece on the side of the Allies was undeniable. The Greek Army was said to have a strength of 200,000; Serbia had also 200,000; with some additional troops from England and France the Allied forces in the Balkans would amount to over half a million. It seemed reasonable to spare a couple of Divisions for such an object. Mr. Lloyd George went in haste to Paris to arrange for co-operation with the French, who undertook to send one Division if we would do the same. Kitchener agreed to this and ear-marked the 29th Division for Salonika.

Scarcely had this arrangement been made when the situation was radically altered. Bulgaria was evidently preparing to join the Central Powers with an army of 250,000. This seemed to put Serbia in a helpless position, especially as no hope could be expected from Rumania or Russia. And if Serbia was crushed out of existence Bulgaria, with perhaps some aid from Austria and Turkey, might proceed to invade Greece. It is scarcely surprising that Constantine retracted his former promise and refused to come in. The definite threat of an invasion weighed more than the vague promises, which were all that the Allied diplomatists could offer.

Up to this point the whole idea of a Balkan campaign had been offensive—a movement of half a million men to invade Austria, to overawe Bulgaria, to encourage Rumania. Without Greece, however, an offensive was out of the question. The proposed expedition was in consequence cancelled.

Negotiations went on throughout the summer of 1915 without any material result. Then Bulgaria made a definite declaration, and the Central Powers decided to crush Serbia. The Germans had been disappointed in their hope of decisive victory in 1914. When the stalemate set in, like ourselves they began to look for a "way round," for a cheap victory to revive the spirits of the people. They were connected with the Balkans by rail; and constant transference of Divisions between France and Russia had brought their railway organization to a high state of efficiency. With this valuable machinery in their hands the German High Command naturally sought to make use of it.

The German move had been foreseen by the War Office in London. The forecast ran on the following lines. A force of 200,000 could be collected opposite Belgrade in a few days and without any warning. The capital of Serbia would be occupied at once—a first success, of no military importance but still a visible success. The Bulgarians would then come in on the south-east and the Serbian Army would have to retreat in haste to avoid being hemmed in. The whole of Serbia would be overrun before the Allies could furnish any assistance—a second success, cheap but spectacular. Greece and Rumania would remain neutral for fear of sharing the fate of Serbia. Subsequent events would depend on the action of the Allies. If an Allied force could be lured to Salonika so much the better. That would weaken the Allied front in France; while, as soon as the Allies were thoroughly committed to a campaign in the Balkans, the German Divisions could be taken back to France, Russia, or anywhere else where they might be needed.

Besides this tremendous military advantage there was yet another which the Germans were probably clever enough to reckon on. The military advisers of the Allies might argue against the campaign, but some of their statesmen would probably argue for it. There would be an acute division of opinion, which at best might cause tension between London and Paris, and at worst would introduce an element of indecision into the Allied strategy. This, far from being a cheap and minor success, would be something of real value. The German objects were therefore clear enough—to take Belgrade and overrun Serbia; to encourage Bulgaria and Turkey; to overawe Rumania and Greece; and to sow dissension in the Allied Councils. The cost was calculated at 200,000 German and Austrian forces, which could quickly be withdrawn by train if required elsewhere.

It is natural to argue that if all this was actually foreseen, it would have been worth our while to make a real effort to prevent it happening. But it was not in our power to plump down 200,000 men at Belgrade at short notice, and without ample warning to the enemy of our intentions. It is of course impossible to say what might have happened if we had embarked resolutely on the adventure before Bulgaria mobilized and before the invasion began. But, as in the case of Gallipoli, it can be said very definitely that a belated attempt was a bad compromise.

The German plans were carefully matured. The wily Monarch of Bulgaria continued to write diplomatic notes which kept up the pretence of neutrality until his mobilization plans were complete; not till all was ready were diplomatic relations with the Allies broken off and the double invasion of Serbia from north and east launched. It began on October 7. The Serbs, menaced in front and in their flank, fell back rapidly. By the 27th they had been driven westwards off the railway towards Durazzo, and Uskub was in the hands of the enemy. It was evident that no troops from England or France could arrive in time to be of any practical use. But something might still be done to save the remnant of the Serbian Army and to keep Greece in a state of neutrality. The ostensible argument for intervention was that our national honour was involved; our Ally, unhappy little Serbia, was at the mercy of the enemy. Whatever the military experts might say, something must be done.

The real argument, however, seems to have had its root in the couloirs of Paris. It is dangerous for an Englishman to pretend to unravel them without assistance. I take temporary refuge, therefore, under the wing of a clever French interpreter, M. Renaud, who did his best to instruct me in these matters at the time.

I cannot resist the temptation to interpolate a picture of Renaud. A typical French Anglophile, he had become well known and very popular in our Brigade. His death from a stray shell in Arras, in 1916 was a real loss to the British

Army. He was a man of considerable ability. After taking high honours at the Sorbonne he had spent a couple of years in Manchester to perfect his English as Frenchmaster in a Grammar School. He loved the English schoolboys who called him "Froggie"; he loved Rugby football; but above everything he worshipped King Edward VII, the greatest monarch that ever wore a crown, "un vrai Roi Soleil." Once, at Longchamps, where he was Secretary to the Racecourse, King Edward had shaken his hand on the occasion of a gala meeting. This was his happiest memory. Up to that glorious day he had waxed his moustache and carried a tuft on his chin. When it arrived he went to a coiffeur and said *"Coupez mois à l'Anglais,"* bought a new top hat (of English make) and practised walking backwards up and down the steps of the Royal box. This was "ver' difficult," but fortunately not required of him. However, he gave us a nightly performance of the whole scene. It became known as the *Répétition Général,* and always got a rousing encore. When war broke out Renaud was forty years of age and too fat for the trenches; also he knew nothing of soldiering, for his two years of compulsory service had been spent as a clerk in the Commandant's Office. Fortunately for us, they made him an interpreter. In the mess he smoked a pipe and English tobacco, and even cultivated a taste for whisky. But for all his Anglophilism he remained a red-hot French patriot, fiercely jealous of his country's honour, and enormously interested in French political movements.

"You ask me of French politics, *mon cher*—we have none. But we have politicians, and each great man has many little men to follow him. So in Paris there are groups. In England you have two great parties with a line between them, and a change of Government means a change of principles, a *renversement*. With us it is different. The Cabinet makes a mistake and must be reformed—*bien,* but there is no change of principles, only an exchange of portfolios; no *renversement,* only a little sidestep one pace to right or left. A group from the right disappears, a group from the left arrives and there is the new Cabinet. Paris is *malcontent* at present because there was not a *bonne bataille* in Champagne." Renaud was talking after the autumn offensives of 1915, "One must not blame the Army. One must, however, blame someone. The groups begin to talk. Now that our Ally in Serbia is attacked, we can talk of that. A group on the left will talk loudly; then there will be a side-step to the left. But do not be afraid—there is no change of principles in the hearts of Frenchmen, only a change in the Président du Conseil."

"But look here, Renaud, what about those newspapers you brought from Paris? They had some nasty things about Joffre."

"Those"—Renaud's contempt was magnificent—"Those *L'Homme enchaîné* and *L'Œuvre*. They are nothing. Or rather they are very useful. You remember your journals have made an attack on Kitchener—and every Englishman was immediately on his side. That was good. And now the same thing happens in France. One reads *l'Œuvre* over the aperitif, and hands it to one's neighbour. 'See, monsieur, how the Boche has been spending money here in Paris to throw stones at our good Joffre. *Nous sommes trahis*. Eh?' But we know better. Let these *scélérats* throw the stones, Joffre will be all the stronger. In fact he could not have written anything himself that will do him more good. We must have a little change. That is all."

The forecast was correct. At the end of October Viviani gave place to Briand, and Renaud declared that the French Army was well satisfied with the change. "He is clever this Briand. He is the friend of Joffre and the Army, but we must stop the talk of the Cailloux group. Alors—an expedition to somewhere, with Sarrail in command. Sarrail has been *dé-gommé*, but he is a friend of the Socialists and must have a command. One must send him somewhere. If he does well, *bon;* if there is nothing, *bon;* at least the Socialists will not be able to talk when their own General has failed. Meanwhile they will let Joffre and the Army alone and we shall have the *bonne bataille* next year. But you English must help. If you refuse there will be too much talk, Briand and Joffre will be in danger."

Of course Renaud knew nothing of the many conferences which were going on in London, Paris, Calais. But the account of the Salonika adventure given by Sir William Robertson agrees very well with my friend's conjectures. Robertson himself was entirely opposed to the scheme. In his opposition he had the support of the General Staff and of French as well as British military opinion. He says:

"As to military opinion practically all the leading French Generals with whom I was brought into contact, including Joffre, Foch, and Pétain, showed, in manner if not in actual words, that they intensely disliked the project from the start and would be glad to see the end of it."

A majority of the Cabinet held the same view, though a few of them were still ready to vote for anything in preference to further offensives in France.

It is important to note that the first proposal from Paris did not concern Salonika; the suggestion was that four French Divisions under Sarrail should support the Gallipoli expedition by making a landing on the Asiatic shore of the Dardanelles. As the French had been totally opposed to the Gallipoli expedition the sudden change of policy was surprising and significant. It confirms the conjecture that a command of some kind had to be found for Sarrail. The proposal was checked by Joffre, who was engaged with his autumn offensive and wanted every man for it; he succeeded in stipulating that the four Divisions should not leave France till after the battles of Loos and Champagne.

Then came the invasion of Serbia. Paris suddenly lost all interest in the Dardanelles and switched on to Salonika. This still further supports the conjecture that the original aim was to find a command for Sarrail and that the actual destination of the expedition was a secondary matter. But if the decision was made in Paris on political grounds, it could, of course, only be recommended to the British Government on strategical grounds.

The new proposal gave rise to furious argument in London. Although the French refused further troops for the Dardanelles, and insisted that we should relieve two Divisions of theirs which were already there, Mr. Churchill still believed in the possibility of reaching Constantinople. The General Staff preferred anything to Salonika and put in a strong memorandum to that effect. Mr. Lloyd George preferred anything to "wasting life in useless attacks in France." Agreement was impossible, and the discussions ended in the astounding compromise that six Divisions should be withdrawn from France and sent to Egypt, their final destination to be settled later.

On October 25 the Chief of the Imperial General Staff, Murray,[1] went over to interview Joffre, who had hitherto been a sturdy opponent of all diversions. Murray certainly expected that Joffre would agree with the Imperial General Staff in opposing the Salonika scheme. But the disappointing result of the autumn offensive at Loos and Champagne had shaken the French Government and had altered the views of the French Commander-in-Chief. Far from opposing the Salonika adventure he now argued that we should reinforce it. Murray failed to make any impression on Joffre, who immediately afterwards came to London and on October 29 produced his plan before some members of the Government. The arguments were the same as before, except that some of the probabilities had now become facts. Where the Allied diplomacy had failed, the mailed fist of Germany had succeeded. Bulgaria had come in; Greece and Rumania would also come in on the German side unless we used force to prevent them. He proposed that the force at Salonika—now consisting of one British and two French Divisions—should be raised to a quarter of a million. When he found that the British Government was opposed to his plans he threatened to resign.

[1] Murray relieved Wolfe Murray as C.I.G.S. in September.

Joffre's visit marks the turning point of our policy in the Near East, and there seems to be little doubt that the strong attitude of the French Commander-in-Chief was the decisive factor. Robertson says:

"General Joffre reduced his first demand for 250,000 to 150,000 men, and realizing that even then he was making no headway he suddenly announced that unless British co-operation was sanctioned he would resign his position of Commander-in-Chief of the French Armies. This threat was the cause of some consternation."

The British Cabinet gave way. After that there was much wrangling over details, how many Divisions should be sent and where they were to come from; how much of the line we would afterwards be able to hold in France; whether steps would be taken to put extra pressure on Greece. Later on the General Staff made several attempts to have the expedition withdrawn entirely. But after the fall of the Viviani Cabinet and while Briand was Prime Minister, there was no possibility of persuading the French. In the event we remained there to the end of the war.

Sarrail, with the first of the French Divisions, disembarked in October. He pushed up along the railway to Krivolak, a distance of a hundred miles, but found that the Serbs had been driven westwards and the whole of the Bulgarian Army was facing him. He fell back and joined the British contingent. The combined forces took up a position about thirty miles north of Salonika, and their strength was gradually increased to eight Divisions. There for three years was maintained a force averaging about 250,000 men, monopolizing an enormous quantity of British shipping. One or two futile attempts were made to take the offensive, but never got further than a few miles.

Briand afterwards maintained that the Salonika Expedition was the decisive factor in the war. The article quoted at the beginning of this chapter ends by saying:

"Enfin, on sait qu'en 1918 ce sont les victoires éclatantes de l'armée d'Orient qu'ont fait capituler la Turquie, la Bulgarie et l'Austriche-Hongrie. Le mur qui protégeait, en Orient, l'Allemagne était tombé. Le maréchal Hindenburg écrivit la fameuse lettre dans laquelle il disait: 'Il ne nous est plus possible maintenant de résister. Il faut demander l'armistice.' "

It was natural that the Germans should seek to find an excuse for their defeat and that Hindenburg, whose wall in France was crumbling under the great attacks of the Allies, should throw the blame of failure on Turks or Bulgars or anybody except his own Prussians. The other side of the argument is that unless Foch and Haig and Pershing had kept up the pressure in France the German wall in the East would not have fallen.

What was Lord Kitchener's attitude towards the Salonika project? When the agreement was made on October 30 to undertake the expedition no decision had yet been reached about the evacuation of Gallipoli. It seems surprising that the Minister of War should have given consent to a second diversion in the East when the first had already involved us in such trouble. As Briand said, it was necessary to triumph over the resistance of Lord Kitchener. Evidently, therefore, he was in complete concord with his General Staff. Yet in the end he gave way to the pressure of Joffre. From a military point of view this looks like indecision and weakness. There was no fresh information, at least on the surface, which demanded a change of plan. Everything had been foreseen and discussed and argued; the declaration of war by Bulgaria did not come as a surprise; the probability of an Austro-German attack was only too obvious. The natural deduction is that we ought to have gone to Salonika sooner or not at all.

The clue to Kitchener's train of thought is to be found in the conversion of Joffre. Up to this moment, October 29, he had been the most violent of "Westerners"—of that there is no possible doubt. Yet now he suddenly changed and threatened to resign unless the Salonika project was supported by the British Cabinet. Perhaps the political undercurrents were deeper and stronger than they appeared on the surface. Henry Wilson was constantly in touch with Joffre, Foch, and some of the French statesmen. As early as August he was very anxious about some alarming rumours which he records.

"*August* 16. I had a long talk with Kitchener about the French political situation. He listened to all I had to say of the dangers ahead ... of these Valois and Caillaux groups wanting in reality to make peace, of the absolute necessity of our doing nothing to upset the French soldiers ... he told me he quite agreed."

Though Kitchener made use of Wilson to keep in touch with the opinion of Paris I do not think he would have based any important decision on the reports of that officer unless they were confirmed from other sources. We cannot tell what other private information was in his possession; what the Caillaux group intended and what power they had. But the important point is that if Kitchener believed in the dangers suggested by Wilson he could not have acted otherwise than he did. He had to make up his mind not on the facts as disclosed by history but on the information he possessed at the moment. If the Germans were seeking to sow the seeds of dissension between the Allies they had a fertile field in Salonika. Kitchener saw this, and his one object was to prevent them gathering that harvest. He knew that from a military point of view the expedition was unsound; it could not hurt the Germans; it would detain many Divisions which were urgently required elsewhere; it would put a heavy strain on our shipping. The one, the supreme, argument in its favour was that it would prevent the interruption of friendship between the French and British Cabinets.

Here we have the big distinction between Gallipoli and Salonika. The first diversion was proposed in the British Cabinet where Kitchener was then supreme; it was opposed by the French. Kitchener must be given a share of the blame, if not for consenting to it at least for failing to insist on proper preparations before the expedition set out. The second diversion was undertaken on the insistence of Joffre.

I hazard the conjecture that we have here a clue to Kitchener's attitude throughout the war. England's full strength could not be put into the field during 1915; he did not believe that victory could be won until the Allies could outmatch the Central Powers in numbers and munitions; until that moment arrived the general policy must be mainly defensive, and the great thing was not to leave unguarded any vital point at which the enemy might penetrate our ranks. Where did the greatest danger lie? Not in the front lines—after the thrusts at Paris and the Channel Ports had been repelled our trenches in France were fairly secure. The real danger lay further back, and the Germans knew it. Kitchener was familiar with the elements of weakness in his own country—the reluctance of Trades Unions to allow men to work overtime at munitions, the disputes over the "dilution of labour," strikes, pacifism, and the rest. Did Joffre's mission imply that there was an element of weakness in France, only to be rendered harmless by the sacrifice of military common sense? The grand old victor of the Marne was too proud to acknowledge the real cause of his anxiety. Did Kitchener see beneath the surface? Was the *mutisme*, which held them apart, in some mysterious way a bond between them?

If this conjecture is near the mark it explains much that is otherwise very hard to understand. The laws of strategy were thrown to the winds. But as Kitchener had said to Churchill, "Unfortunately we have to make war as we must, and not as we should like to."

CHAPTER XXV

THE WINTER OF 1915–16

AT THE beginning of November the Secretary for War set out on his mission to Gallipoli, arriving at Mudros on the 10th. The problem before him was complicated by the fact that we were now committed in so many other directions.

The autumn offensive in France, which included the battles of Loos and Champagne, had been started on September 20 and came to an end on October 15. There were no complaints about shortage of men or munitions in this case but a promising beginning on the first day was spoilt by the late arrival of the reserves, for which the staff has been sharply criticized. Once more the battle fizzled out. The casualties of the Allies were heavy—300,000 in the first week—but we know now that the Germans were badly shaken; from this time onward they could not afford to weaken their line in France. Kitchener had given his assent to the attack, chiefly on the ground that Russia was in trouble, but he had otherwise little to do with it.

With Mesopotamia he had still less to do. That campaign was in the hands of the Indian authorities, on whose representation the War Council decided on an advance to Baghdad. Kitchener uttered a warning that larger forces would be required—a warning that fell on deaf ears. The Cabinet was anxiously seeking a success to counterbalance disappointments in the other fields of war. General Nixon was authorized to go ahead.

Russia was short of munitions and could do nothing; Italy seemed to have found another stalemate beyond the Izonzo; Egypt was disturbed by the Senussi on the west; we were committed to Salonika, where the Greek Army might turn against us.

Such was the general posture of the war, when Kitchener arrived at Mudros. The problem which he had to solve was one of extreme difficulty. The dangers of holding on were many and serious. The Turks were in superior numbers, well entrenched. Without larger reinforcements an offensive was out of the question. Even to maintain the defensive was hazardous. Since Serbia had been overrun the railway to Constantinople was at the disposal of the Central Powers, and could be used to supply the Turks with munitions and gas, even perhaps reinforcements. The Germans might snatch advantage of the lull on the Russian front to stiffen the Turks with some of their own troops. A quite small addition to the enemy's forces would give him a good chance of throwing us into the sea. Our position, bad for attack, was still worse for defence because it had no depth. Our lines of communication lay upon the sea. The landing-places were on open beaches exposed to the blast of winter gales which might isolate the troops for days at a time. The shipping was under the peril of submarines.

Kitchener consulted long with the naval and military Commanders; he went round the lines and talked with officers and men; he looked at the crowning height of Achi Baba hedged in with rows of wire. The decisive factor in his decision was the fear of German reinforcements. That evacuation was necessary he could have no doubt; and he allowed no bitterness of regret to interfere with his decision or colour his mind. I believe that no writer, with the exception of Mr. Churchill, has questioned the wisdom of his decision.

Munro had not had time to make a complete study of a plan for getting the troops away. But Birdwood had been there from the first; he knew the ways of the Turks and he could be trusted to suggest the best means of keeping them in the dark while the movement was in progress. There was one comforting feature. Kitchener saw that the withdrawal would not be as costly as the first estimates had led us to fear.

THE WINTER OF 1915–16

The next problem was that of the effects which the evacuation would have. An army of about 125,000 Turks would be set free for operations elsewhere, and would probably be directed by the Germans against the Suez Canal. This was a matter of definite calculation. What could not be calculated was the effect of evacuation on the Mohammedan races of the Near East—Turks, Arabs, Egyptians. With all his experience in that part of the world Kitchener might have been expected to forecast this more accurately than he did. Events showed that his anxiety was exaggerated. But he was right to take every precaution, for the Suez Canal and Egypt were the vulnerable points which must be protected at all costs.

His plan was for an expedition to Ayas Bay on the coast of Asia Minor. A landing at that point would present no difficulty, and would be within reach of the railway which runs from opposite Constantinople south-eastwards to Alexandretta and thence southwards through Damascus into Palestine. By cutting this railway we should be able to hinder the advance of Turkish forces towards the Canal and we should be on the flank and rear of any which passed to the southwards.

From a military point of view this was a most inexplicable proposal. The defence of the Suez Canal was certainly all important. But the General Staff pointed out that the scheme had all the disadvantages of the Salonika project. The railway was not a vital point in the Turkish Empire, as Gallipoli had been; a force at Ayas Bay would not be within reach of Constantinople. The Turks, advised by the Germans, might, and probably would, leave us there in peace and turn their attention to Russia. A large British force would be locked up and unable to pull its weight. Shipping, munitions, supplies, all urgently required elsewhere, would continue to be diverted for no useful purpose. Nothing could suit the Germans better than the dissemination of our forces; already we had too much on hand outside the main theatre of war in France. Against these arguments Kitchener contended that the defence of Egypt on the Suez Canal was unsound. But the War Council supported the General Staff. He accepted the decision and started homewards, paying brief visits to King Constantine and the King of Italy on his way.

For some time it had been evident that a change must be made in the command of the forces in France. The blunder at Loos removed all reason for further hesitation. The Government took care to make the fall of Sir John French a light one—more care than he had taken himself in the case of Smith-Dorrien. He received a peerage, and was appointed Commander-in-Chief of the Home Forces. Sir Douglas Haig took over the command in France. This decision was made while the Secretary of State was abroad; Kitchener approved it. He would, indeed, have been forced to take the same step himself if it had not been done for him. But he must have felt glad that it was done in his absence.

The shuffle of high posts made it possible to bring Sir William Robertson home to the War Office as Chief of the Imperial General Staff. That was the beginning of a partnership which worked smoothly till Kitchener's death put an end to it. The task before the two men was not an easy one. The Government was showing its anxiety. Ministers were asking themselves why the soldiers could not produce some success to lighten the gloom. Unable to elicit any hopeful forecasts from the War Office, they went to work on schemes of their own; as Mr. Churchill artlessly says, "It was left to members of the War Council to write papers on the broad strategic view of the war."

Robertson knew something of the difficulties in front of him. He was an optimist, with great confidence that the Allies possessed both the will and the means which would ultimately lead to victory; he had unbounded admiration for the work Kitchener had done in raising the New Armies. At the same time he felt that the C.I.G.S. had not been given sufficient authority in shaping our military policy. He was not prepared to accept responsibility as professional head of all the land forces of the Empire unless he had the sole right of presenting schemes for the approval of the War Council. This subject was discussed fully and frankly with Kitchener in an interview which Robertson put on record.

"In the course of our conversation, which lasted for nearly two hours, he assured me that no action of his should prevent the condition from being fulfilled, and he asked me to disregard the prevailing gossip that he insisted upon keeping exclusive control of everything in his own hands. On the contrary he would be only too glad to rid himself of some of the work he had hitherto been compelled to do, if he could but find someone to relieve him of it. He described to me the tiresome and protracted discussions which took place in the Cabinet upon practically every question that came up for consideration, and the consequent delays experienced in obtaining decisions. He also referred to the hostility of some of his colleagues, who were continually endeavouring to thwart and discredit him in the eyes of the people, and were bent upon ousting him from the Cabinet at the first opportunity that offered.

"No soldier could be aware as I was, of the difficulties and personal animosities against which he was contending without wishing to assist him in surmounting them. It seemed desirable, however, before going to the War Office, that I should set down on paper for him to see what, in my opinion, the duties of the General Staff in future ought to be. He at once assented." [1]

After another conversation in Paris the Memorandum on the future status of the C.I.G.S. was finally approved. Its main points were three in number. First, the War Council was to be the supreme authority for the formulation of policy. Secondly, in order that the War Council

[1] Robertson, I, p. 164.

should be able to come to quick decisions all advice on military operations was to reach it through the channel of the C.I.G.S. Advice emanating from any other source was to be sifted and examined by the C.I.G.S. before being accepted by the War Council. Finally, all orders for putting into execution the policy adopted were to be issued by the C.I.G.S.

The most urgent question demanding attention was that of man power. The 70 Divisions were already in existence either at the Front or in training camps. But the wastage of men was calculated at something over 100,000 a month, and for some time it had become evident that voluntary recruiting would not supply the necessary drafts. Under the National Registration Act, which had been passed in July 1915, a roll was compiled of all persons in Great Britain (not in Ireland) between the ages of sixteen and sixty-five. On the basis of this information an estimate could be made of the numbers available for military service. In October an effort was made by means of the "Derby Scheme" to prolong the voluntary system, but with only spasmodic success. In January 1916 the first Military Service Act was passed, enforcing conscription on all single men and widowers between the ages of eighteen and forty-one.

Asquith, whose Cabinet was divided on this issue, had felt much reluctance in taking a step which might arouse opposition and give a handle to agitators. Workmen getting high wages, even for unskilled labour, might be expected to resist any legislation which would take them away from lucrative employment. The task of the Government would have been made easier if Kitchener and Robertson had consented to come forward with a definite categorical demand for universal service. But this they refused to do.

Robertson's attitude was natural and logical. As chief military adviser to the Government he repeated more than once a warning that the recruiting returns were insufficient, that units were below strength, and that the plans of Com-

THE WINTER OF 1915–16

manders were hampered by their ignorance of the numbers on which they could depend. When he was asked what force would be required to finish the war, his reply was "every available man." But in the same way that he disliked civilian incursions into the field of strategy he disliked military incursions into the field of politics. If statesmen would mind their own business he would mind his. It was their business, not his, to provide the men. His business dealt with training and strategy.

But Kitchener had not the same excuse for standing aloof. Though he was a soldier, like Robertson, he had accepted office as Minister of War; and with it the duty of providing for the upkeep of the Army. He himself had been the first to demand a national effort. He had made a personal appeal to the country, and he had fixed the establishment at 70 Divisions. It was therefore essentially his business to see that those Divisions were maintained at full strength. At one time he seems to have been ready to shoulder this responsibility. According to Sir George Arthur, who was certainly in a position to know, he had intended to take the matter into his own hands and demand the necessary legislation. He got into touch with the Labour Member of the Cabinet, Mr. Arthur Henderson, and secured a pledge that his proposal should not be opposed by the Labour Party as a whole. But before putting it forward he wished to exhaust all the possibilities of the voluntary system. In the meantime certain hot-headed patriots called clamorously on the Government to enforce universal service at once. Thereupon Kitchener practically washed his hands of further responsibility.

"I have been watching since January very carefully," he said, "for the moment when it would be necessary to come forward and it has been to me a most deplorable fact that this agitation has broken out, because, whatever I say now, I do not speak with as much force as I should have done had this agitation not arisen."

Sir George Arthur goes on to say:

"A difficulty was thus rendered still more difficult by the action of well-meaning zealots, and Kitchener's only course was to inform the Prime Minister of his precise military requirements, and leave it to him to frame the necessary political measures." [1]

This premature agitation was no doubt regrettable; it robbed his intended demand of the dramatic and personal touch which had been so great a factor in August 1914. But surely it cannot have been unexpected. Over two million recruits had been attested; their relations and friends, and the relations and friends of killed and wounded men, were certain to denounce the unfairness of a system which asked everything from volunteers and gave everything to shirkers. Compulsory service was, in fact, a burning question in the country at large, and the only surprising thing about the agitation was that it had not been more marked. If Kitchener remained unaware of it in the early months of 1915 he must have been very badly informed. Apart from this, the fact that the country was becoming aware of its duty was no reason why he should drop the matter. He could of course plead that statesmen of experience were better equipped than he was to deal with many of the problems of man power, such, for example, as the effect of conscription upon the vital industries. Yet if he looked upon conscription as a necessity—as he did—he ought not to have refused the responsibility of advocating it.

It is difficult to get away from the suspicion that he was influenced, no doubt unconsciously, by his conflict with the civilian members of the Government. While he was in Gallipoli an unmistakable hint had been given that they did not want him in the Cabinet. The War Council refused to accept his proposal for an expedition to Ayas Bay. He was well aware of their feeling towards him and told Robert-

---

[1] Arthur, III, p. 316 and footnote.

THE WINTER OF 1915-16

son that "his colleagues were continually endeavouring to thwart and discredit him in the eyes of the people, and were bent on ousting him from the Cabinet." He could scarcely be expected to make things easy for colleagues who regarded him with unmasked hostility. Let them find their own way out of their troubles.

Fortunately there could be no argument about strategy during the crisis which came early in 1916. Reliable information showed that the Germans were preparing a big offensive; Haig was instructed to support Joffre in any way that would suit the plans of the French. The battle burst on Verdun with all its fury on February 21. Pierrefeu has painted a vivid picture of the scene at Grand Quartier Général at Chantilly as the reports came in—the anxious whispers of the staff, the coming and going of Generals, Joffre, imperturbable, sitting astride a chair with his arms over its back, awaiting the news and issuing his orders. Those were anxious days, but Haig and Joffre were equal to the situation. The British Army took over trenches on both sides of Arras, thus making our line continuous from Ypres to the Somme. The French troops thus released were rushed to the danger-point, and the situation was saved.

It was unfortunate that Haig could do no more than take over the extra stretch of line. His big attack on the Somme could not be launched till July 1; had it been ready in March it would have caught the Germans before they had time to recover their breath. But his forces were too widely spread. The Divisions which had gone to Salonika left gaps which must be filled, and the last of the New Armies did not join him till the end of May. Eager as he was to strike he had no option but to hold his hand.

Even so, the French have admitted that without the help which Haig was able to give it would have gone hard with them at Verdun. At the beginning of 1916 the British Army in France numbered 1,210,000. Unless Kitchener had laid the foundation of the shadow armies at the very outset of the war it would not have amounted to more than a fraction of that total. Had he not done so the Germans might well have been victorious in 1916. Therefore it is not too much to say that France owed Verdun, and much more than Verdun, to Kitchener's foresight.

But, while Verdun was saved, another and a deadlier disaster was preparing elsewhere.

If we could forget for a moment the dark tragedy of Russia there would be amusement in comparing our notions of that country in the early days with what we know of it now. Before the war there was little love lost between the British and the Muscovite Empires. Our fathers had fought in the Crimea; we were brought up on stories of the horrors of Siberia, and Russian designs upon India. During the Japanese War our sympathies were all on the side of Japan until it became evident that Russia would be beaten. Hostility then became mild contempt for our hereditary enemy's lack of organization and military skill.

Suddenly in August 1914 we found that the Tsar had become our Ally, and hastened to revise our former impressions. During the first winter we cherished a pathetic faith in the steam-roller which was to pound its way into Germany from the east. When news from France was scanty and depressing we turned eagerly to the columns which military writers filled with praise of the Russian army, of its Generals who had learned the lessons of Manchuria, of the Grand Duke Nicholas—the first strategist of Europe, of the courage of Russian soldiers and the magnificent qualities of the Cossack cavalry. When the steam-roller appeared to be going the wrong way, we said that Russia was short of munitions—a shortage that would soon be remedied. Even after the crash of the Revolution it was believed that "Free Russia," having got rid of its traitors, would show her true value in the field.

The Secretary of State for War must have smiled grimly as he read some of those articles. Colonel (now General

THE WINTER OF 1915–16

Sir A.) Knox was Military Attaché at Petrograd. He knew as much then as we all know now, and his knowledge was, of course, communicated to the Government. It was a tale of treachery in high places, bribery and corruption everywhere, and a general condition of ignorance amongst the rank and file which made them easy prey for the forces of anarchy. When I went to the Russian Front just after the Revolution I was appalled by a degree of disorganization and indiscipline, in evidence on all sides, for which I was wholly unprepared. But a few hours in the office of the Military Attaché showed me that Whitehall had known everything from the first.

It must for ever remain a matter of doubt whether the Allies could have saved the situation by advice or any other form of help. The Russians, like ourselves and everybody else, needed a quick and brilliant success to keep up their spirits. Constantinople was always the object of their desire, and they wanted the Allies to keep up pressure in that direction. They failed to understand that if Germany was defeated all the rest would follow. They were hotly jealous of anything that savoured of interference. An Allied Mission, including Lord Milner and Henry Wilson, went to Petrograd in the winter of 1916–17, only a couple of months before the Revolution. They were feasted and covered with decorations, but they could do no more than suggest plans for co-operation and exchange compliments with their hosts.

Would Kitchener have done any better? He knew how serious the situation really was; he would not have been put off by bland assurances; his figure towered above all the other great men of the war. His word must have carried great weight. He knew, moreover, that the greatest weakness of the Russians lay not in their technical deficiencies—great as these were—nor in the front line. It lay in the absence of any middle party, strong enough to retain power, if the Tsarist despotism were deprived of it. If once the pendulum began to swing it would go unchecked right over; sudden freedom would only mean license and anarchy. Could Kitchener have prevented the pendulum from swinging?

A year later I knew well some of the early leaders of the Revolution, especially Miliukoff and Shoulgine. These men were actuated by patriotic motives. Their revolt was a revolt against treachery and incompetence exemplified in the higher ranks of the Army and by such officials as Sukhomlinoff, Sturmer, Polivanoff. When Russia laid down her arms in 1917 they bitterly repented that they had taken the first steps which led to that disaster. Miliukoff thought that if Kitchener had talked seriously with the opposition leaders he might have persuaded them to defer the Revolution at least until after the war; his assurances would have been accepted when those of Russian Ministers were scouted. The masses who refused to believe anything which came from official quarters had a curious, almost superstitious, faith in the word of the great English soldier. But it is hard to believe that Kitchener would have been allowed to get into touch with anybody outside the Court circle. All this is mere speculation. What matters is, that Kitchener recognized in Russia the weak link of the Allied chain. It became his business to see if he could strengthen it.

CHAPTER XXVI

THE LOSS OF THE *HAMPSHIRE*

SIR GEORGE ARTHUR says that "Kitchener—the secret of whose journey had been betrayed—was to fall into the machinations of England's enemies and to die swiftly at their hands." [1] It would seem that the author, who had the best sources of information, must have based this statement on some unrevealed evidence. But its vagueness has led to a number of quite unfounded conjectures. In view of these and of the many extraordinary stories which were current at the time of the disaster, it is still commonly supposed that some strange mystery surrounds the death of Lord Kitchener. There is, in fact, no mystery; and there was no connexion between the sinking of the *Hampshire* and any triumph of German espionage.

The dates are important. Early in May the Tsar sent Kitchener an invitation to visit Russia. On the 27th of that month a reply was dispatched to the Chief of our Military Mission in Russia stating that Kitchener hoped to arrive at Archangel on June 9. This notification was of course handed to the Russian Court, and as nothing could be kept secret in Petrograd at that time, in all probability it came to the knowledge of the enemy. But that could not have happened before May 28.

On June 4 Kitchener and his party travelled to Thurso by train and on the morning of the 5th crossed to Scapa Flow. He lunched with the Admiral, Sir J. Jellicoe, in the flagship, H.M.S. *Iron Duke* and afterwards embarked in the *Hampshire* (Captain Savill).

There were three possible courses for the *Hampshire* to take on the way to Archangel. The first, and most direct,

[1] Arthur, III, p. 354.

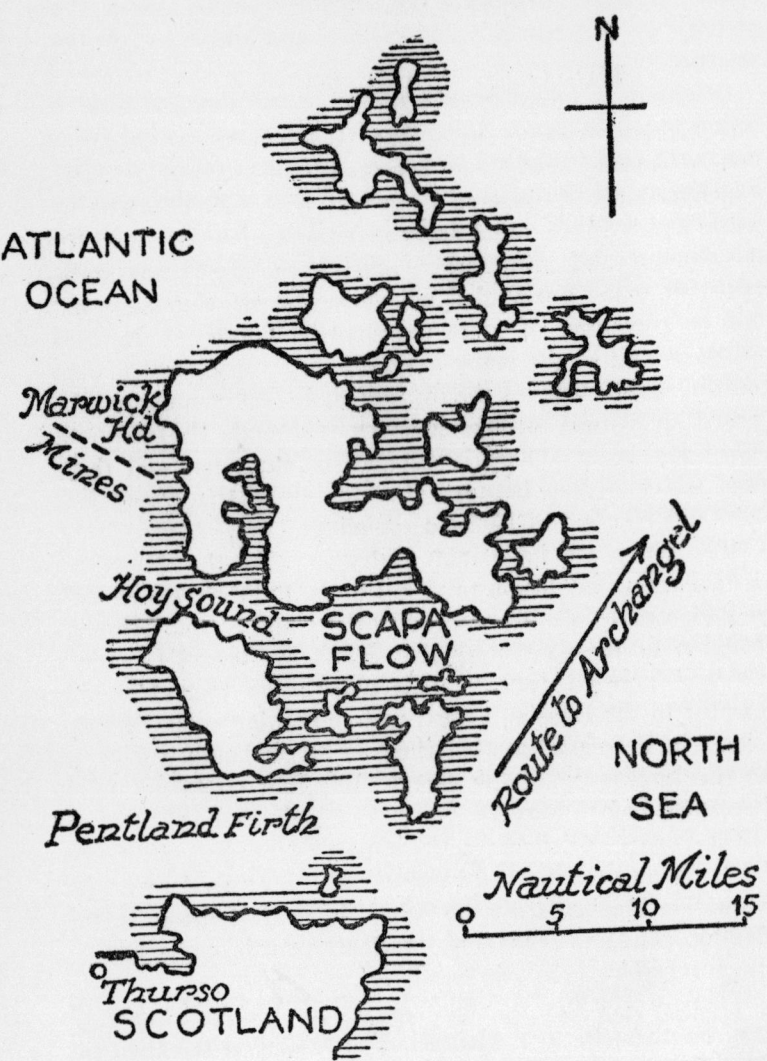

THE LOSS OF THE *HAMPSHIRE* 333

lay east of the Orkneys. The second lay westwards through the Pentland Firth to Cape Wrath and thence northwards. The third lay close along the west of the Orkneys. The choice of route depended on reports received about the activity of the enemy's submarines and the state of the weather.

Originally Captain Savill's sailing orders directed him to follow the first route. But during the morning a wind from the north-east freshened to a gale. An officer on duty in the flagship called the attention of the Admiral to the increasing heavy weather, but was told that Lord Kitchener would not hear of any delay. After serious consideration, however, the admiral altered his instructions and ordered Captain Savill to take the second route, which would be to some extent under the lee of the Islands.

The ship, with Kitchener's party on board,[1] got under way at a quarter to five in the afternoon of the 5th. She was escorted by the destroyers *Unity* and *Victor*. A little later the wind backed into the north and west, and as the head sea which it raised was too much for the destroyers Captain Savill ordered them back.

At about 7:40 p. m. there was an explosion which seemed to tear the centre of the ship right out, and in a few moments she went down. The disaster occurred about a mile and a half from Marwick Head, where the coast is wild and forbidding with dark cliffs rising sheer from the waves. Only fourteen of the crew escaped on Carley rafts, and of these two died from exposure before rescue parties could reach them. Some of the survivors stated that they saw a group of military men in the gunroom flat just after the explosion; another that he heard voices crying "Make way for Lord Kitchener," and another that Captain Savill's last anxiety was to get him into the galley.

---

[1] The party included Brig.-General W. Ellershaw, Lieut.-Colonel O. A. G. Fitzgerald (Mil. Sec.), Mr. H. J. O'Beirne, of the Foreign Office, Sir H. F. Donaldson, Mr. L. S. Robertson of the Ministry of Munitions, and Second-Lieutenant R. D. Macpherson.

The German official account, Vol. V, pp. 201-2, gives details about the laying of the mine. The High Sea Fleet was preparing to come out for the move which led to the battle of Jutland on May 31. The British Grand Fleet would of course concentrate to meet it. The object of the Germans therefore was to lay mines at the various exits from Scapa Flow in the hope of interfering with this concentration. The submarine U75 (Lieutenant-Commander Kurt Beitzen) was one of those detailed to watch the British base. On the night of May 28-29 he laid twenty-two mines off Marwick Head and it was one of these that the *Hampshire* struck.

From these facts,[1] which have been thoroughly investigated by the Admiralty, it is evident that the mine was laid a week before the disaster, at a time when no information could have reached the U75 about Kitchener's projected voyage. Throughout the war the enemy's submarines haunted the neighbourhood of the Grand Fleet. There was always danger. Kitchener knew it. In deciding to go to Russia he took what proved to be a fatal risk. It is something to know that he died by the ordinary hazard of war, and not by any act of treachery.

By a strange coincidence the last of the 70 Divisions was on the way to France when their creator embarked on his fatal voyage. It has been suggested by more than one writer that Kitchener's death came at the moment when he had completed his great contribution to the war; that it was, for England, less a real than a sentimental disaster. I do not agree with this view, much less with any harsher judgment. He had raised England to the rank of a first-class military power and it was only at this moment that she could take up her full share of the common burden. Up to this moment it was only reasonable that we should conform as far as possible to the policy of our Allies; their territory had been invaded and they stood in the more im-

[1] See O.H., Naval Operations, by H. Newbold, IV, p. 20-1.

mediate danger; theirs were the troops which had borne the brunt of the first German onslaughts. But, as Kitchener himself had said, the last million men would decide the war. In spite of entrenchments and barbed wire a time would come when human nerves could stand the strain no longer. Sooner or later those impregnable lines must give way in one direction or the other. The French reserves were practically exhausted. It fell then to the British to find the next million and it should have fallen to them to say where and how they should be used.

This was where the loss of the *Hampshire* was irreparable. In matters of administration Kitchener could bequeath his task to successors; the new armies were already in line; arsenals and workshops were pouring out guns and shells. But nobody could inherit his authority or speak in the Allied Councils as he could and would have spoken.

Lord Esher, in the *Tragedy of Lord Kitchener,* argues that his authority had weakened; physically and mentally the victor of Omdurman had passed his prime; he was bewildered by the political net in which he found himself enmeshed. The picture drawn is one of indecision and wavering. It is a shortsighted view, disproved by the broad facts.

From the moment when Kitchener first entered the War Office he made no secret of his belief that the struggle would be a long one and that the British strength could not be fully developed until 1917. The intervening time must therefore be regarded as a period of preparation. If he had been a student of military history—which he was not—he might have compared his policy with that of Wellington in the Peninsular War. For over four years the Iron Duke had to maintain a struggle against forces which were in many ways superior to his own. He knew he could not inflict a decisive blow which would destroy Napoleon's power. His object was to hold the Grand Alliance together, his immediate object to avoid a defeat. Each year he advanced, fought and drew the French Marshals on to him; each year he retired again into Portugal. When Napoleon in 1812 took away the best French troops for the invasion of Russia, Wellington struck hard; he stormed Cuidad Rodrigo and Badajos, defeated Marmont at Salamanca and forced the enemy to leave Madrid. Yet with calm deliberation he was content to retreat once more in order to complete his preparations before the final advance. During those four years he had to exercise forbearance towards his Allies, who were demanding huge subsidies and giving very little in return. Scarcely less troublesome was the Government in London, parsimonious, peevish, always expecting immediate and decisive results.

The Great War was of course on a much bigger scale, yet the circumstances were not dissimilar. Throughout the two years of his power Kitchener was looking forward. In Egypt and South Africa patience and foresight were the outstanding factors in his policy. With tireless persistence he spent three whole years in working his way up the Cataracts and across the desert to Omdurman; he spent two whole years in building the blockhouse lines which finally broke the resistance of the Boers. The obstacles in either campaign would have defeated a man of smaller will power. The same stern consistency unites all his actions in the Great War. During the period of preparation the supreme necessity was to hold the Allies together. He rushed to Paris to save the Entente; he allowed Joffre to over-ride his military judgment of the Salonika Expedition in order to maintain goodwill with the French; he lost his life on a mission to Russia. Bad as the failure in Gallipoli and the reverses in Mesopotamia were, he did not allow them to occupy too large a space in his mind. They were, after all, side-shows. The Germans had suffered worse. Meantime his own armies were maturing. Like Wellington, he could afford to disregard the vexations of the moment because his plans were laid for the future.

It was unfortunate that he could not instil the same patience and confidence into his colleagues. He had no gift of eloquence, no turn for optimistic prophecy. They found him an inarticulate and uncomfortable member of their councils, and before long they would have been glad to get rid of him. But the very fact that they could not do so is the strongest possible evidence that his authority was in no way diminished.

Nothing had happened to weaken his authority with the French. On the contrary, those who could see below the surface were gradually coming round to his point of view. At first they had found him difficult to understand, irresponsive, impassive. He refused to squander the new armies before he considered them ready for the field; he had not endorsed the opinion of Joffre and Sir John French that the German lines could be broken; he did not seek for popularity by indulging in roseate dreams of immediate success. But the British strength had risen from a hundred thousand to over a million, and the French could not fail to see that the shadow armies on which they had once placed little reliance had become a real factor in the war. When the years of preparation were over he could have asserted an authority which would not have been resisted.

Contrary to the general belief, Kitchener was not a good organizer. Though the campaign of Omdurman is often quoted as an example of perfect organization it would be more correct to say that its success was due to close and personal attention to details. The true test of organization is the power to employ all available resources to the best advantage and to appoint every man to work where the best use can be made of his individual ability. During the Great War Kitchener failed in both these respects. Far from making use of the experience and knowledge of other people he discouraged advice and avoided discussion. During his whole career there is no instance of his carrying through any conception which had its origin outside his own brain. The Sudan campaign, the Peace with the Boers, the reforms in India, the New Armies—all were his own work, conceived by him and brought into being by his personal strength of will. When his schemes were anticipated and exploited by other people—as in the case of compulsory service—he lost interest in them simply because they were no longer his own.

This absorption in his own plans and indifference to those of other men probably accounts for his strange lack of interest in the Territorial organizations, created by Lord Haldane, and the means of expansion which it provided ready to his hand. It accounts, too, for more than one serious mistake, of commission and omission. Thus he allowed the finest "officer material" of which several Territorial battalions were composed, to be wasted in the ranks during the early stages of the war.[1] In the administration of large forces there are several branches in which technical military knowledge is of less importance than business experience. But no attempt was made to exploit specialized civilian ability. No provision was made for the training of an adequate staff for the great armies he was preparing. Nor was attention paid early enough to those few who foresaw the mechanization of modern warfare.

He had, in fact, the defects of his qualities and of his experience. Driving-power, not less than patience and foresight, was the quality which crowned his plans with success. His experience had been autocratic; his autocracy successful. He had found that men could usually do what they thought impossible if they were driven hard enough. This experience stiffened his natural tendency to avoid discussion. Discussion meant the consideration of difficulties, the admission of doubt. His method had been to determine the objective and to compel his lieutenants to overcome the obstacles which lay before it. Such a method cannot admit doubt. In the magnitude and complexity of the war, and in the political embarrassments of his office it at once served and betrayed him. It enabled him to sow his "dragon's teeth"

[1] Smith-Dorrien, who had much experience of the Territorial Forces, held a very high opinion of them and urged Kitchener to use them as the basis of expansion. See pages 369, 374, 375.

THE LOSS OF THE *HAMPSHIRE*

and reap the iron harvest with magical rapidity. But it aroused the resentment of men like Sir John French and Sir Henry Wilson, and of most of his political colleagues. It led him also into the disastrous *cul de sac* of Gallipoli. Difficulties were ignored which would have come to light in a discussion among experts; there was no co-operation between the naval and the military efforts; troops were detailed, ships provided, and all arrangements made before the General Staff had been called into consultation; the Commander was appointed at the last moment and had no opportunity to study the problem before him until after premature naval bombardment had destroyed more than half his chances of success. In cases of this kind no amount of driving power can compensate for lack of organization. But Kitchener failed at first to recognize this. In his Oriental way he assumed that it was for him to command and for others to obey. It took time for him to realize that a method which succeeded in the limited fields of Egypt and South Africa could not be applied to the conduct of a world war.

There was in fact a strain of Orientalism in his character which showed itself in his relations both with his subordinates and with his political colleagues. To the former he appeared ruthless, inconsiderate, sparing of praise. By the terror which he inspired he sometimes failed to get the best out of those below him. He knew, of course, that men were afraid of him, and the knowledge was a lever which he deliberately used. But the legend of an inhuman Kitchener is as far from the truth as the legend of the superhuman organizer. By nature he was neither ruthless nor inhuman; he made use of his reputation for these qualities with the object of enhancing his driving power.

To his colleagues in the Cabinet he showed reserve because he knew that they were incapable of sharing his views. This appeared to them as a lack of candour, and in the end cost him their confidence. It is not quite correct to think of him as the simple-minded soldier alone among the subtle politicians. Though he had little knowledge of the political machine he was not without subtlety himself. But with the exception of the support which he always had from Asquith he was alone in the Cabinet. Its members began by relying on his omniscience and ended by doubting his ability. He was not omniscient. The war was too big for him as it was for everybody else. He had to grow into it. Perhaps it would have been better if he had treated the members of the Cabinet with greater confidence and confessed the limitations of his own knowledge from the beginning. But this he never did, and probably it was not in him to do so. It is easy, however, to understand his point of view. He distrusted their power of taking a broad view of the military situation; he distrusted their ability to keep their information to themselves; he distrusted their fertility of ideas, their passion for short cuts and long ways round, their unprofessional judgment. As his quarrel with Curzon had shown in India, he was no match in debate with clever civilians, and he would not risk his opinion against theirs in a battle of words.

The twenty-one months of the war had taught him much. He had been subjected to continuous badgering and baiting in the Cabinet and to public criticism in the Press, but the total result was to enhance his prestige in the eyes of the country. The new experience tried his temper to some extent, yet those who were closest to him in the War Office found him easier to work with towards the end than he had been at first. He had learned something of his power and something of his limitations. While confidence in his own judgment remained undiminished he had learned that staff work, in the fullest sense of the word, was indispensable for the conduct of a world war. Though he held the confidence of the army he had never been in close touch with it till Robertson came to the War Office as Chief of the Imperial General Staff. Robertson had a deep knowledge of the personal factor from the highest to the lowest rank, and was in every way an organizer. Afraid of nobody, he was outspoken in his views. He could have saved the Secretary of

THE LOSS OF THE *HAMPSHIRE*

State from blunders like Gallipoli. While Kitchener determined the objective and supplied the driving power the General Staff would have taken care that the machinery was not thrown out of gear.

The loss of the *Hampshire* was a tragedy for England. The Kitchener of 1914 had grown into the Kitchener of 1916, the military despot into the Secretary of State. The long period of preparation was over. His armies and munitions were ready. His staff was in working order. His authority at home and abroad stood higher than that of anybody, soldier or civilian, on either side. He was approaching the maximum of his utility. Nor would his services have ended with victory in the field. The man who had urged peace with the Boers in 1901 and criticized Milner's views as just but vindictive might have saved Europe from the worst features of the Peace of Versailles. But this is speculation. What remains certain is that once again in England's history the hour had found the man, and that by his foresight and iron patience he had saved his country from the greatest danger she has ever known.

1849

B KITCHE, H.
Ballard, Colin R. (Colin
Robert), 1868-1941.
Kitchener,

DATE DUE